Governance, Resistance and the Post-Colonial State

The manifestation of the colonial nation-state as a legal-bureaucratic-police structure – an exploitation tool – undermined customary modes of governance in colonies. When post-World War II independence of colonies transferred ownership of the state structure to the colonized elite, electoral and civil society politics battled for capture of this post-colonial state. Meanwhile, the state was also forced to build its legitimacy in the face of customary governance practices seeking rehabilitation and decolonization in the midst of civil wars and strife. This "state-building social movement" was further complicated with the global spread of neoliberalism and neocolonialism, and herein lies the significant difference between the post-colonial nation-state and the Western nation-states.

This book fills the gap in literature and argues that it is necessary to foreground discussions of the nature of the post-colonial nation-state in examining resistance and provides a window into the dynamics of the post-colonial state and its implication in everyday organizing and resistance.

Jonathan Murphy works as a scholar and practitioner in the areas of democratic governance and international management. He has led democratic development projects in more than 20 countries in Africa, Asia, Europe and the Americas, and has been a faculty member at Cardiff Business School in Wales as well as the University of Alberta, Canada. Currently, Jonathan is a UN official in Kiev, Ukraine.

Nimruji Jammulamadaka is an associate professor with the organization behavior group at the Indian Institute of Management (IIM) Calcutta. She is also co-chair of the critical management studies division of the Academy of Management for 2016–2017, and the author of *Indian Business: Notions and Practices of Responsibility*.

Routledge Studies in Management, Organizations and Society

This series presents innovative work grounded in new realities, addressing issues crucial to an understanding of the contemporary world. This is the world of organized societies, where boundaries between formal and informal, public and private, local and global organizations have been displaced or have vanished, along with other nineteenth-century dichotomies and oppositions. Management, apart from becoming a specialized profession for a growing number of people, is an everyday activity for most members of modern societies.

Similarly, at the level of enquiry, culture and technology, and literature and economics, can no longer be conceived as isolated intellectual fields; conventional canons and established mainstreams are contested. **Management, Organizations and Society** addresses these contemporary dynamics of transformation in a manner that transcends disciplinary boundaries, with books that will appeal to researchers, student and practitioners alike.

For a full list of titles in this series, please visit www.routledge.com/series/SE0536

Recent titles in this series include:

The Organization of the Expert Society
Staffan Furusten and Andreas Werr

Foucault and Managerial Governmentality
Rethinking the Management of Populations, Organizations and Individuals
Edited by Alan McKinlay and Eric Pezet

Dance and Organisation
Integrating Dance Theory and Methods into the Study of Management
Brigitte Biehl

How Speech Acting and the Struggle of Narratives Generates Organization
Thorvald Gran

Governance, Resistance and the Post-Colonial State
Management and State Building
Edited by Jonathan Murphy and Nimruji Jammulamadaka

Governance, Resistance and the Post-Colonial State

Management and State Building

**Edited by Jonathan Murphy
and Nimruji Jammulamadaka**

Routledge
Taylor & Francis Group

LONDON AND NEW YORK

First published 2017 by Routledge

2 Park Square, Milton Park, Abingdon, Oxfordshire OX14 4RN
52 Vanderbilt Avenue, New York, NY 10017

Routledge is an imprint of the Taylor & Francis Group, an informa business

First issued in paperback 2019

British Library Cataloguing-in-Publication Data
A catalogue record for this book is available from the British Library

Library of Congress Cataloging-in-Publication Data
A catalog record for this book has been requested

ISBN: 978-1-138-68137-8 (hbk)
ISBN: 978-0-367-37466-2 (pbk)

Typeset in Galliard
by Apex CoVantage, LLC

"To Shree Ram for being there and constantly reminding me of my duty"

Nimruji

"To my father"

Jonathan

Contents

Illustrations

Figures

Tables

Contributors

Mário Aquino Alves is an associate professor on civil society and nonprofit organizations at FGV-EAESP (Brazil), where he is also the associate dean for the PhD program in public administration and government. Mário is interested in critical perspectives on civil society and state relations. His research focuses on how the institutional context influences civil society organizations' ability to promote advocacy.

Ivor Chipkin is the founder and executive director of the Public Affairs Research Institute (PARI), based at the University of the Witwatersrand.

Raqib Chowdhury taught at Dhaka University from 1997 to 2004 as a lecturer and an assistant professor and then joined Monash University, where he currently teaches, upon completing his PhD in 2008.

Paulo Faveret is a senior analyst and the former human resources director at Brazilian Development Bank.

Marcus Vinícius Peinado Gomes is a lecturer on organization and sustainability at the University of Exeter Business School. Marcus is interested in critical perspectives on business and society. His research focuses on the development of governance mechanism regarding environmental degradation and human rights through negotiations between civil society, states and corporations.

Md Khalid Hossain is the Economic Justice Resilience Programme manager at Oxfam in Bangladesh. He oversees the coordinated activities of rural, urban, private sector linkage and youth programs of Oxfam in Bangladesh. His research focuses on climate change adaptation for multinational corporations.

Nimruji Jammulamadaka is an associate professor with the organization behaviour group at the Indian Institute of Management (IIM) Calcutta. She is also co-chair of the critical management studies division of the Academy of Management for 2016–2017, and the author of *Indian Business: Notions and Practices of Responsibility*.

Ariful H. Kabir is an associate professor teaching sociology of education at the Institute of Education and Research at the University of Dhaka, Bangladesh.

Rajiv Kumar is an associate professor of organizational behaviour at the Indian Institute of Management (IIM) Calcutta. His research interests include a variety of areas in organizational behaviour. His research has appeared in peer-reviewed outlets such as journals, edited books and conference proceedings.

Virpi Malin is the pedagogical director and a lecturer at the Jyväskylä University School of Business and Economics, Finland. She is an active member of the CMS division and has acted as an organizer/facilitator for CMS sessions at the Academy of Management and has run workshops at the CMS International Doctoral Consortium in Halifax, Canada.

Arpita Mathur is a fellow in the sociology department, Indian Institute of Management (IIM) Calcutta, and an assistant professor at SRM University School of Management, Chennai. Her research interests include theorizing the state, corruption, border thinking, post-colonial theory and anticorruption policy.

Jonathan Murphy works as a scholar and practitioner in the areas of democratic governance and international management. He has led democratic development projects in more than 20 countries in Africa, Asia, Europe and the Americas, and has been a faculty member at Cardiff Business School in Wales as well as the University of Alberta, Canada. Currently, Jonathan is a UN official in Kiev, Ukraine.

Teke Ngomba is an associate professor at the Department of Media and Journalism Studies, Aarhus University, Denmark. His research is in the fields of journalism and media studies, political communication and communication and social change.

Biswatosh Saha is an associate professor with the strategic management group of the Indian Institute of Management (IIM) Calcutta. He had a brief stint in the public-sector steel industry before he joined academics. His current academic interests revolve around strategy-as-practice, critical management studies, digitization and complexity, institutional/organizational change and innovation and technology and society.

Acknowledgements

We would like to acknowledge IIM Calcutta and Cardiff Business School for the support provided; our families for supporting us through the making of this book; the authors for being part of the project; our students and colleagues at IIM Calcutta, at Cardiff Business School and at the Critical Management Studies Division of the Academy of Management for conversations which revealed the scope for this work.

We would also like to express our appreciation to Terry Clague and Samantha Phua of Routledge for believing in this project and supporting us all the way in making the book a reality, as well as Kate Fornadel and everyone involved in the copyediting and production process.

1 Governing and managing the post-colonial

Nimruji Jammulamadaka and Jonathan Murphy[1]

The rise in populism in most parts of the world highlights that the state is far from dead, despite the reign of neoliberalism. The state is an essential feature of this global world. This very same populism infused with contestations around identities also suggests that it is not just a universal neoliberal state, but *states*, states which have evolved in highly diverse contexts and carry with them varying sets of expectations. A fundamental feature of these different evolutions is the distinct trajectories of post-colonial states and European[2] states. What do these different trajectories imply in the post-colonial situation? Unlike Eurocentric nation-state theories that posit the state as a guarantor of rights, the colonial nation-state manifested as a legal-bureaucratic-police structure was the colonizer's instrument for exploiting the colony. This structure undermined customary modes of governance in the colonies. The post–World War II independence of colonies transferred ownership of the state structure to (post)-colonialized elites.

On one hand, electoral and civil society politics has battled for capture of this post-colonial state structure; on the other, this state itself has been forced to build its legitimacy in the face of customary governance practices seeking rehabilitation and decolonization in the midst of strife and even civil wars. This "state-building social movement" of the post-colonial condition is further complicated with the global spread of neoliberalism in a context of neocolonialism. Herein lies the significant difference between the post-colonial nation-state and the Western nation-states, a difference that suggests important implications for everyday organizing, and for alternatives and resistance to capitalist control.

For critical scholars of management and organization studies to surface such implications, it is necessary to foreground discussions of the nature of the post-colonial nation-state in examining organizing, governance and resistance. This edited book is an attempt to fill in this gap in literature and to provide a window into the dynamics of the post-colonial state and its implication in everyday organizing and resistance.

The essentially political nature of the post-colonial state derives from the different interests, influences and dynamics at work in constituting the post-colonial state. We outline in particular four such influences – customary forms of governance, incumbent bureaucracy, nation-building and the rise of neoliberal ideology.

While these influences appeared in a chronological order, in the contemporary world they coexist and simultaneously influence the state.

Customary forms of governance

In all pre-colonial societies, there were customary forms of governance of social life and conduct. Customary does not imply that these forms of governance were necessarily rigid, totalitarian or unchanging. These societies were constituted of diverse communities sharing different civilizational experiences, resulting in governance systems more or less flexible, responsive and open to contestation and transmutation (Birla, 2008). The colonial state adopted different strategies in establishing its governance over these societies and furthering imperial interests; ranging from essentializing custom, delegitimizing custom, co-opting custom and even attempting to destroy both custom and peoples (Mamdani, 1996; Birla, 2008). European modernity entered the colonies through these governance processes (Chatterjee, 1986; Kaviraj, 2009) and such colonial governance even helped constitute European modernity (Mignolo, 2012). While these strategies have done much to subjugate the colonized, customs have survived in various forms including as hybrids (Bhabha, 2012) and in subterranean social life waiting for expression at opportune moments (Nandy, 1989). Modernity also influenced struggles for independence, wherein nationalists drew on certain elements of customary resources and pride in constructing images of the native *nation* as the *other* of the colonial state and paradoxically as justification for the foundation of a modernizing post-colonial state. For example, Nehru, the first prime minister of India, characterized institutions of modern scientific and industrial development such as the Bhakra Nangal Dam as "temples of modern India." Independence has also been construed as a means of rehabilitating silenced customary practices.

Incumbent bureaucracy

To varying degrees, the colonial state introduced a bureaucratic apparatus that enabled it to exploit and govern the colonized societies. These bureaucratic structures were elaborated according to the perceived importance of the colony in the empire. Transfer of power at the dawn of independence meant transferring this bureaucracy and civil-police structure into native control. Given the colonial administration's repression of pre-existing governance structures, this bureaucratic and civil-police structure represented the only vehicle for the newly independent nations to govern themselves. Newly independent countries varied widely in the sophistication, complexity and power of these inherited bureaucratic structures. For instance, in parts of West Africa the inherited bureaucratic structure was extremely sparse, whereas, on the other hand, the Indian subcontinent had a very elaborate bureaucracy with a separate class of civil service officers. To the extent that the inherited structure was sparse, it affected the stability of the post-colonial state and its ability to manage internal conflict and strife. And in cases like the Indian subcontinent, bureaucracy achieved an autonomy largely independent of electoral politics (Alavi, 1972; Kumar, 2005). Throughout the postcolonial world, "the elites that the colonial education created inherited the government following independence and continue to use their privileged position to monopolize the control of African states" (Ntiri, 1993).

Thus, on one hand, post-colonial states inheriting skeletal state structures have faced difficulties implementing a development and nation-building agenda and have frequently been subject to instability and state capture by factions such as of armed forces. On the other, states with well-developed structures such as India have been able to quickly implement a developmentalist agenda, but also have encountered bureaucracy as a self-interest-driven, entrenched power centre. These different post-colonial bureaucratic inheritances have resulted in divergent and path-dependent development trajectories and outcomes.

Nation-building

Picking up the pieces in the aftermath of colonial plunder, the newly independent nations embarked on a grand journey of nation-building, particularly emphasizing industrialization. Given the tall order of the task, scant domestic private capital and poor industrial base, industrialization was necessarily driven by the state, largely through state-owned enterprises in various fields. Private domestic capital welcomed and at times demanded such participation. For instance, in India in 1944, respected native industrialists came together in anticipation of independence and proposed the Bombay Plan for economic development. In this Plan "the state was to play a critical role as a central directing authority. It was to exercise control over the distribution of industries, to minimize regional disparities, to develop public utilities and basic industries, and to undertake nonremunerative enterprises" (Kudaisya, 2014: 124). The state-owned enterprises which were consequently set up had very clear agendas of social development, redistribution of wealth and self-reliance in addition to the usual economic objective of wealth creation (Bhattacharya, 2006). For instance, the 1956 industrial policy of India spells out state-owned enterprise objectives as "to promote *redistribution of income and wealth, to promote balanced regional development, save and earn foreign exchange for the economy*" (cited in Bhattacharya, 2006: 40). In some countries, these state-owned enterprises emerged as the largest and most powerful enterprises and also employers. By 1975, the jute sector of Bangladesh which provided employment to 25 per cent of the population was entirely under public-sector ownership (Alamgir, 2013). These state-owned enterprises need to make profits in order to survive and provide for the government, but their mission is not to maximize financial return. State enterprises also help in establishing state presence through outposts of state departments/enterprises throughout the national territory. This is particularly important because the moment of independence drew arbitrary national boundaries that often cut across traditional communities (Englebert, 2000). Post-colonial states therefore often have a daunting challenge in maintaining state integrity.

Despite substantial external pressure to comply with Washington Consensus strictures on privatization and marketization, the state-enterprise sector remains important to post-colonial states as a source of employment, as a tool for political control and as a tool of national sovereignty. In addition to completely government-owned enterprises are hybrid public-private enterprises as well as privately owned but nationally significant corporations. While these companies are in one way part of the "private sector," their strategic and historic importance results in their being provided explicit or implicit protection to assure continuity and the integrity of the national project.

Rise of neoliberal ideology

From the 1970s, Keynesian economic ideology was gradually supplanted through the rise of neoliberal ideas initially associated with Hayek and the Mont Pelèrin Society, and the Chicago University economics school. Whereas the approach of Keynesianism was in many ways consistent with the national economic development strategies adopted by the newly independent post-colonial states, neoliberalism – which privileges free market transnational trade and a reduced role for the state – challenged the nation-building and welfarist ideologies of these states. Neoliberals emphasized transnational economic growth, leading to the development of global value chains. A number of post-colonial states slowly emerged as the shop-floor of the world, although the bulk of added value continues to be realized in Western countries, particularly through their dominance of the financial sector and control of intellectual property (Smith, 2012). Indigenous knowledge also has been captured and privatized by transnational corporations (Brush, 1993).

By the late 1970s and early 1980s, neoliberal ideas had come to dominate the international development banks which had previously provided significant capital resources for the industrial and infrastructural development of the post-colonial states. Under neoliberal ascendency, the international development banks replaced infrastructural lending with "policy-based lending," in other words, loans to be provided in return for governments agreeing to implement neoliberal reforms. The menu of required neoliberal reforms- known as structural adjustment – became increasingly codified until congealed into the universal policy prescription of the Washington Consensus (Williamson, 2000). Most post-colonial states adopted some or all aspects of the neoliberal prescription. State-owned enterprises which earlier were viewed as indispensable for nation-building came under attack for inefficiency and unfair competition with transnational corporations, leading to pressures for divestment.

The actual implementation varied considerably across states. The more powerful ones were able to negotiate protection for certain sectors, retention of state-owned enterprises and extended implementation periods for reforms. Even where states were not in a position to directly confront the new orthodoxy, policies were often implemented more on the surface, leaving the deeper mechanisms intact (Gervais, 1992). The more powerful states were more or less able to instrumentalize neoliberal policies in order to further national interests. Whereas countries such as China and India have been able to gain access to Western markets without generally relinquishing the ability to protect their own strategic industries, smaller and poorer countries have been forced to relinquish even food security in order to orient their economies towards export crops. For example, Mali and other West African cotton-producing countries have become highly dependent on food imports at the same time as they are forced to compete in cotton exports against major powers, including the United States and China, which heavily subsidize their own cotton farmers. Therefore, neoliberalism has become part of the pastiche of pressures on the state and a tool that some post-colonial states have been able to strategically incorporate.

In the face of these multiple and sometimes contradictory influences, the post-colonial state is subject to constant and varying expectations and pressures, leading to tensions within the state itself, between the state and citizens, and between the state and global forces. Post-colonial states have displayed varying abilities and strategies to successfully manage these tensions. Some of these strategies might hold broader lessons for states and citizens outside the post-colonial world as they too attempt to cope with the tensions unleashed by neoliberalism and globalization.

Expectations of the post-colonial state

Expectations of itself

The state itself as an organization seeks to perpetuate and reproduce itself (Selznick, 1949; Perrow, 1970). Given that the post-colonial state is an external implant, it faces constant legitimacy threats on one hand, while on the other, neoliberalism seeks to reduce its relevance; in the face of these challenges, the state attempts to preserve and reproduce itself. It seeks to do this by expanding its influence and control of public life through technologies such as active redistribution, guaranteeing security and maximizing its surveillance and governmental capacities.

Resistance of the bureaucratic state to external reform is often presented as a weakness; however, the self-perpetuation of the state also provides the possibility and the space for preserving autonomy from domination of transnational capital and hegemonic states. In an ironic way, this makes the state's preservation and bureaucratic self-perpetuation a pre-condition for political and economic independence; two examples follow.

When the South African government licensed the distribution of low-cost generic antiretroviral therapies in 1997, it not only engaged in redistribution, creating access and protecting its citizens from profiteering of transnational corporations, but it was also justifying its existence and relevance. This decision asserted South African sovereignty vis-à-vis the new World Trade Organization which was attempting to force developing countries to provide global pharmaceutical companies with long-term patent protection (Hoen et al., 2011). Similarly, almost twenty years later another post-colonial state was symbolically justifying its existence as a punisher of lawbreakers – "looters" in popular parlance. In November 2016, the prime minister of India, Modi, announced the demonetization of high-value currency as a "war on black money." The policy's ability to actually combat black money[3] was seriously suspect – most is in the form of non-cash assets. The policy also severely inconvenienced the poor, rural and informal sector workers dependent on cash who constituted almost 50 per cent of the population; it disrupted their ability to fulfil their daily needs. Nevertheless, the policy appeared to receive general public approval as the gesture was seen as punishing lawbreakers, thus demonstrating the symbolic efficacy and utility of the state.

Expectations from people(s)

As for all nation-states, post-colonial states provide a platform for public dialogue and arbitration of diverse group interests. This process can be particularly challenging in post-colonial societies which are building a sense of both identity and diversity from the repressive legacy of colonialism. For example, language policy and languages used in education are frequently a thorny subject. In many post-colonial states, choosing a national language was a fundamental early interrogation. There was a tension between the choice of a language which would be shared by the entire country – which was almost inevitably the language of the former colonizers – an indigenous language which would not be spoken by all of the country's citizens or would be perceived as favouring one language group over the others. In most former French colonies in Africa, the French language was chosen as the official language and the language of education, but this increased disparity between the post-colonial elite (who had usually been schooled in French) and the masses of the population who did not master the language (waThiong'o, 1987). Similarly, in Latin America, the issue of language and education is closely intertwined with relationships of power where even though bilingual education is often implemented, "indigenous education has always been looked upon with concern and distrust, practically from the moment our countries became independent and adopted the principles of classical European liberalism" (Lopez, 2008).

Another particular challenge facing the post-colonial state is the demands for rehabilitation of silenced customary practices of governance that surface from time to time. Such demands often imply that the political self of the state works against its bureaucratic self. For instance, India has had a traditional form of local governance known as *panchayats*. Since independence there were demands for restoring this mode of governance. It was finally restored through the seventy-third amendment of the constitution in 1992. However, the actual amendment resembled the traditional form more in name than content, with limited devolution of powers from the centre to the local level (World Bank, 2000).

The initial impulse of the post-colonial leaders was to build a strong, centralized state in which difference was downplayed in favour of national unity. This approach has come under increasing challenge as states have confronted globalization and pressure for integration into global markets on one hand, and popular demand for community autonomy on the other. The market pressures for homogenization inherent in neoliberalism lead to a popular reaction to assert group identities whether linguistic, regional or ethnic (Appadurai, 2000). The challenge of addressing difference is exacerbated by the arbitrary nature of post-colonial national boundaries which have frequently cut across ethnically similar groups and/or combined ethnically diverse populations into one nation-state. Post-colonial states are often forced into efforts to build a national imaginary from scratch, while at the same time providing diverse communities with political freedoms and autonomy, even to the extent of challenges to the integrity of the state (Deshpande, 2003). For example, Pakistan's initial territory was divided geographically into two entirely separate territories with diverse ethnic and language communities and the unity of this post-colonial entity could not be maintained, leading eventually to the secession of Bangladesh. In Nigeria, efforts to create an independent state of Biafra led to a civil war between 1967 and 1970 with up to 2 million civilian deaths before the insurgency was quelled.

International expectations

A key tenet of the neoliberal Washington Consensus is the requirement of developing countries to open their economies to transnational capital. Countries were expected to liberalize trade, to permit inward foreign direct investment, to abolish regulations restricting market entry, to provide legal security for property rights and reduce taxes on business. These expectations on one hand weakened the scope for post-colonial states to pursue national welfarist strategies, such as national industrial strategies, agricultural self-sufficiency and import substitution; at the same time, however, the policy dictates of the Washington Consensus made this same post-colonial state a pre-condition for delivery of neoliberal expansion because only the state could guarantee that its markets would be open.

The structure of the new international economic regime also provides space for rent-seeking behaviours of elites within some post-colonial states, undermining the possibility for accountability of leaders to their populations. In some cases, this has even resulted in violent repression. For example, in the process of exploiting oil in the Niger delta of Nigeria, Shell and a Nigerian military dictatorship colluded in suppressing the local Ogoni population's demands for a fair share of royalties and mitigation of environmental damage. The Nigerian regime ultimately executed Ken Saro-Wiwa, a leader of the Ogoni campaign. Royal Dutch Shell eventually paid US$15.5 million to the families of Saro-Wiva and other victims (Pilkington, 2009).

The neoliberal expectation was that states would develop policies of economic concentration to optimize integration into the global economic order. Developing countries were forced to focus economic activities in a few export-oriented sectors, and the rest of their needs, including many basic needs, were to be fulfilled by trade, which increased their trade dependence. They therefore became extremely vulnerable to declines due to external shocks such as falls in global commodity prices, recession in export markets and oil price shocks (Ruggie,

1982). Enforced integration into global markets greatly reduced post-colonial states' margins for manoeuvre to protect their citizens from the fall-out of economic shocks.

International expectations on trade and governance posed a particularly vexing bind for post-colonial states. Often as a condition for accession to international treaties and conventions they were expected to put in place various legal regimes to afford protection to workers, the environment and citizens. Sometimes, states themselves also started such efforts in responding to national popular demands. On the other hand, entry of transnational capital is frequently conditioned upon its exemption from complying to such laws. Many post-colonial states managed this challenge by creating mechanisms of exception such as Special Economic Zones, where virtually all welfarist laws were suspended to encourage investment, as well as investment agreements which override current and future national legislation.

> Foreign investment gives considerable leverage to corporations and enables them to use their economic power to discipline states. For example, an ExxonMobil executive was quoted as saying to [the] *Wall Street Journal* (October 14, 1997) that "Poor developing countries cannot afford environmental protection. If they insist on such measures, foreign investment might go elsewhere" (cited in Environmental Defense Fund, 1999: 2).
>
> (Sikka, 2011: 814)

The global neoliberal economic order brought new actors into transnational governance. This period has been marked by the rise of non-state actors such as international NGOs and advocacy groups. These groups have pressured domestic governments into adopting policies intended to address perceived concerns about issues such as child labour, working hours and conditions, empowerment etc. However, the priorities of international NGOs are frequently developed without engagement with the affected communities. This can result in the imposition of foreign values on communities. In the rehabilitation of women in war-torn Afghanistan, humanitarian agencies have promoted the model of women's economic independence. This can result in disruption to prevailing family- and marriage-based rehabilitation practices, and can lead to the loss of social capital from family and kinship networks (Daulatzai, 2008). The priorities of advocacy groups can sometimes be at variance from those of the local people. In Nicaragua, where the indigenous communities living on forest edges were interested in control over their resources, international environmentalist groups instrumentalized the local population as the human face of the NGOs' global strategies of sustainability. In this environmental narrative, Indians became "guardians of the forest" and "people dwelling in the nature according to nature," rather than actors seeking control over resources (Nygren, 1999). However, as Gomes and Alves show in their chapter on the environmental impact of the global beef supply chain, there are cases where the post-colonial state and international NGOs function synergistically.

Sometimes international NGOs have directly facilitated the undermining of post-colonial state capacity through lobbying for the transfer of resources from the state sector to civil society, on the grounds that developing country administrations are corrupt and inefficient (Edwards and Hulme, 1996; Hudock, 1999). Clayton (1998) notes that, particularly in some African countries, international NGOs implement much larger programmes than those provided by poorly resourced local authorities and thus wield "too much power and influence in the local context." This exaggerated role for NGOs that can undermine state capacity as well as service accountability is frequently facilitated by international institutions such as the World Bank, the Ford Foundation and USAID.

The problem

The specificity of the post-colonial state has not been sufficiently considered, particularly in the neoliberal context. The post-colonial state appears outwardly to take the same form and have the same mandates as the European state. However, in practice it operates within a very different context, subject to multiple different pressures and constituencies, leading to priorities and objectives at variance with the European state. Indeed, the external pressures to mimic the European state that the post-colonial state has faced, have frequently led to irreconcilable tensions with the desires and interests of its subject populations.

The first generation of post-colonial state leaders had a clear vision for the state. While that vision has largely ceased to be operative, little consideration has been given to how the state can evolve in the new context. Post-colonial countries have, to varying extents, become increasingly important in the global economy, and, according to current trends, will outstrip the West within the next few years. The major post-colonial states such as the BRICS have started to flex their muscle in global politics. However, this growing muscle does not yet translate into an authorial role in defining the state and its roles and functions in society. It is paradoxical that despite being home to most of the world's population and an increasingly large share of the world economy, these states continue to lack an authoritative voice. This lack of voice is clearly reflected in the field of management and organizational scholarship, where management and business schools in the post-colonial states continue to transmit Western ideology and knowledges. This has been noted across the major post-colonial states, including India (Jammulamadaka, 2016), South Africa (Nkomo, 2006, 2011), Brazil (Cooke and Alcadipani, 2015) and China (Murphy and Zhu, 2012).

The increasingly important role of the post-colonial countries in the global arena will "necessitate changes not only in the rules and structures for international/geopolitical governance but also in the rules and structures that govern the production of scholarly knowledge" (Prasad, 2015: 161).

What should be shocking is that even though the increasing economic capabilities of the post-colonial state have merited scholarly interest in the form of a focus on emerging markets, it still is the scholars of the West who retain the right to speak about these "markets"! Scholars of the sociology of knowledge have repeatedly commented about this unequal production of knowledge. Europe and North America account for 90 per cent of social science knowledge production (Boshoff, 2010; Gingras and Mosbah-Natanson, 2010). This is compounded by the continuing sense of inferiority created through the colonial encounter (Alatas, 2000; Akena, 2012).

The loss of voice is not simply a geographic problem; it is also an epistemic problem, because modern Western social science is intimately linked to a separation of social life into distinct and autonomous spheres like economy, polity, society, culture, public, private etc. These categories are generally taken as *a priori* to the phenomenon under investigation. But this leads to problems of distortions and interpretations when examining phenomena in societies such as the post-colonial states, where social life does not present itself in these a priori categories, but exists in a permeable, diffuse manner which is at once economic-political-social-cultural and so on (Escobar, 1995; Birla, 2009; Prasad, 2015). The Western social science logic of disciplinary separation subordinates ways of life to particular logics of capital (Birla, 2009).

One prominent social science disciplinary category of growing importance in the neoliberal world is management studies. As Ibarra-Colado notes, management studies is the most important form of epistemic coloniality in the past 150 years. This form of knowledge has "ordered and simplified the world by means of instrumental rationality. Thus, it is necessary to recognize the 'coloniality of knowledge' as the root of coloniality of power" (2006: 464). This management studies has largely left the state in all its manifestations outside the theorizing of "organization" and its "management"; Pearce (2001) notes that there has been very little work on governments in management and organization studies. Marens (2008) in his essay on how government matters, also argues that management studies has generally neglected any engagement with government, and goes on to show how government is crucial to business. Arellano-Gault and colleagues (2013), in their special issue of *Organization* on "Bringing Public Organization and Organizing Back In," rue the disappearance of public organization from organization studies and attribute this phenomenon to increasingly exclusive interest in the corporation and the tendency for organization and management scholars to be located in business and management schools rather than in social science faculties. This in turn can be linked to the rise of neoliberalism with its disregard or outright hostility towards the autonomous power and authority of the state. Even within critical management studies, concern with neoliberalism has tended to be directed towards corporate practices, while sidelining the relevance of the state. This book shows that, particularly in the post-colonial context, the state remains simultaneously a crucial actor and a site of contestation.

As we have discussed, the post-colonial state is capable of sustaining democratic pluralism and mediating between different interests. It negotiates spaces of community autonomy while preserving the coherence of the nation-state. It acts as the gate-keeper of national interest in the face of international pressures, including the demands of transnational business. It also mediates between customary forms of life and governance and exigencies of the modern capitalist economy. Each of these roles has significant implications for the organization of social life and productive activity. The post-colonial state should therefore be a central concern for management and organization studies.

Conclusion

In conclusion, we therefore argue that firstly, the Western category of the state attempts to impose a fixity of the definition of "what is the state." This fixity is questionable even in the West where the role of the state has changed and continues to change. However, in the post-colonial context, the state is not simply a contest for the right to manage implementation of an already consensual political-economic project, but a contest over the state's very character, substance and form, with different influences both from within, outside and inside itself, trying to create and recreate it in their image and interests. The post-colonial state is at once a boundary, a site and an actor in a contest where the three roles exist in dynamic tension and need to find a balance with each other. Conventional treatments of the state as either neutral, static and monolithic, or even an elitist ally actually de-recognize this foment of state-building. Such de-recognition further amounts to another continuation of the colonial encounter, where metropolitan treatments of the nation-state are superimposed over native experiences and understandings of state and treated as sacrosanct.

Secondly, we have argued that the state needs to be brought back in, but it needs to be conceptualized as part of the societies' emic understanding of governance, even as the post-colonial state necessarily exists within the Westphalian nation-state framework. The post-colonial state needs to exist as a political category, but it is at the same time a cultural-social and economic category.

Thirdly, the concept of state-building itself needs to be problematized. The post-colonial state cannot be reduced to a set of institutions or buildings or rigid rules. The state-building project is never finalized and in fact, its essence lies in its never being finalized. It is in this inherent possibility of change and reinvention that the hope and scope for de-colonial and plural futures lie. By keeping the state-building project open to dialogue, engagement and change, the state ensures not only its continuity, but also its legitimacy in the face of multiple contradictory influences and pressures.

The state too is being "enacted" (Weick et.al, 2003) in an ongoing manner. It is this realization that the state is "being enacted," "being made," that opens up the doors for making critique "do" something. While this realization of the state as being "built," as constituted by various actors, may be new to management and organization studies, it has been discussed and elaborated in several other domains like political sociology, development studies and primary social movement literature itself.

Management and organization studies will be better equipped to pursue the epistemic project of benefitting humankind through embracing the study of the post-colonial state and its context as an integral and important part of its work.

Management studies has often engaged in decontextualized prescriptions of efficiency. These prescriptions are directed at "administering the state," "managing the economy and organization," to even "managing struggles or movements against both state and economy." Notwithstanding the practical benefits in establishing solidarity amongst diverse local struggles transnationally and translocally, and the temptation to merge all these struggles into the grand flow of the global anti-globalisation/anti-capitalist protest in the pursuit of solidarity, it is necessary for management to recognize these struggles as situated in the specific histories of these post-colonial nations and the still continuing processes of decolonization. The colonizers may have departed, but they left behind their legacies of legal, political, social, economic and knowledge systems which often have and continue to conflict with pre-existing and indigenous notions of all these and other categories. In fact, some of these conflicts are at the levels of these categories themselves. For management studies to be truly effective in the human sense of the word, it needs to move beyond de-contextual prescriptions. It needs a more grounded and interconnected epistemology that stems from an appreciation of these "other" worlds both as post-colonial states and as societies. Appreciating the context would even mean opening up academia to questions of 'who is a scholar' and 'what is scholarship'. Although certain categories of professionals and academicians are currently acknowledged as scholars with the right to knowledge, there is a need to further open this space. This for instance would include creating opportunities for those with traditional knowledges and currently outside university or business to also share their insights within the scholarly world.

We see this book as an illustration of looking at the state in the holistic sense. This book is thus not an interdisciplinary work that seeks to bring concepts of political science into management. Instead, it views management, business and public administration, governance and resistance within the post-colonial condition to be intricately interwoven, feeding each other. It is an attempt to problematize and politicize the neoliberal de-politicization of both management and the state. De-politicization of management and the state – which are themselves part of the technology of post-colonial neoliberalism – is the strategy of predetermining the role of the state according to neoliberal ideological prescriptions and the interests of the dominant states, with this prescription presented as taken-for-granted "technical necessities" into technologies of neoliberalism. This book draws attention to the struggles of the making of the post-colonial state.

About this book

This book comprises ten chapters in addition to this introductory chapter. These chapters reflect experiences from diverse post-colonial contexts – South Asia, Africa and Latin America. They also reflect varied dimensions of governance and resistance from the very local village level to the transnational level. They encompass issues of knowledge struggles in administering the state and its constituents. They also explore legitimacy dilemmas of state and governance both internally and transnationally in the making/unmaking of governance.

The book is divided into three sections. The first section, *Knowledge struggles*, includes three chapters which discuss the implications of ideologies and managerial knowledges in governance. The second section, *Legitimacy challenges*, includes three chapters which draw attention to the legitimacy challenges government faces at the local, national and transnational levels. The third section, *Making/unmaking governance*, looks at neocolonial, neoliberal and de-colonial forces driving governance and resistance in the post-colonial state.

In Chapter 2, the first chapter of the first section, Ivor Chipkin reads the discourse of corruption and state capture in contemporary South Africa as an ideology of the form of the state. Contrasting the liberal conceptions of the state as nonpartisan and neutral with the decolonizing post-apartheid conflation of the South African state's administration with the African National Congress, Ivor argues for a more nuanced treatment of corruption. Thus, corruption discourse is also a power struggle by groups who been excluded in previous regimes. He suggests that while the current debate on corruption and compliance to rules and politicization of administration may be important in its own place, it misses the essence of the political struggles in South Africa. The ideology of governance and corruption more importantly reflects public sentiment and disappointment with party officials and political leadership that fail to play their legitimate roles.

In Chapter 3, Paulo Faveret explores the Brazilian Development Bank, with a particular focus on the bank's human resources policies and practices. He underlines the hybrid character of the bank, in which the objectives of national development and of financial sustainability must both be addressed. This specific developmental approach diverges, of course, from the neoliberal organizational trope in which the only interest of the organization is to maximize market profit (or in the case of the new public management organization, to attain pseudo-market targets). The dual obligation of the development bank to remain financially solvent while meeting national social and economic objectives has to be tailored to the emergent characteristics of the bank's loan portfolio, ranging from large and individually tailored and negotiated investments to more standardized divisions of the portfolio. The chapter effectively highlights the inappropriateness of the one-size-fits-all model for economic development privileged by fundamentalist neoliberalism and evangelized by international financial institutions such as the World Bank.

In Chapter 4, Rajiv Kumar reflects on the process of the transfer of organizational behaviour (OB) knowledge in the provision of consulting services to an Indian state police service. Through a fine-grained exploration of the issues that arise when "classic" OB concepts are applied to a specific post-colonial organizational environment, he demonstrates both how disconnected OB theory actually is from organizational practice in general, and the interiorized Western assumptions that are inherent in OB theory. Kumar argues that the attraction of Western, particularly North American, management concepts derives from the predilection of post-colonial elites to reproduce the management perspectives and worldview they themselves have absorbed through their own typically Western education. In common with several other chapters, Kumar highlights how post-colonial governance emerges from and remains influenced by a global knowledge hierarchy in which indigenous knowledge is subordinated to hegemonic Western discourses.

In Chapter 5, the first chapter in the *Legitimacy challenges* section of the book, Md Khalid Hossein focuses his enquiry on the dilemmas and contradictions arising from the state's global claims for environmental justice contrasting with specific internal environmental practices of the state. Hossein's chapter centres around three examples of urban environmental management in Bangladesh, a country seriously threatened by global climate change and whose government has pursued justified demands for climate justice in international fora. Hossein reveals a disconnect between the international claims of the Bangladesh state and the practices of national urban environmental management. In the latter cases, environmental justice is frequently sacrificed in order to suit the economic and social interests of national elites at the expense of disadvantaged groups within the population. Hossein underlines that the potential for the Bangladesh state to secure global environmental justice will be enhanced if internal and external practice and discourse are consistent.

In Chapter 6, Teke Ngmoba contextualizes the responses of South Africa's leading trade union, COSATU, to the killings by police shooting at Marikana's platinum mine. He shows that despite being a key actor in South Africa's political struggle against apartheid, COSATU's subsequent participation in national governance not only posed challenges to its legitimacy but also limited its ability to pursue extensive criticism against the post-apartheid government. The chapter highlights the specific nature of outside support to government formation that is often seen in post-colonial states. On one hand, this approach maintains the union's capacity to criticize government even as it participates directly and indirectly in government. It is this specific character which enables COSATU to criticize the neoliberal policies of mining companies and the state. On the other hand, COSATU attempts to assert hegemony within the labour movement, adopting dissent-suppressing strategies to manage legitimacy challenges arising at least in part from its close proximity with the ANC national government.

In Chapter 7, Arpita Mathur shifts the focus from the nation-state to a village community in India and interrogates the practice of corruption. In this ethnographic account, she reports about long-standing customary social norms and social relationships in a village that legitimize corruption. She traces the prevalence of contingent and unfixed hierarchies of norms governed by mutual interdependence, reputation and social status in the village, which cut across diverse communities within the village, at the same time highlighting the ways in which these norms are made illegal by modern colonial anti-corruption laws. Her study demonstrates continuities from the colonial period into the present time, both in village life and in the legal-administrative structure of the state. She argues that the continuing (post-)colonial character of the state turns acts classified as legally corrupt into acts of resistance against a distant and modern nation-state that does not recognize the structures, ties and networks of the people.

In Chapter 8, 'Making/unmaking governance', the first chapter of the third section, Marcus Gomes and Mário Alves examine the environmental impact of the global beef supply chain, the construction of resistance and the negotiation of environmentally sensitive governance of the supply chain. The chapter thus highlights the ways in which the global economic order has also provided space for transnational resistance through astute issue framing by organizations such as the global environmental NGO Greenpeace, parallel to the Brazilian state prosecutor's office (MPF) enforcement of national laws controlling deforestation.

In Chapter 9, Ariful Kabir and Raqib Chowdhury discuss the governance of education in Bangladesh. They examine the interplay between the Bangladeshi state, NGOs and international education development policy driven by neoliberal economic strategies of international institutions. They demonstrate how governance is intimately tied to ideas of national, secular and religious identities; sovereignty; neoliberalism and markets. Kabir and Chowdhury identify how a form of network governance is emerging between donor agencies, NGOs and the ruling political elite. A particular feature of neocolonial educational policy is the enlisting of NGOs to further a global neoliberal agenda, to break down resistance within the state and its educational sector, and to transform education in Bangladesh to prepare the national labour force for integration into the global economy. The chapter provides an interesting contrast to Chapter 8, demonstrating the diversity of positions that civil society organizations can take in transnational governance, ranging from the building of international campaigns to limit post-colonial countries' exploitation in global supply chains as in Gomes and Alves's study, to the instrumentalization of NGOs to further a neoliberal agenda as detailed by Kabir and Chowdhury.

In Chapter 10, Jonathan Murphy and Virpi Malin discuss the process of dialogue entailed in constitution building after a democratic revolution in Tunisia. The chapter identifies the difficulties encountered in articulating divergent visions of the state drawn from the multiplicity of influences and visions for society encountered within a post-colonial state. The chapter argues that Tunisians' capacity to overcome discursive blockages provides an example not only for other post-colonial states, but more generally for citizens attempting to redefine what role the contemporary state should play in the face of the global existential crisis of the neoliberal state.

In the final chapter, Nimruji Jammulamadaka and Biswatosh Saha trace the development of two anti-corporate protests in India – one successful, the other with limited success. Written in an autobiographical style, the chapter not only performs a comparative analysis of these protest movements to explain variation in outcomes, but also emphasizes the importance of researcher subjectivity in unearthing the peculiar character of such movements in the post-colonial state. It thus underscores this book's entreaty to overcome epistemic obstacles in understanding governance and management in post-colonial nation-states. The chapter draws attention to a continuing colonialism in the legislative system, and argues that anti-corporate protests are not just directed against transnational capital, but are significant contributions to state-building, through decolonizing the legal structures through which the nation-state operates. Ironically, it is the insertion of colonial difference into the legal structure during the founding moments of the post-colonial nation-state that enables present-day decolonization.

Notes

1 Names in alphabetical order. Both authors contributed equally.
2 As an imaginary and not a geography.
3 Income illegally obtained or not declared for tax purposes.

References

Akena, F. A. (2012). Critical analysis of the production of Western knowledge and its implications for Indigenous knowledge and decolonization. *Journal of Black Studies*, *43*(6), 599–619.

Alamgir, F. (2013). Conflicting regimes of legitimacy of the state: exploring rights-centric management. Paper presented at the 73rd Academy of Management Conference, Orlando.

Alatas, S. H. (2000). Intellectual imperialism: definition, traits, and problems. *Asian Journal of Social Science*, *28*(1), 23–45.

Alavi, H. (1972). The state in post-colonial societies Pakistan and Bangladesh. *New Left Review*, *74*, 59.

Appadurai, A. (2000). The grounds of the nation-state: identity, violence and territory. Nationalism and internationalism in the post–Cold War era, in Goldmann, K., Hannerz, U. and Westin, C. (Eds.), *Nationalism and internationalism in the post–Cold War era*. New York, Routledge, 129–143.

Arellano-Gault, D., Demortain, D., Rouillard, C. and Thoenig, J.C. (2013). Bringing public organization and organizing back in. *Organization Studies*, *34*, 145.

Bhabha, H. K. (2012). *The location of culture*. London, Routledge.

Bhattacharya, A. (2006). Role of government, in Dewan, S. M. (Ed.), *Corporate governance in public sector enterprises*. New Delhi, Dorling Kindersley, 39–60.

Birla, R. (2008). *Stages of capital: law, culture, and market governance in late colonial India*. Durham, NC, Duke University Press.

Boshoff, N. (2010). South–South research collaboration of countries in the Southern African Development Community (SADC). *Scientometrics*, *84*(2), 481–503.

Brush, S. B. (1993). Indigenous knowledge of biological resources and intellectual property rights: the role of anthropology. *American Anthropologist*, *95*(3), 653–671.

Chatterjee, P. (1986). *Nationalist thought and the colonial world: a derivative discourse*. London, Zed Books.

Clayton, A. (1998). *NGOs and decentralised government in Africa*. INTRAC. Oxford.

Cooke, B. and Alcadipani, R. (2015). Towards a global history of management education: the case of the Ford Foundation and the Sao Paulo School of Business Administration, Brazil. *Academy of Management Learning and Education*, *14*(4), 482–499.

Daulatzai, A. (2008). The discursive occupation of Afghanistan. *British Journal of Middle Eastern Studies*, *35*(3), 419–435.

Deshpande, S. (2003). *Contemporary India: a sociological view*. New Delhi, Penguin.

Edwards, M. and Hulme, D. (1996). Too close for comfort? The impact of official aid on nongovernmental organizations. *World Development*, 24(6), 961–973.

Englebert, P. (2000). Pre-colonial institutions, post-colonial states, and economic development in tropical Africa. *Political Research Quarterly*, 53(1), 7–36.

Environment Defense Fund USA. (1999). *The Chad–Cameroon oil and pipeline project: putting people and the environment at risk*. Washington, DC: Environment Defense Fund. www.edf.org/documents/728 ChadCameroon pipeline.pdf.

Escobar, A. (1995). *Encountering development: the making and unmaking of development*. Princeton, NJ, Princeton University Press.

Gervais, M. (1992). Les enjeux politiques des ajustements structurels au Niger. *Revue canadienne des études africaines*, 26, 2, 226–249.

Gingras, Y. and Mosbah-Natanson, S. (2010). Where are social sciences produced? *Europe*, 47(43.8), 46–51.

Hoen, E., Berger, J., Calmy, A. and Moon, S. (2011). Driving a decade of change: HIV/AIDS, patents and access to medicines for all. *Journal of International AIDS Society*, 2011(14), 15.

Hudock, A. C. (1999). *NGOs and civil society: development by proxy*. Cambridge, Polity.

Ibarra-Colado, E. (2006). Organization studies and epistemic coloniality in Latin America: thinking otherness from the margins. *Organization*, 13(4), 463–488.

Jammulamadaka, N. (2016). A postcolonial critique of Indian's management education scene, in Thakur, M & Babu R. (Eds.) *Management education in India*. Singapore, Springer, 23–42.

Kaviraj, S. (2009). The post-colonial state: the special case of India, in *Critical encounters: a forum of critical thought from the Global South*. https://criticalencounters.net/2009/01/19/the-post-colonial-state-sudipta-kaviraj/

Kudaisya, M. (2014). "The promise of partnership": Indian business, the state, and the Bombay plan of 1944. *Business History Review*, 88(1), 97–131.

Kumar, V. B. (2005). Postcolonial state: an overview. *The Indian Journal of Political Science*, 66(4) 935–954.

Lopez, L. E. (2008). Top-down and bottom-up: counterpoised visions of bilingual intercultural education in Latin America, in Hornberger, N. H. (Ed.). *Can schools save indigenous languages? Policy and practice on four continents*. London, Palgrave Macmillan, 42–65.

Mamdani, M. (1996). *Citizen and subject: contemporary Africa and the legacy of late colonialism*. Princeton, NJ, Princeton University Press.

Marens, R. (2008). Getting past the "government sucks" story: how government really matters. *Journal of Management Inquiry*, 17, 84.

Mignolo, W. (2012). *Local histories/global designs: coloniality, subaltern knowledges, and border thinking*. Princeton, NJ, Princeton University Press.

Murphy, J. and Zhu, J. (2012). Neo-colonialism in the academy? Anglo-American domination in management journals. *Organization*, 19, 915–927.

Nandy, A. (1989). *Intimate enemy*. Oxford, Oxford University Press.

Nkomo, S. M. (2006). Images of "African leadership and management" in organization studies: tensions, contradictions and revisions. Inaugural lecture presented at the University of South Africa, Pretoria, 7 March.

Nkomo, S. M. (2011). A postcolonial and anti-colonial reading of "African" leadership and management in organization studies: tensions, contradictions and possibilities. *Organization*, 18(3), 365–386.

Ntiri, D. W. (1993). Africa's educational dilemma: roadblocks to universal literacy for social integration and change. *International Review of Education, 39*(5), 357–372.

Nygren, A., (1999). Local knowledge in the environment–development discourse: from dichotomies to situated knowledges. *Critique of Anthropology, 19*(3), 267–288.

Pearce, J. L. (2001). How we can learn how governments matter to management and organizations. *Journal of Management Inquiry, 10,* 103–112.

Perrow, C. B. (1970). *Organizational analysis: a sociological view.* Stamford, CT, Wadsworth Publishing.

Pilkington, E. (2009). Shell pays out $15.5m over Saro-Wiwa killing. *The Guardian,* 8 June 2009, accessed at www.theguardian.com/world/2009/jun/08/nigeria-usa on 20 November 2016.

Prasad, A. (2015). Toward decolonizing modern Western structures of knowledge, in Prasad, A., Prasad, P., Mills, A. J. and Mills, J. H. (Eds.), *The Routledge companion to critical management studies.* London, Routledge, 161–199.

Ruggie, J. G. (1982). International regimes, transactions, and change: embedded liberalism in the postwar economic order. *International Organization, 36*(2), 379–415.

Selznick, P. (1949). *TVA and the grass roots: a study of politics and organization* (Vol. 3). Berkeley, University of California Press.

Sikka, P. (2001). Accounting for human rights: the challenge of globalization and foreign investment agreements. *Critical Perspectives on Accounting, 22,* 811–827.

Smith, J. (2012). The GDP illusion: value added versus value capture. *Monthly Review, 64*(3), 97–114.

waThiong'o, Ngugi (1987). *Decolonising the mind.* Harare, ZPH.

Weick, K. E., Sutcliffe, K. M. and Obstfeld, D. (2005). Organizing and the process of sensemaking. *Organization Science, 16*(4), 409–421.

Williamson, J. (2000). What should the World Bank think about the Washington Consensus? *The World Bank Research Observer, 15*(2), 251–264.

World Bank. (2000). *Overview of rural decentralisation in India.* Washington, DC, World Bank.

Part I

Knowledge struggles

2 Corruption's other scene

The politics of corruption in South Africa

Ivor Chipkin

Introduction

The term 'state capture' is suddenly widespread in political and social commentary in and on South Africa. It has become the description of choice in relation to reports that the Gupta brothers, businessmen associated with the South African president, Jacob Zuma, and his family, influenced the appointment of cabinet ministers and senior officials and also benefitted from huge state tenders (Munusamy, 1 June 2016, 6 June 2016; Thamm, 10 March 2016, 16 March 2016, 7 April 2016, 8 July 2016). 'State capture' is also invoked to discuss the influence of elements of 'white capital' on government in general and more particularly of certain families, notably the Kebble and Rupert families, amongst others (Cronin, 13 April 2016; Shivambu, 24 March 2016). Migrating from economics, the expression describes an especially severe form of corruption. Whereas traditional definitions of corruption focus on acts of illegality and/or the breaking of rules by politicians or officials in order to subvert the public good in favour of private interests, 'state capture' occurs when the rule-making process is itself 'captured'. The World Bank, for example, in a report that likely popularised the expression, defined it as occurring when state institutions, potentially including the executive, state ministries, agencies, the judiciary and the legislature, regulate their business to favour private interests. In this sense, 'state capture' is different from traditional 'corruption' in that many of its activities may be legal. It is regarded as a form of corruption, nonetheless, because private influence is exercised illicitly in public affairs, subverting and even replacing transparent and legitimate forms of intermediation.

What 'state capture' and 'corruption' have in common as analytical terms is a certain concept of the state. Frequently, when corruption is discussed in this regard, it is understood as an especially important vehicle for elite accumulation and class (Bayart, 1993). The purchase of this analysis is deemed very wide, explaining, *inter alia*, why, relative to other parts of Europe, Italy and Spain are so much more corrupt (della Porta and Vannucci, 1999; Heywood, 1997); why corruption persists in Mexico, Brazil, Venezuela and Argentina (Weyland, 1998) and why there is corruption in the United States (Galbraith, 2005). In South Africa, such an approach informs studies of how the state has become a vehicle for 'class formation' (Von Holdt, 2010; Von Holdt and Murphy, 2007), for arguments about the emergence of political elites (Netshitenzhe, 2012) and about analyses of 'service delivery protests' (Von Holdt, 2011). In all these cases, the focus is on the struggles over who can get hold of the instruments and resources of the state and use them for their own purposes.

In the tradition of comparative, historical sociology inspired by Theda Skocpol and Peter Hall, where the task is to understand why some economic or political practices take root in certain environments and not in others, corruption is frequently given as an answer for why some countries perform poorly economically. For example, more and more economists attribute economic failure or poor economic performance in countries to corruption. It is not so much that public officials do not know what the right policies or interventions are, the argument goes, but that policies are distorted to favour the personal interests of politicians, legislators and/or bureaucrats (Coolidge and Rose-Ackerman, 1997; Grossman and Helpman, 1994). Corruption, on these terms, is said to happen when politicians and officials lose sight of the public interest or public good and serve their own narrow needs and desires.

The problem with such approaches is that they treat corruption as devoid of politics. I do not mean that these scholars write as if corruption is not about the pursuit of interests and the exercise of power. They do precisely that, often very well. They frequently obscure, however, that corruption has a politics that is also about virtue in politics and about the proper organisation of the state. In other words, corruption has a politics *qua* ideology. In this regard, the moralising tone of the term ('corruption!') and what is progressive is important. This chapter will argue that corruption is not the sign simply of an absence, like ethics in conduct of government affairs or of 'good governance', but also of a presence: different ideologies (ideas and practices) of the state.

I will make this argument by considering the case of South Africa. We will see that the struggle against corruption in South Africa is really a struggle about the form of the state. In this sense the term names a field of ideological contestation. On one side are proponents of a liberal idea of the state. On the other are those who defend *patronage* in the name of 'state transformation' or the 'theory of national democratic revolution'. We will see that it is difficult to appreciate the tenacity of corruption in South Africa and elsewhere unless we appreciate that corrupt practices are also discursive practices, that is, that they express political-ideological commitments.

The state of corruption in South Africa

In 2015, civil society organisations and trade unions launched a 'Unite Against Corruption' campaign, which organised under the slogan that R700 billion (roughly $46 billion at 2016 exchange rates) had been lost to corruption since 1994. Apparently, this represented 20 per cent of the country's GDP over 20 years. The figure has a tortuous history, but likely originates in a 2006 handbook by Transparency International that estimated that 'between 10% and 25%, and in some cases as high as 40 to 50%' of the country's procurement budget is lost to corruption (Africa Check, 30 September 2015). Africa Check, a non-governmental organisation that promotes accuracy in journalism, notes that the report never mentioned South Africa specifically, nor did the statistic refer to corruption as a percentage of GDP. Nonetheless, the figure of R700 billion, or R25 billion per annum) stuck in the public discourse. It has been mentioned by officials from the National Treasury and even by officials from one of South Africa's anti-corruption agencies, the Special Investigating Unit (SIU). Yet there is no empirical basis for the figure other than generalised speculation about what middlemen demand of a contract's value. Africa Check concluded that the figure was a 'thumbsuck', an arbitrary guess (30 September 2015).

The idea that between R25 and R30 billion has been lost to corruption each year since 1994 more likely reflects public sentiment than actual loss. Transparency International, in its global Corruption Perception Index (CPI) for 2013, revealed that South Africa had dropped 29 places since 2001. South Africa is currently ranked number 61 out of 168 countries.[1] A number of local surveys also show that the public has the perception of high levels of corruption. The Human Sciences Research Council found in 2012 that the vast majority of those surveyed (91 per cent) believed that corruption was a serious problem in South Africa (HSRC, 2012). Whereas only 9 per cent of respondents in 2003 believed that corruption was in the top three of South Africa's most serious challenges, by 2011, this number had grown to 26 per cent.

Attempts in South Africa to arrive at hard numbers for corruption usually draw on reports of the Auditor-General South Africa (AGSA), an independent constitutional entity tasked with monitoring and reporting on the proper management of public money. Between 2010/11 and 2014/15, the AG found that 'irregular' expenditure in national and provincial departments had increased from more than R16.5 billion to R25.7 billion, a jump of 36 per cent in four years. Unauthorised expenditure had come down, as had fruitless and wasteful expenditure. Irregular expenditure in local governments reached R11.4 billion in 2014/2015. In the whole of government (excluding state-owned enterprises), the total figure for irregular expenditure in 2014/2015 stood at more than R37 billion.

The category of irregular expenditure is frequently treated as a proxy category for corruption because it indicates noncompliance with government processes or regulations, where the assumption is that deviations are for corrupt purposes. So a dramatic increase in this area is reported as corruption out of control. This is not necessarily the case, however. As the work of the Public Affairs Research Institute (PARI) frequently shows, noncompliance has many causes, including that operational processes are poorly designed and/or that personnel are not adequately trained on how to follow them (2012). Nonetheless, it is fair to assume that some of this represents abuse of office for private gain – though it is difficult to know how much.

One of South Africa's largest law firms reports that on the basis of documented fraud and malfeasance cases presented to the parliament and those reported by the Public Service Commission, more than R1 billion was lost in 2011/12, an increase from R130 million in 2006/07. It is impossible to generalise from these figures because they are only based on reported cases (Tamukamoyo and Mofana, 2013). Even if the figure is 1,000 per cent higher, it would still mean that less than a third of irregular expenditure is for corrupt purposes. If it is difficult to gauge accurately the scale of corruption in South Africa, it is likely that the problem is smaller than often reported. We will see, however, that the discourse on corruption betrays a real concern about the loss of autonomy of public administrations.

The definition of corruption

As an idea, 'corruption' has a varied conceptual history. Contemporary definitions of the term are a late eighteenth-century innovation. If we use Montesquieu to stand in for the 'classical' period, then corruption, on his terms, is a feature of any polity (democratic, aristocratic, monarchic or despotic) when its leaders fail to act on the basis of its core or foundational principles (Buchan and Hill, 2007). This sense finds its way into contemporary private and public conversations, though it remains at a distance to 'modern' definitions of the term.[2]

It is in the late eighteenth-century work of Edmund Burke and Adam Smith that corruption came to be associated with specific activities that threatened to subvert the *integrity of public office* (especially bribery, graft and electoral fraud) (Buchan and Hill, 2007). This is the sense in which it continues to be defined in, for example, international charters, national legislations and, in particular, South African law (see, for example, the UNDP's Corruption and Good Governance report of 1997, the various Corruption Barometers by Transparency International and South Africa's Prevention and Combating of Corrupt Activities Act, 2004). Typically, definitions of corruption identify an act of private abuse or private misuse or private appropriation at the heart of the phenomenon of corruption. Drawing on J. S. Nye's formative work, the World Bank, for example, defines corruption as the 'abuse of public office for private gain' (2006). This phraseology carries with it a sense of misuse of office with violent or injurious intent (think of spousal abuse, abuse of alcohol). Nye's own phraseology was more subtle, allowing a broader range of activities to be included in the notion of corruption. He refers not to 'abuse', but to 'deviation from the formal duties of public role for private gain' (1967, p. 419). The subtlety is important because it brings into play practices of noncompliance with internal rules and procedures where malicious intent may be absent. Brooks discusses it in similar terms: the 'misperformance or neglect of a recognised duty or the unwarranted exercise of power, with the motive of gaining some advantage, more or less personal' (1910, p. 46).

Burke and Smith would have no difficulty recognising the terms of the current debate about corruption; for, in a basic sense we remain, or are rather once again, within their conceptual universe – more than 200 years later. Central to their understanding of corruption was a distinction between *private* interests and *public* duties. This distinction would soon become the hallmark of liberal thinking.[3] The renewed interest in corruption, coming as it does at the end of the Soviet period,[4] reflects the ascendancy of liberalism as an economic ideology as much as a *constitutional framework*. Indeed, this last aspect, though often overlooked, is more important. Modern definitions of corruption are not necessarily tied to liberal or neoliberal economic policy prescriptions, but they are closely tied to a *liberal conception of the state*.

The neutral state

A distinctive feature of the liberal idea of the state is its emphasis on *neutrality* – that the state should provide a neutral framework within which different conceptions of the good life can be pursued (Galston, 1991; Kymlicka, 1989; Raz, 1986). Weber's (1966) distinctive contribution to liberalism was to conceptualise it as a form of state and not simply as a political ideology or political system. We should see the distinction between government and bureaucracy as an important theoretical development in this regard. It makes it possible, that is, to distinguish hermeneutically between the political system and the administrative system, so that governments that are not liberal politically (including monarchies and dictatorships) may have liberal elements at the level of their administrations.

Governments, especially in a liberal democracy, represent particular interests and make claims about the content and the conditions of the good life. That is their prerogative. Yet the state in the form of the bureaucracy does not make such claims; it is supposed to implement the policies and programmes of the government of the day. This is the sense in which the state is neutral.

Weber understood that such neutrality was always an ideal and that in practice bureaucrats had a tendency to develop their own interests. On these terms, corruption refers to:

- any kind of bias or partisanship that bureaucrats practise either towards themselves (Weber's major concern) or to a social class or group (Burke's objection),
- any deviation in the work of bureaucrats from the policies and programmes of the government of the day.

Nonetheless, central to Weber's conception of bureaucracy is that the state can be organised in such a way that it 1) more or less operates neutrally *vis-à-vis* any social class or group of individuals and 2) that it can become a reliable instrument for whoever is in government. Neutrality, on Weber's terms, depended on the following design elements: loyalty to rules/office, a rule-bound and routinized decision-making structure, recruitment of officials through a universal entrance exam, training and incentives in the forms of career development, salaries and status and a professional *esprit de corps*.

What we call bureaucracy today can, therefore, be understood as a set of techniques of government to reduce the opportunities for officials to pursue their own interests. They substituted for practices based on bio-power. In the Ottoman Empire, that is, civil servants were often European slaves, captured in war.

Their lack of pedigree in Ottoman society made it nearly impossible for them to pursue wealth and status by marriage into powerful dynasties. Similarly, across Asia, from China to Korea to Vietnam, various dynasties used eunuchs in the royal household as officials. So too did Indian sultanates (Finer, 1997).

Therein lies the 'secret' of meritocratic recruitment (and other bureaucratic measures). It goes some way to attract smart and qualified officials for their posts in government, but that is not its primary function. The universal entrance exam disrupts recruitment through personalistic networks (of class, of kinship, of political party). In this regard its purpose is transcendental: to create the conditions for a neutral civil service.

The adoption of measures in European states in the late nineteenth century transformed their public administrations. Napoleon disrupted ancient regime practices by throwing appointments to the civil administration 'open to the talents'. Drawing on Jesuit translations of Confucian texts, Prussian jurisprudential scholars like St Justi introduced such principles into the design of the German administrative practice of cameralism (Lee, 2013). After the Trevelyan reforms of the 1850s, Britain similarly made the holding of public office dependent on suitable merit, rather than on aristocratic breeding. Rubenstein discusses this as the slow shift from what he calls the 'Old Corruption' to modern bureaucracy in Great Britain (1983). As these measures were introduced in England through the nineteenth century, the proportion of the rich owing their revenue to state offices dropped dramatically (Rubinstein, 1983, pp. 73–74). We will see shortly that the twentieth-century 'developmental states' too have incorporated some of these features in their administrative designs.

A partisan state

For most of the twentieth century, however, the idea that the bureaucracy could be neutral relative to dominant social groups or classes was rejected out of hand. The neutrality of the civil service relative to political authority was tackled head-on in the months after Russia's February Revolution in 1917. Lenin's pamphlet *State and Revolution* set the terms for much writing and political activity on the left for the past century (Wright, 1983, p. 195). Erik-Olin Wright summarises the debate thus:

> Should the state be considered an essentially neutral apparatus that merely needs to be 'captured' by a working-class socialist political party for it to serve the interests of the working class, or is the apparatus of the state in a capitalist society a distinctively capitalist apparatus that cannot possibly be 'used' by the working class, and as a result, must be destroyed and replaced by a radically different form of the state?
>
> (1983, p. 195).

Lenin provided an emphatic answer. The state must be smashed and a new kind of apparatus built. A similar question posed itself in anti-colonial movements.

Could liberation groups seize power and use the colonial-era civil administration to serve the interests of formerly colonised populations? In South Africa, a Leninist view of the state prevailed in the anti-apartheid movement. The African National Congress argued that not only had successive National Party governments implemented racist laws and policies, but that the very structure of the state itself worked to advance white interests. In language reminiscent of Lenin's, the ANC declared in *The State, Property Relations and Social Transformation* document of 1998 that:

> We [the National Liberation Movement] have inherited a state which was illegitimate and structured to serve the interests of a white minority. [. . .] To attain all these and other objectives, it became the seedbed of corruption and criminal activity both within the country and abroad. [. . .] The NLM cannot therefore lay hands on the apartheid state machinery and hope to use it to realise its aims. The apartheid state has to be destroyed in a process of fundamental transformation. The new state should be, by definition, the antithesis of the apartheid state.
>
> (1998)

Underpinning this Leninist discourse was a nationalist politics that, especially under the influence of Thabo Mbeki, conflated the general interest with the policies of the ANC. Election majorities since 1994 served merely to confirm what was believed to be true *a priori*, that the organisation was the authentic representative of the 'people' (see Chipkin, 1997, 2015). As we will see shortly, the purpose of state transformation has not been to create a *neutral* state. The purpose has been to bring the state under the political direction of the party. What is striking is just how far the ANC government went to politicise the public administration.

Public sector reform in South Africa: 1994–2000

The apartheid-era bureaucracy was regarded as unfit to carry out the orders of the democratic government. In the first place, it was staffed at senior levels by largely white, Afrikaans-speaking men – the very people responsible for implementing the racist programmes of the former government (Picard, 2005, p. 302). Transformation of the state thus required 'extending the power of the NLM over all levers of power: the army, the police, the bureaucracy, intelligence structures, the judiciary, parastatals, and agencies such as regulatory bodies, the public broadcaster, the Central Bank and so on' (ANC, 1998). At stake was a massive effort to change the racial profile of the post-apartheid administration.

In 1994, senior personnel in state departments were overwhelmingly white and male, 94 per cent and 95 per cent, respectively. However, by September 2011, the racial composition of the administration had almost been reversed. According to the most recent report of the Department of Public Service and Administration (DPSA), of the 1,327,548 officials in national and provincial departments (excluding local government), 760,501 (57.29 per cent) were female, while 567,047 (42.71 per cent) were male. Africans now make up 1,050,692 (79.15 per cent) of positions, Coloureds count for 110,929 people (8.35 per cent) and Asians a further 43,187 (3.25 per cent). White officials now represent less than 10 per cent of public servants (122,740) (DPSA, 2013, p. 32). These figures do not include municipalities, where the changes are no less dramatic.

Affirmative action and demographic change in the public service were accompanied by only rudimentary measures to recruit on the basis of merit. Indeed, the African National Congress has gone very far in the other direction. The idea of introducing a universal entrance exam for would-be public servants was mooted shortly after 1994, but only in the context of dismissing it. The 1997 Green Paper on Employment, for example, in comparing 'best practice' recruitment practices concluded that 'foreign countries' were 'flexible' in their recruitment instruments, preferring principles of fairness, reliability and objectivity to those of merit or experience (Green Paper, 1997: 14.2.1, 14.3.1).[5] In a *coup de grace* for the idea of an entrance exam, the DPSA argued that 'equality of opportunity [does] not give recognition to the inequalities of South Africa's educational system nor [does it] take into account past racial barriers to employment opportunities' (DPSA, 2013: 14.3.2).

In the end, South Africa opted for an 'open career system' where appointments and promotions were advertised inside and, especially, outside the public service. The drift to a political mode of recruitment did not stop there, however. Responsibility for recruitment was taken away from statutory bodies (the Public Service Commission, for example) and/or from the human resource units in government departments. Instead it was handed over to ministers and their provincial government equivalents. It is worth pausing here to consider this more closely. It constitutes a dramatic choice that does not simply follow from the desire to expedite affirmative action in the post-apartheid public service.

South Africa has a system of government with strong federal features. In addition to the national government, the country's nine provinces have their own elected governments made up of a premier and an executive committee – the name of the provincial cabinet. Section 3(7) of the Public Service Act assigns to ministers at the national level and members of the executive committees (MECs) – provincial cabinet ministers – the *power of appointment* (Public Service Commission, p. 29).[6] This responsibility is sometimes delegated by ministers or MECs to senior officials in their departments, but frequently it is not, creating what the Presidential Review Commission and later the National Development Plan called tensions in the 'political-administrative interface'. The PRC meant by this a conflictual situation arising from the fact that senior officials, especially directors-general and superintendent generals and heads of departments who were responsible for operationalising policy, could not recruit staff in terms of their plans – unless this power was delegated to them by the responsible minister or MEC. This is not always forthcoming. This arrangement is, actually, a structural constraint on bureaucratisation in government, by privileging political calculations in the making of appointments and granting promotions over professional and administrative considerations.

Consider the recruitment process itself. The process starts with the creation of a post. Each post or group of posts must include a job description and a job title that explains its main objectives, what skills are required to perform it and what the holder of such a post will need to achieve in order to be promoted (PSC, 2014, p. 27). These are technical tasks that were performed historically by the Public Service Commission together with the administrative heads of the relevant departments and in line with the needs and mandate of the department itself. Yet in post-apartheid South Africa, 'discretion for setting the job specifications rests with the relevant minister' (PSC, 2014, p. 27). The job is then advertised and a selection panel is assembled to evaluate shortlisted candidates. Candidates do not sit for an exam, though for senior appointments they have to undertake a 'competency assessment'. Instead, a selection committee interviews them. The 1998 report of the Presidential Review Commission into the public service described the process in the following unflattering terms:

> The overall impression [. . .] was that hardly any good practice guidelines exist to assist selection panel members with the shortlisting and interviewing processes. [. . .] Similarly no guidelines exist for the selection of panel members in any of the departments that were surveyed. In many cases panel members seem to be selected at the last minute without being given much information about the nature of the job. [. . .] Scoring systems are generally vague and unclear and it is not clear how decisions are reached. Similarly, guidelines on the use of referees are vague. [. . .] Selection decisions often seem to be made on the basis of the interview alone and *without a clear linkage to the requirements of the job*.
> (Presidential Review Commission, 4.4.6.3) (emphasis added)

There are thousands of selection committees across the public service (PSC, 2014, pp. 12–13). Given, furthermore, that such committees are designed to maximise political discretion in appointments and that they rely on subjective considerations, they have resulted in tremendous unevenness in the quality of appointments. Frequently, the Public Service Commission notes, people are appointed without the skills, knowledge or experience to do their jobs (PSC, 2014, p. 13).

Taken together, political discretion, not simply in the recruitment process, but in the very design of posts, coupled with the absence of an entrance examination or career advancement on the basis of subject-related tests, means that the public service after 1994 has been organised with a view to reduce its administrative autonomy as much as possible.

In 2014, the Public Service Commission made a very gentle bid to reclaim some of its former glory. As the Presidential Review Commission of 1998 noted, bodies like the PSC exist essentially to 'protect and advance the principle of merit' (PRC, 1998, p. 2.5.5). That such a principle had become 'politically and emotionally loaded' after 1994 meant that the PSC in South Africa had lost its *raison d'etre*. Indeed, the Presidential Review Commission was at pains to determine what role it could play in the new system. The PSC itself made a savvy bid for relevance. It compared South Africa's recruitment process with those of other 'developmental' states to affirm the value of meritocratic selection. The ANC government has since the late 1990s described itself as a 'developmental state' in terms of its economic policies and also in terms of its international relations. The PSC highlighted four major differences:

- 'Appointments are not made on the basis of political and other primordial considerations' (PSC, 2014, p. 22).
- 'Top managers are technocrats appointed from within the public service' (PSC, 2014, p. 23). Even in countries like China and Singapore, where civil servants are 'cadres', that is, members of the ruling party, the PSC insists that they are nonetheless appointed on the basis of qualification and the ability to do the job (PSC, 2014, p. 22).
- 'Educational qualification is a crucial factor for entrance into the bureaucracy' (PSC, 2014, p. 24). It notes that 92 per cent of public servants in China had a four-year degree and most (60 per cent) had a master's degree. Even in Brazil, 50 per cent of officials were university graduates. In South Africa, the PSC lamented, only 3 per cent of officials had a basic degree or diploma.
- 'Merit is achieved through open, transparent and competitive examinations' (PSC, 2014, p. 24).

Noting that the public service was today largely representative, the Commission wondered aloud if it was not time to return to a 'career system' where appointments were made largely from within the public service in and through a process run by the PSC itself. It was not so much that political appointments in civil administrations are uncommon – they are. Elsewhere, including the United States or even China and Singapore, they are restricted to specific positions[7] and are still normally subject to competitive and meritocratic evaluations. What the PSC was pointing to was that in South Africa, a political as opposed to a bureaucratic logic permeated the entire system indiscriminately.

In particular, the PSC recommended that responsibility for advertising jobs be taken back from what it termed the Executive Authority (ministers and MECs) and be lodged with heads of departments and that internal candidates be considered before advertising the job externally. It also proposed that candidates be considered for promotion only after they had served an adequate amount of time at their current level and that their suitability be assessed through a grade exam. Most dramatically, the PSC raised the possibility of recruiting middle managers (feeders to senior positions) via an entrance examination. As a sign of just how controversial such an idea was, the PSC immediately offered all sorts of caveats, including that there were instances when a political appointment process was advisable. The Commission's gentle attempt to nudge South Africa away from an 'open bureaucracy' was like a cry in the wilderness (PARI, 2014, p. 47).[8]

Battalions of revolutionaries

In 1997, Nelson Mandela gave the final address to the ANC's fiftieth national conference in Mafikeng. He had just stepped down as president of the ANC in favour of Thabo Mbeki. In addition, Jacob Zuma was elected deputy president. They would soon after go on to become president and deputy president of the country, respectively. In 2005, Mbeki fired Zuma for corruption, triggering a storm of events that would ultimately destroy his presidency, while propelling his nemesis into the seat of power. Still, in December 1997, it was too soon to anticipate how terribly this arrangement would come apart.

These events have tended to overshadow the significance of the conference for another reason. It marked the formal launch of the ANC's policy of 'cadre deployment'.

The expression had been part of the ANC's vocabulary at least since 1985, when it was used to refer to the discipline of members in relation to the struggle against apartheid. In 1996, Joel Netshitenzhe, a key advisor to Mbeki who would soon after head up the policy and advisory unit in the presidency, recast it in relation to the exercise of state power. Writing in the ANC's internal journal, *Umrabulo*, Netshitenzhe suggested that 'deployment' of ANC cadres to all 'centres of power', including the economy, education, sports, arts and the media, be carried out so as to secure ANC control and hegemony. The document urged the ANC to set up a database of cadres and their skills so that their deployment could be more organised. It also suggested that the first accountability of ANC members should be to the party. Further, the document stated: 'We must have a clear understanding of the system of supervision and decision-direction [. . .] to ensure that our army of cadres discharge their responsibilities in accordance with decisions which the movement has made' (Netshitenzhe, 1996, pp. 4–6).

The final report to the fiftieth national conference explained why this was necessary. 'We have experienced serious resistance to the transformation of the public service, with *representatives of the old order* using all means in their power to ensure that they remain in dominant positions. Some among these owe no loyalty to the new constitutional and political order nor to the government of the day, and have *no intention to implement our government's programmes* aimed at reconstruction and development' (ANC, 1997, Report of the 50th Conference) (emphasis added).

This 'counter-revolutionary network', it continued, was based in the public administration and was engaged in 'disruptive actions', including the 'weakening and incapacitation of state machinery' and the 'theft of public assets, arms and ammunitions'. In this context, the ANC proposed deploying 'battalions of revolutionaries' to 'local, provincial and national legislatures and governments, [to] ANC structures at all these levels, [to] the public service and the economy' (ANC, 1997, Report of the 50th Conference).

This *political logic* goes some way to explain features of the South African public service as discussed earlier. In particular, a model of recruitment that privileged political considerations over administrative ones in the selection process served, as Geraldine Fraser-Moloketi, the minister of public service and administration in the Mbeki cabinet, put it, to 'establish control over the bureaucracy and to inculcate a new value system and philosophy, in tune with the agenda of the ruling party' (Fraser-Moleketi, 2006, p. 20).

Such an explanation does not go all the way in explaining the rejection of bureaucratic modes of government, however. Another logic imposed itself at this time, whose origin and vocabulary came not from within the ANC, but from the emerging field of 'public management'.

Neoliberalism and neutrality

Within only a few years of the first democratic election, there was growing concern in parts of government that something was terribly wrong in the public service. The 1998 Presidential Review of the Public Service, for example, begins awkwardly that 'to a considerable extent [. . .] the essential ingredients of good governance are still missing, including the development of an effective culture of democratic governance' (PRC: 1.5).[9] The report itself is a wide-ranging document that considers structures and functions within the public service, human resources management and development, financial management and planning and information management, systems and technology. Its first recommendation was that 'radical change' was needed in respect of 'creating a professional public service, under professional leadership and within a professional ethos' (PRC: 7.2.1.1).

In particular, the commission worried about what it called 'confusion' at the 'political-administrative interface'. The problem was that the responsibilities of ministers and MECs on one hand and senior officials on the other were not clearly defined or delineated. 'If ministers and MECs act as managers, involving themselves in details of administration, and if senior officials act as politicians, involving themselves in political processes outside their departments, this is to the detriment of their proper and necessary roles,' the Commission suggested somewhat soberly (PRC: 2.1.6). The report is noticeably vague about what it means by political overstretch and, unlike what the Public Service Commission will later recommend, says nothing about political control of the recruitment process. The implication is that a misunderstanding currently exists between politicians and officials about the limits of their respective roles. Yet as we have seen earlier, there was no such 'misunderstanding' in the ANC or in the administration of Thabo Mbeki. With the exception of the economic institutions (the Reserve Bank, the National Treasury and the South African Revenue Service (SARS)), the intention was to politicise the administration through 'cadre deployment'. It is hardly surprising, therefore, that the same concern about the 'political-administrative interface' was raised 15 years later in the National Development Plan.

The Presidential Review came up with numerous recommendations about how to improve the performance of the public service, including establishing a 'centre of government' to monitor and coordinate between departments and to ensure that they were following through on cabinet decisions (PRC: 7.2.1.4). It further recommended a dramatic 'rightsizing' of the public service, noting that it was unnecessarily large and risked consuming more and more of government revenue (PRC: 7.2.1.3).[10] The centrepiece of the review's proposals, at least as it was interpreted by the Department of Public Service and Administration (DPSA), was for what it called a 'Professional Management Corps" (PRC: 7.2.1.10). The proposal was to:

- move away from the traditional, career-based model of the public service in favour of contract-based employment for the entire management echelon;
- to develop all-round managers with experience in a range of portfolios, by creating opportunities for greater mobility;
- to develop a managerial *esprit de corps* through joint workshops and training opportunities.

It is possible that the PRC intended that such a *corps* would act neutrally in relation to executive authority, though the term is not used once in the whole document. What it definitely did intend was a reform away from bureaucratic practices. Therein lay part of its appeal.

The DPSA acted quickly to implement the PRC's recommendation. It established the Baskin Commission in 2000 to determine what it might involve and then in 2001 launched the Senior Management Service (SMS) – its name for the 'professional management corps'. The move to *public management* in South Africa has an uncanny history, which I have explored elsewhere (Chipkin and Lipietz, 2012). For the moment it is only necessary to say that it has its origin in the Thatcherite and post-Thatcherite (Tony Blair's Third Way) critique of the welfare state. By the time of South Africa's transition to democracy a cluster of metaphors had come to dominate in the field of public administration. Patrick FitzGerald and Anne McClennan, both influential at the time, give a sense of the mood in South Africa:

> Public administration teaching and theory in South Africa is experiencing a paradigm shift. There is an attempt to move away from a descriptive, academic approach which emphasises processes and procedures to a *value-oriented public management approach*.
> (FitzGerald and McLennan, 1991, p. 8) (emphasis added)

At stake was a critique of 'bureaucracy' as an organisational form. Geraldine Fraser-Moleketi completed her master's degree whilst in political office. In her thesis, bureaucracies are said to be wasteful and inefficient. Ultimately, they are 'out of date' – a term used frequently in the academic and policy literature at the time as well. In contrast, 'public managers' are freed up from 'red tape'. They are innovative and enterprising. They are focused on outputs and outcomes, rather than on following rules. In summary, public management is 'modern' (Fraser-Moleketi, 2006).

Ultimately, the creation of the senior management service was associated with a host of measures to *dis-embed* senior officials from routine and rule-based practices and to give them discretion over as wide-ranging a set of activities as strategizing how best to discharge the department's function (in South African parlance, the design of the 'service delivery model'), determining the structure of their own departments and financial management. The Public Finance Management Act (PFMA), passed in 1999 to regulate financial affairs in the national government and in provincial governments, for example, wanted to 'let managers manage' by giving heads of departments wide discretion over spending (PFMA: chapter 5, S36(a), S38). Senior managers were also to be highly paid. Indeed, the International Monetary Fund (IMF) reports that today, South African public servants are amongst the best remunerated in the developing world (2016, p. 76). Yet the crucial element in this mix, recruitment of staff, remained a political prerogative, creating, as we have seen, conflict in the 'political–administrative' interface.

It is not hard to see why the idea of a senior management service was approved quickly in the cabinet. It was an attractive vehicle through which the ANC government could drive political control of the administration. What is more, it resonated with international 'best practice'. Political control, in other words, did not have to come at the expense of efficiency and effectiveness. So it seemed, anyway. Originally intended to have no more than 3,000 members, it already had 7,283 people by 2005, most of them in national departments (DPSA, 2006, p. 37). Although there are no published figures about 'cadre deployment' in South Africa, it is likely that most ANC officials are placed at this level.

Decentralisation

If public management was the vehicle through which regions of the public service were politicised, decentralisation, especially in the procurement space, provided a way of using the state to take forward the project of economic transformation.

At least since 1998, the South African government has been interested in using government resources to create a class of black capitalists. Let us follow the logic of the Mbeki presidency. I am drawing again on *State, Property Relations and Social Transformation*, an important theoretical intervention from this period. One of the tasks of the ANC, it argues, is to change property relations in South Africa, including patterns of ownership, of investment and of procurement. How can this be done when capital is held overwhelmingly in white hands? The solution is deemed to lie in the creation of a black capitalist class; one created essentially through government procurement practices and regulatory interventions requiring minimum quota for black equity in private (white) firms.

> In a systematic way, the NDR has to ensure that ownership of private capital at all [. . .] levels [. . .] is not defined in racial terms. Thus the new state – in its procurement policy, its programme of restructuring state assets, [its] utilisation of instruments of empowerment, pressure and other measures – promotes the emergence of *a black capitalist class.*
>
> (ANC, 1998) (emphasis added)

In this way, a government that worked by contracting out its tasks to private companies could leverage its procurement budget to advance the project of economic transformation.

The Public Affairs Research Institute (PARI) has done leading-edge work on procurement in South Africa, and I will draw here on its research.[11]

Historically, the PARI notes, the system of procurement in South Africa was highly centralised. Prior to 1994, various South African governments followed the international norm in establishing and running a state tender board. In addition, the then four provinces had their own provincial tender boards. The process of decentralisation would proceed in earnest after 2003. The various tender boards were abolished and the Framework for Supply Chain Management was published as part of the regulations for the PFMA. Responsibility for procurement was devolved down to the departmental level. We have already seen that in terms of the PFMA, departmental heads became 'accounting officers' with wide financial discretion, including responsibility for the procurement of goods and services. The implementation of the new system has been associated with two major developments:

Firstly, notes the PARI report, 'procurement has become one of the largest tasks, arguably the single largest function, of government departments' (PARI, 2014, p. 34). Today the estimated expenditure by government departments on goods and services is about R500 billion ($34 billion), more than half of national expenditure (after debt repayments). In other words, the lion's share of government's day-to-day responsibilities are outsourced to third-party service providers, usually private companies.

Secondly, 'the procurement of goods and services takes place through a system that is highly fragmented and decentralized. In some cases, the very outsourcing function is itself outsourced' (PARI, 2014, p. 34). The result is that in South Africa today, 'there are literally tens of thousands of sites and locations where tenders are issued and awarded and where contracts are managed for the performance of all manner of services and functions' (PARI, 2014, p. 34).

The extent of decentralisation is extraordinary relative to South Africa's past. Furthermore, the procurement system is widely held responsible for massive unevenness in the performance of government units – so much depends on how well departments can select and manage contractors – and for corruption in government. Until recently, for example, public servants could themselves tender for government contracts. The trouble, claimed the Public Service Commission in 2010, was that 'while some of these contracts might have been awarded fairly, the scale of the revelations [. . .] suggests that there was much impropriety, and subsequently damage to 'the public trust' (PSC, 2010, p. 9). 'This begs the question', the Commission continued, 'should public servants or their spouses be allowed to do business with government?' (PSC, 2010, p. 9). Its answer: yes. What mattered for the Commission was that contracts were awarded according to procedure.

This surprising answer reflected the political mood. As much as the move to supply chain management followed from the supposed efficiency gains of decentralisation, this major concession to the market in the performance of government affairs had another *raison d'etre* as well. It was an opportunity to engineer the government to serve the political project of the day, black economic empowerment.

Things fall apart

What we have seen is the coincidence of two reform logics, the first political and the second managerial, coming together, sometimes by chance and sometimes by design, to weaken and to block the bureaucratic organisation of the post-apartheid state. That is, the ANC's ideology of the state, coupled with briefly hegemonic public management discourses in the 1990s, has served to weaken administrative procedures and mechanisms to discipline public officials and to reduce the likelihood of them pursuing their own interests.

Let us recall that in the bureaucratic model, officials are subject to the disciplinary regime of the administration, from organs responsible for meritocratic appointment, to rules and routines of work. In South Africa since 1994, such mechanisms have been forsaken by choice or deliberately weakened. The current organisation of the public service is not, however, without its own measure of neutrality. Officials are still expected to be subject to the discipline of the party. Therein lies the bitter twist in the current model.

Today, reports of corruption are met with the usual consternation from opposition parties and from civil society and the media. What is new is that the ANC expresses deep concern too. This is a far cry from the way that former president Thabo Mbeki reacted to claims of corruption in the arms deal in 2006. 'Some in our country', he warned in a column published on the ANC website, 'have appointed themselves as "fishers of corrupt men"' (Mbeki, 2003). Those who made such claims, he argued, sought to entrench the stereotype that 'Africans as a people [. . .] are corrupt, given to telling lies, prone to theft and self-enrichment by immoral means, a people that are otherwise contemptible in the eyes of the "civilised"' (Mbeki, 2003).

What has changed? It does not reflect an ideological concession to liberalism. What it reflects is that the 'wrong' people are seen to be benefitting from tenders and public expenditure. The organisational renewal document notes, for example, that within the ANC there has been 'a silent retreat from the mass line to palace politics of factionalism and perpetual in-fighting' (ANC, 2012, p. 9).

> The internal strife revolves around contestation for power and state resources, rather than differences on how to implement the policies of the movement. This situation has shifted the focus of the cadres and members of the movement away from societal concerns and people's aspirations. These circumstances have produced a new type of ANC leader and member who sees ill-discipline, divisions, factionalism and in-fighting as normal practices and necessary forms of political survival.
>
> (ANC, 2012, p. 9)

On the ANC's terms, when this 'new type of cadre' – self-interested and prone to pursue their self-interest through divisive alliances – benefits from government and party interventions, there has been a 'misuse' of public resources, that is, there has been corruption. Note the deviation here is relative to the ANC's own culture, that is, to its norms and traditions. That is why for the ANC, the solution to corruption lies in *internal organisational renewal*: to reinforce the organisation's own culture and to attract members invested in the broader vision of the organisation (ANC, 2012, p. 34). The ANC thus proposes the following internal reforms:

- building a new corps of cadres with political and ethical as well as academic and technical acumen;
- strengthening Luthuli House to be able to manage not only the exercise of political power and constitutional statecraft as well as the multitudes of members and supporters, but also how to relate to civil society – including intellectuals, artists and media – not as victim and protestor, but as leader;
- operationalis[ing] the decision on the Integrity Commission: a commission that will have the legitimacy and authority to call to order members who stray;
- a radical shift in the management of leadership contestation so we can dispense with the current pretence that everyone is waiting for October when nominations will start, while people are actually organising factional meetings about slates in the middle of the night (Netshitenzhe, 2012).

Joel Netshitenzhe goes even further, suggesting that ANC members wanting to stand for positions should be 'vetted' by branches and regions (2012). He describes the current problems with ANC membership as a 'sin of incumbency' resulting from the transition. South Africa's peculiar character as a colonial society of a special type meant that coloniser and colonised inhabited the same territory. As a result, argues Netshitenzhe (2012), black South Africans, especially those returning from exile and/or those from the 'middle strata', had to 'contend with lifestyles of the erstwhile metropolis (essentially the white community) that are profoundly pervasive. Such lifestyles', moreover, 'are based on a standard of living that is artificially high compared to today's global "middle class", in terms, for instance, of assets, number of cars per household, domestic assistants, swimming pools, emulation of the European "gentry" and so on'.

> This mainly First Generation middle and upper strata quite legitimately aspire and pursue the *artificially high standard of living* of the metropolis. [. . .] Yet, unlike their white counterparts, these emergent middle strata do not have historical assets, and they have large nuclear and extended families to support. As a consequence, they have to rely on massive debt and/or patronage.
>
> (Netshitenzhe, 2012) (my emphasis)

Under these conditions, many ANC cadres and black 'middle elements' became indebted and ultimately vulnerable to corruptible practices and people. Why ANC cadres and others felt compelled to live by 'white' standards requires an explanation in its own right.[12]

In summary, talk of 'corruption' in South Africa increasingly refers to members of the ANC acting in ways contrary to what is expected of them, either by the standards of the ANC as a political organisation or by the standards of public service. In having displaced responsibility for the discipline of officials from the public service to the ANC itself, the organisation has lost control of the process.

Conclusion

This chapter has argued that the definition of corruption rests, in South African law as well as that used by most international bodies, from Transparency International to the World Bank, on a liberal conception of the state, distinguishing sharply between private interests and the public good. On these terms, state power is an 'empty place' that is temporarily filled when a political party wins an election and forms a government to give expression to its idea of the public good. The role of the civil service is to implement the policies of the government of the day and not to faithfully develop its own interests. To secure such neutrality, a variety of techniques have been developed – from meritocratic recruitment to rule-based routines. These techniques are what Weber called bureaucracy. Corruption happens, on these terms, when civil servants depart from these administrative standards and rules to pursue actions that benefit themselves personally, their families and/or the private associations and/or political parties that they support.

In South Africa since 1994, however, we have seen that this conception of the state has frequently been rejected in favour of another. The ANC has long believed that as the authentic representative of the 'people', it has a privileged right to define the public good (Chipkin, 2007, 2015). This is why concrete steps have been taken to reduce the autonomy of public administrations in relation to executive authority. When officials break the law, or violate departmental rules in response to a political commandment, we have not so much a moral or ethical failure as an act of political discipline. Hence, what is corruption on liberal terms is often construed as public virtue from the ANC's perspective. If we treat corruption simply or mainly as the absence of public mindedness in government by officials or politicians, then we miss corruption's other scene.

Since 2009, the ability of the ANC to control its own government, officials and cadres in government has declined remarkably. There is growing contestation about who has legitimate authority in the organisation and where, moreover, power lies. It is not simply that the party leadership is sometimes in conflict with the government – the situation during Thabo Mbeki's presidency – but that there are today multiple and fluid 'kitchen cabinets' in government, the movement and outside. There are accusations, moreover, that President Jacob Zuma has allowed his family and their business associates (such as the Gupta family) to 'capture' key institutions. The unexpected dismissal of the finance minister in December 2015 was widely interpreted as an attempt by factional interests to seize control of the National Treasury (Pearson, Pillay and Chipkin, 2016).

What all these intrigues have in common is that they centre on reducing the autonomy of state institutions and/or displacing those who currently control them in favour of a new configuration of forces. This politics of purge and displacement has wracked the law and order departments (the police, the directorate for specialised crimes (the 'Hawks'), the National Prosecutions Authority, the South African Revenue Services (SARS) and some of the state-owned enterprises, most recently Denel, a state arms company.

In a context where state power is seen as personal and in some cases has become so, these efforts are viewed as legitimate attempts to break the hold of existing groups and alliances to make way for new interests. In particular, Jacob Zuma gives expression to the aspirations of rural and traditional elites, regional forces outside the big cities and those who have not benefitted from English-medium schools and/or tertiary education – precisely those largely excluded from the patronage that began under Thabo Mbeki.

Notes

1 Transparency International: www.transparency.org/cpi2014/results (accessed April 2014).
2 Discussions about apartheid corruption are frequently cast in these 'classical' terms, where the reference point is a norm of universal and egalitarian citizenship. In this sense the apartheid government was corrupt because it refused political, civic and social equality on the grounds of race and actively pursued measures to produce racial inequality, with the attendant violence that this required.
3 It is not unreasonable to see in Burke's campaign against the corruption of the East India Company in the late eighteenth century the foundation of British, nineteenth-century, *liberal* ideas of government.
4 For all its apparent ubiquity in the twentieth century, corruption rose to prominence on the international policy agenda only in the late twentieth century. In 1996, the World Bank, then under the leadership of James Wolfensohn, put the issue firmly on the agenda as part of a broader focus on 'good governance' (see Doig and Theobold, 2000, p. 1). Hodgson and Jiang attribute the conflation of corruption with the public sector to the hold of libertarian and individualistic political ideologies that see the state as a restraint on individual freedom. In other words, they see the focus on corruption from the 1990s as the handmaiden of a liberal politics of rolling back the state. 'From this individualistic and libertarian perspective [. . .] the solution to the problem of corruption [is] the reduction of the State' (2007, p. 1047). Was this not the intention of the structural adjustment exercises undertaken by the World Bank and the International Monetary Fund in many African countries in the 1980s?
5 It privileged those countries, especially New Zealand, at the forefront of what became known as the new public management, a new reform credo heavily critical of 'bureaucratic' modes of organisation.
6 Section 9 of the Public Service Act of 1994 gives the power of appointment to the executive authority subject to certain conditions. These include that the person is a South African citizen or a permanent resident and is 'fit and proper'. Evaluation of persons based on 'training, skills, competence, knowledge' needs to be

balanced with the need 'to achieve a public service broadly representative of the South African people, including representation according to race, gender and disability'. In 1997 this Act was amended, inter alia, to allow the Executive Authority to delegate the right of appointment to other officials, with in the same limits as mentioned earlier.

7 In the United States, most civil servants 'exempt' from the standard recruitment practices administered by the Office of Personal Management of the federal government, the equivalent of South Africa's Public Service Commission, are employed in intelligence or national security departments or agencies.

8 PARI defines an 'open bureaucracy' as such: 'Open bureaucracies are those where politicians retain substantial lawful discretion over the appointment, promotion and, in extreme cases dismissal, of public servants. This can enable politicians to go beyond formal and impartial rules in imposing their will upon public administrations. Politicians with power over appointments and promotion can place close associates into key positions and collude with them in non-compliant behavior' (PARI, 2014, p. 47).

9 The Presidential Report available online does not have page numbers. I have referred to the section number instead.

10 During the Thabo Mbeki period, there were moves to reduce the size of the public service, but after 2009 and the election of Jacob Zuma as president, the size of government grew dramatically. There were 28 ministers in Thabo Mbeki's cabinet. This rose to 35 ministers and 37 deputies in the current administration. Moreover, between 2005 and 2012, the public service wage bill grew by 145.6 per cent and the number of government employees climbed by 27.3 per cent (Africa Check, 2014). The public sector wage bill is today the second largest item in the budget after debt servicing today.

11 The lead researcher in this study was Ryan Brunette.

12 In the mass democratic movement of the 1980s and 1990s, there was an often stinging critique of 'white' and/or 'bourgeois' living and an explicit rejection of its norms. This is why suburbs like Yeoville in Johannesburg, for example, developed an iconic status. It was not simply that its racial mixity offered a preview of what non-racialism after apartheid might look like. No less important was that its residents often explicitly rejected 'white' norms – sometimes expressed as a rejection of middle-class values (about family, about sexuality, about consumption), sometimes as a rejection of racism and racialism, sometimes as a combination of both.

References

Africa Check (30 September 2015). July 2016. 'Has South Africa lost R700 billion to corruption since '94?' *Daily Maverick*, https://africacheck.org/reports/has-sa-lost-r700-billion-to-corruption-since-1994-why-the-calculation-is-wrong/ (accessed 30 May 2016).

Africa Check (16 October 2014). 'Does SA really employ more civil servants than the US?', *Daily Maverick*, www.dailymaverick.co.za/article/2014-10-16-africa-check-does-sa-really-employ-more-civil-servants-than-the-us/#.V4CzuFefTVo (accessed 9 July 2016).

African National Congress (ANC) (16 December 1997). *Report by the President of the ANC, Nelson Mandela to the 50th National Conference of the African National Congress*, Mafikeng, www.sahistory.org.za/archive/report-president-anc-nelson-mandela-50th-national-conference-african-national-congress-mafik#sthash.GSJKjmXg.dpuf (accessed 30 May 2016).

African National Congress (ANC) (1998). 'The state, property relations and social transformation', *Umrabulo*, Third Quarter (5).

African National Congress (ANC) (1999). *Building a National Democratic Society. Strategy and Tactics*, adopted at the 52nd National Conference of the ANC.

African National Congress (ANC) (10 April 2012). *Organisational Renewal: Building the ANC as a Movement for Transformation and a Strategic Centre of Power*, a Discussion Document Towards the National Policy Conference.

Auditor General of South Africa (AGSA) (2011). *Consolidated General Report on the Audit Outcomes of Local Government*, 2010/2011 (Pretoria: Auditor General of South Africa).

Bayart, J. F. (1993). *The State in Africa: The Politics of the Belly* (London: Longman).

Brooks, R. (1910). *Corruption in Politics and American Life* (New York: Dodd, Mead and Company).

Buchan, B. and Hill, L. (2007). *From Republicanism to Liberalism: Corruption and Empire in Enlightenment Thought* (Adelaide: University of Adelaide, School of History and Politics).

Chipkin, I. M. (1997). *Democracy, cities and space: South African conceptions of local government*. MA thesis, University of Witwatersrand, Johannesburg.

Chipkin, I. (2007). *Do South Africans Exist?* (Johannesburg: Wits University Press).

Chipkin, I. (2015). Public Affairs Research Institute). Enlightenment Thought. onal-confe215-227.

Chipkin, I., and Lipietz, B. (2012). *Transforming South Africa's Racial Bureaucracy: New Public Management and public sector reform in contemporary South Africa*, PARI Long Essays, Number 1 (February). (Johannesburg: Public Affairs Research Institute).

Coolidge, J., & Rose-Ackerman, S. (1997). *High-level rent-seeking and corruption in African regimes: Theory and cases* (No. 1780). The World Bank.

Cronin, J. (13 April 2016). 'State capture's not a new thing', in *Independent Online*, www.iol.co.za/dailynews/opinion/state-captures-not-a-new-thing-2008576 (accessed 19 June 2016).

Della Porta, D. and Vannucci, A. (1999). *Corrupt Exchanges: Actors, Resources, and Mechanisms of Political Corruption* (New York: Aldine de Gruyter).

Department of Public Service and Administration (DPSA). (2006). *Senior Management Service: Overview of Reports 2000–2006*, www.dpsa.gov.za/dpsa2g/docu ments/sms/publications/SMS_Resource_pack_1.pdf (accessed 9 July 2016).

Department of Public Service and Administration (DPSA). (2013). *Public Service Affirmative Action and Employment Equity Report (2011–2012)* (Pretoria: DPSA).

Doig, A. and Theobold, R. (Eds.) (2000). *Corruption and Democratization* (London: Frank Cass).

Elias, N. (1969). *The Civilizing Process, Vol. I: The History of Manners* (Oxford: Blackwell).

Finer, S. (1997). The History of Government from the Earliest Times (Oxford: Oxford University Press).

Fraser-Moleketi, G. J. (2006). Public Service Reform in South Africa: An Overview of Selected Case Studies From 1994–2004. Masters of Administration. School of Public Management and Administration, Faculty of Economic and Management Sciences, University of Pretoria.

Galbraith, J. K. (2005). *The Economics of Innocent Fraud* (Boston, MA: Penguin Books).

Galston, W. (1991). *Liberal Purposes: Goods, Virtues and Diversity in the Liberal State* (Cambridge: Cambridge University Press).

Government of South Africa (1997), *Green paper on a New Employment Policy for a New Public Service*, accessed at http://www.dpsa.gov.za/dpsa2g/documents/acts&regulations/frameworks/green-papers/employ.pdf.

Grossman, G., & Helpman, E. (1994). *VProtection for sale*. V American Economic Review, 84(4), 833–850.

Hamadziripi Tamukamoyo and Reitumetse Mofana, *Those heading the National Prosecuting Authority and the Special Investigating Unit should be appointed for their skills, expertise and integrity, following a transparent recruitment process*, ISS, 7 May 2013, accessed at https://issafrica.org/iss-today/south-africa-needs-credible-leaders-at-the-helm-of-its-criminal-justice-system.

Heywood, P. (1997). 'Political corruption: problems and perspectives', *Political Studies*, 45(3), pp. 417–435.

Hodgson, G. M. and Shuxia, J. (2007). 'The economics of corruption and the corruption of economics: an institutionalist perspective', *Journal of Economic Issues*, XLI (4), pp. 55–80.

HSRC (2012), *Business unusual: Perceptions of Corruption in South Africa*, accessed at http://www.hsrc.ac.za/en/review/june-2012/business-as-usual-perceptions-of-corruption-in-south-africa.

International Monetary Fund (IMF) (June 2016). *Case Studies on Managing Government Compensation and Employment – Institutions, Policies, and Reform Challenges* (Washington, DC: IMF), www.imf.org/external/np/pp/eng/2016/040816ab.pdf (accessed 11 July 2016).

Kymlicka, W. (1989). *Liberal individualism and liberal neutrality*. Ethics, 99(4), 883–905.

Lee, E.-J. (2013). 'Cultural transfer "Eurasian" style: Johann Heinrich Gottlieb von Justi's perception of China and the reception of cameralism in Meiji Japan'. *African-State Formation and Bureaucracy in Comparative Perspective*, Programme for the conference, September 16–18, University of the Witwatersrand, Johannesburg, Public Affairs Reasearch Institute.

Lenin, V. I. (2004). *State and Revolution* (Whitefish, MT: Kessinger Publishing).

Lodge, T. (2002). 'Political corruption in South Africa, from apartheid to multiracial state'. In A. J. Heidenheimer and M. Johnston (Eds.), *Political Corruption, Concept and Contexts*, Third edition (New Brunswick, NJ: Transaction Publishers).

Mbeki, T. (2003). 'Letter from the president: Bold steps to end the "two nations" divide', *ANC Today*, 3 (21), 30 May.

McLennan, A. and FitzGerald, P. (1991). 'Administration initiative and the Mount Grace Consultation'. In A. McLennan and P. FitzGerald (Eds.), *The Mount Grace Papers: The New Public Administration Initiative and the Mount Grace Consultation* (Johannesburg: Public and Development Management Programme [P&DM]: University of the Witwatersrand Press).

Munusamy, R. (1 June 2016). 'Captura continua: Guptas triumph as ANC shuts down state capture probe', www.dailymaverick.co.za/article/2016-06-01-captura-continua-guptas-triumph-as-anc-shuts-down-state-capture-probe/#.V49jq2V0XR0 (accessed 20 July 2016).

Munusamy, R. (6 June 2016). 'Get Guptas, duck Zuma: SACP's obstacle race on state capture', *Daily Maverick*, www.dailymaverick.co.za/article/2016-06-06-get-guptas-duck-zuma-sacps-obstacle-race-on-state-capture/#.V49jpmV0XR0 (accessed 20 July 2016).

National Treasury (2012). *Diagnostic Research Report on Corruption, Non-compliance and Weak Organisations*, Project Number 671, a report prepared for the Technical Assistance Unit by the Public Affairs Research Institute (PARI), August.

Netshitenzhe, J. (1996). 'The national democratic revolution – is it still on track?' *Umrabulo*, Fourth Quarter (1), pp. 4–6.

Netshitenzhe, J. (15–21 June 2012). 'Competing identities of a national liberation movement and the challenges of incumbency', *ANC Today*.

Nye, J. S. (1967). 'Corruption and political development: a cost-benefit analysis', *American Political Science Review*, 61 (2), pp. 417–427.

PARI. (August 2012). 'Diagnostic research report on corruption, non-compliance and weak organisations', a report prepared for the *Technical Advisory Unit* (TAU), Pretoria: National Treasury.

PARI. (2014). *The Contract State: Outsourcing and Decentralisation in Contemporary South Africa* (Johannesburg: Public Affairs Research Institute).

Pearson, J., Pillay, S., & Chipkin, I. (2016). *State-building in South Africa after apartheid: The history of the national treasury*. Johannesburg, PARI, accessed at http://pari.org.za/wp-content/uploads/State-Building-in-South-Africa-The-History-of-the-National-Treasury-1.pdf.

Picard, L. (2005). *The State of the State: Institutional Transformation, Capacity and Political Change in South Africa* (Johannesburg: Wits University Press).

Presidential Review Commission (PRC) (1998). *Report of the Presidential Review Commission on the Reform and Transformation of the Public Service in South Africa*, www.gov.za/documents/report-presidential-review-commission-reform-and-transformation-public-service-south (accessed 11 July 2016).

Public Finance Management Act (PFMA), Act No. 1 of 1999.

Public Service Act, Proclamation 103 published in GG 15791, 3 June 1994.

Public Service Commission (PSC) (2010). 'Reflections on an ethical public service', *News: Official Magazine of the Public Service Commission*, November/December.

Public Service Commission (PSC) (2012). *Trends Relating to Corruption in the Public Service*, presentation to the Portfolio Committee on Public Service and Administration, 7 November.

Public Service Commission (PSC) (2014). *Building a Capable, Career-Oriented and Professional Public Service to Underpin a Capable and Developmental State in South Africa: A Discussion Document* (Pretoria: PSC).

Raz, J. (1986). *The morality of freedom*. London, Clarendon Press.

Rubinstein, W. D. (November 1983). 'The End of "Old Corruption" in Britain 1780-1860', *Past & Present*, No. 101, pp. 55–86.

Shivambu, F. (24 March 2016). 'State capture: it's criminal, and it is nothing new', *Daily Maverick*, www.dailymaverick.co.za/opinionista/2016-03-24-state-capture-its-criminal-and-it-is-nothing-new/#.V5TeW2V0XVo (accessed 19 July 2016).

Thamm, M. (10 March 2016). 'State capture: did the Guptas offer treasury's top job to Deputy Minister Jonas?', *Daily Maverick*, www.dailymaverick.co.za/article/2016-03-10-state-capture-did-the-guptas-offer-treasurys-top-job-to-deputy-minister-mcebisi-jonas/#.V49jj2V0XR0 (accessed 20 July 2016).

Thamm, M. (16 March 2016). 'State capture: the floodgates open as Deputy Finance Minister Jonas admits Guptas offered him top job', *Daily Maverick*, www.dailymaverick.co.za/article/2016-03-16-state-capture-the-floodgates-open-as-deputy-minister-jonas-admits-guptas-offered-him-top-job/#.V49jiWV0XR0 (accessed 20 July 2016).

Thamm, M. (7 April 2016). 'State capture: banking and business screws on the Guptas tighten considerably', *Daily Maverick*, www.dailymaverick.co.za/article/2016-04-07-state-capture-banking-and-business-screws-on-the-guptas-tighten-considerably/#.V49jimV0XR0 (accessed 20 July 2016).

Thamm, M. (8 July 2016). 'State capture: Thuli's final quest for the truth – investigating the Guptas' political influence', *Daily Maverick*, www.dailymaverick.co.za/article/2016-07-08-state-capture-thulis-final-quest-for-the-truth-investigating-the-guptas-political-influence/#.V49jhGV0XR0 (accessed 20 July 2016).

Transparency International (1996). *The TI Source Book*, www.Transparency.de/document/source-book/ (accessed 19, 20 and 22 October 2012).

Transparency International (2001). *Global Corruption Report*, www.Transparency.de/document/source-book/ (accessed 19, 20 and 22 October 2012).

Transparency International (2003). *Global Corruption Barometer*, www.Transparency.de/document/source-book/ (accessed 19, 20 and 22 October 2012).

UNDP (United National Development Program) (1997). *Corruption and Good Governance*, UNDP Management Development and Governance Division discussion paper n. 3. (New York: UNDP).

Von Holdt, K. (2010). 'Nationalism, bureaucracy and the developmental state: the South African case', *South African Review of Sociology*, 41 (1), pp. 4–27.

Von Holdt, K. (2011). *Insurgent citizenship and collective violence: Analysis of case studies*. Centre for the Study of Violence and Reconciliation (CSVR) & Society, Work and Development Institute (SWOP), The smoke that calls: Insurgent citizenship, collective violence and the struggle for a place in the new South Africa: Eight case studies of community protest and xenophobic violence, 5–32.

Von Holdt, K., and Kirsten, A. (2011). *The Smoke that Calls: Insurgent Citizenship, Collective Violence and the Struggle for a Place in the New South Africa. Eight Case Studies of Community Protest and Xenophobic Violence* (Johannesburg: Centre for the Study of Violence and Reconciliation (CSVR) and Society, Development and Work Institute (SWOP)).

Von Holdt, K. and Murphy, M. (2007). 'Public hospitals in South Africa: stressed institutions, disempowered management', in S. Buhlungu, J. Daniel, R. Southall and J. Lutchman (Eds.), *State of the Nation 2007* (Cape Town: HSRC Press).

Weber, M. (1966). *The Theory of Social and Economic Organisation* (edited by T. Parsons) (New York and London: The Free Press and Collier-Macmillan Limited).

Weyland, K. G. (1998). 'The politics of corruption in Latin America', *Journal of Democracy*, 9 (2), pp. 108–121.

World Bank (2000). *Anticorruption in Transition: A Contribution to the Policy Debate* (Washington, DC: World Bank).

World Bank (2006). *Strengthening Bank Group Engagement on Governance and Anti-corruption*, Paper DC2006–0017 prepared for the 18 September 2006 Joint Ministerial Committee of the Boards of Governors of the World Bank and the International Monetary Fund on the Transfer of Real Resources to Developing Countries (Washington, DC: World Bank).

Wright, E. O. (1983). *Class, Crisis and the State* (London: Verso).

3 Change and continuity at the Brazilian Development Bank

Paulo Faveret

It should be clear from the outset that the Brazilian Development Bank (BNDES) has an unavoidable dual nature, expressed in a group of apparently contradictory pairs: state–market; public–private; financial sustainability–social benefits; economic–social; national–global; and so on. The organization and its employees are always fighting to balance these dimensions. If one of these poles becomes predominant, instability takes place and the long-term mission is in jeopardy.

BNDES: a hybrid organization

BNDES is a class of organization virtually ignored by management literature, especially in the Anglo-Saxon tradition. Academics have difficulty with state-owned enterprises, often considered as distortions in relation to the private standard. There are fewer studies on development banks than on state companies in general, which are a more common subject of academic investigations. Even if the academic world does not properly recognize the development bank, it exists. According to Luna-Martínez and Vicente (2012), there are 90 development banks in 60 countries, 39 percent established after 1990, meaning that it is not a group on the way to extinction.

My hypothesis is that BNDES is "halfway," or "in the middle," a kind of hybrid organization. It is a governmental entity, 100 percent controlled by the federal government with access to tax resources. At the same time, the Bank is a company incorporated under private law that hires employees, not public officials, and performs as a typical private financial entity, lending for and investing in private companies.

It is a bank that needs to make profit in order to survive, but whose mission is not to maximize financial return. Rare as it may seem, its strategy map, or balanced scorecard, defines "support competitive and sustainable development" as the higher dimension. The financial dimension, usually the most important for companies, is just below as the basis for the realization of the ultimate goal, which lies outside the organization (Table 3.1).

Trying to cope with duality, BNDES developed a kind of hybridism, combining elements of both sides. In a way, the Bank has become an "amphibious" organization, adapted to its business context, operating in the blurry boundaries between state and market. One of the consequences of this feature is that HR

Table 3.1 BNDES's strategic map in 2014

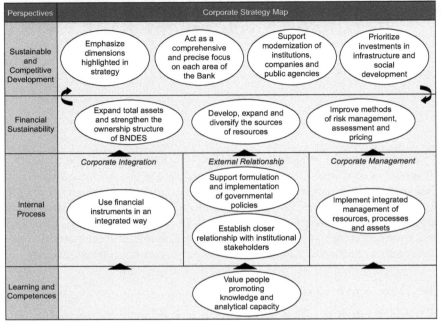

Source: BNDES.

practices, strategies and institutional strictures are quite distinct from mainstream management approaches.

This chapter attempts to analyze how traditional HR practices in BNDES were deemed not enough for supporting business needs in the new development context and how a set of reforms was launched to "modernize" management of this state-owned enterprise.

Theoretical support

This chapter deals with the disjunctive that Pettigrew mentions in his influential article on the transformation of the firm. According to him, "empirically and theoretically, change and continuity need one another. Action and structure are inextricably linked" (1987, p. 149). It is in this context that a "transformational leadership" must operate to achieve its strategic goals. This theoretical approach, later developed in this chapter introduction, is useful to understand the transformational journey in the Brazilian Development Bank – BNDES.

This chapter is not normative, nor does it try to find some general rules, applied *urbi et orbi*. It is a reflection on emergent and intrinsic dilemmas when an organization decides to dive into a transformational journey. It is important to underline that the author is not in a neutral position. On the contrary, I have been right in the middle of a plethora of projects and its accompanying conflicts and frictions. Again, Pettigrew offers an insight when he states, "there is the problem of perspective, where we sit not only influences where we stand, but also what we see" (1987, p. 649).

There is a conscious option for analyzing the transformational projects framed by the major context of the firm and the country. As Pettigrew suggests, it is necessary to "conceptualize major transformations of the firm in terms of linkages between the content of change and its process and to regard leadership behavior as a central ingredient but only one of the ingredients, in a complex analytical, political, and cultural process of challenging the core beliefs, structure, and strategy of the firm" (1987, p. 650).

Whenever possible, I try to highlight the internal and external elements that combine in different proportions to produce an iterative, multilevel process of organizational change, as Pettigrew puts it. I hope to provide a vivid explanation of change-continuity in BNDES, without falling into a schematic and rigid academic approach.

For various reasons, the Bank launched many modernization projects in the period 2007–2015. Traditional processes and rules were considered outdated and in need of reformulation. The scope and number of projects mark a radical change in the Bank's internal management approach. In the past, there have been a few wide initiatives of modernization, but never for so long and so spread throughout the organization. Table 3.2 is self-explanatory and gives a good idea of the nature and extension of a certain managerial "frenzy."

Table 3.2 Projects and initiatives related to modernization and control (2006–2014)

Name	Start	Scope	Leadership	Time length	Main Focus	Origin
Processes and systems integration, including SAP	2006	Broad	IT	Permanent	Control	Internal
Strategic planning	2007	Broad	Planning area	Permanent	Strategy and control	Internal
Strategic HR, including organizational design	2008	Broad	HR area	Permanent	Strategy and control	External
Risk management	2008	Broad	Risk management area	Permanent	Control	External
External supervision	2010	Broad	Presidential office	Permanent	Control	External
Financial model validation	2011	Local	Validation department	Permanent	Control	External
Institutional relations	2013	Broad	Presidential office	Permanent	Control	Internal
Access to information law	2013	Broad	Presidential office	Permanent	Control	External

Source: author, based on internal primary data.

This modernization wave fits very well into Pettigrew's (1987, p. 658) conceptual framework. The large set of ambitious projects and initiatives produces change as well as continuity, and is the result of interaction between actions and structures, endogenous and exogenous factors, not to mention chance and surprise.

BNDES's organizational context

The name of the game is "development"

Ethics, Commitment to Development, Public Spirit and Excellence are the four values of BNDES. After six decades of existence, the Bank has acquired a large social capital through the actions of its employees, guided by these core values. At various times in the history of Brazil, Bank staff could identify the main socioeconomic trends, adopt compatible behaviors and policies and develop new technical skills and innovative solutions to fulfill the mission.

With a privileged financial position at each stage in recent history, the Bank achieved a respect in Brazilian society that stemmed mainly from a highly technical approach to the "business" of development, albeit dialoguing with the main political constraints. Managing public resources in a context of recurrent social, political and macroeconomic turmoil often required management and employees to adopt stringent ethical standards in order to gain and maintain legitimacy.

Technical and ethical criteria guided operations, helping the Bank to secure privileged access to the resources needed for its operations. The constant preoccupation with requirements for the development of Brazil throughout history manifested in the Bank's commitment to a development value. From its founding until the 1990s (Table 3.3), BNDES has concentrated its efforts in supporting state infrastructure and basic industries. Despite some diversification, the focus remained almost unchanged from the 1950s until the late 1980s, as the prevailing model of industrialization through import substitution, in which the main role of the Bank was to finance capital-intensive sectors.

The crisis of the previous development model and its replacement by a more open and less regulated one led to reviewing the role of BNDES. Over the past 20 years, yet without abandoning its original connections to industry, the Bank increased its scope of action, incorporating new sectors, roles and, consequently, new interlocutors. In the twenty-first century, the agenda of so-called crosscutting themes has been gaining prominence. Attention is growing on sustainability and innovation, which overlap and change, without discarding the traditional sector approach. Management, especially people management, in BNDES is undergoing significant transformation. The main sources of change are both external – the environment in which the Bank operates – and internal – generational change and modernization of systems and processes. Traditional methods of management, based on personal interactions and leading by example, are still valid, but more formal and structured instruments complement them. To deal with these challenges, in 2008, BNDES's Board of Directors decided

Table 3.3 BNDES's timeline

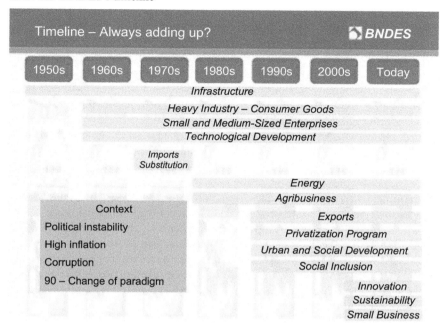

Timeline – Always adding up? © BNDES

| 1950s | 1960s | 1970s | 1980s | 1990s | 2000s | Today |

Infrastructure

Heavy Industry – Consumer Goods
Small and Medium-Sized Enterprises
Technological Development

Imports
Substitution

Energy
Agribusiness

Context
Political instability
High inflation
Corruption
90 – Change of paradigm

Exports
Privatization Program
Urban and Social Development
Social Inclusion

Innovation
Sustainability
Small Business

Source: author, based on internal primary data.

to set up the Human Resources Area (ARH). The core agenda of the new unit was the implementation of a human resources policy centered on competencies management.

As the table shows, the Bank's main business focus has always been the financing of investment, i.e., the expansion of productive capacity, increasing productivity and job creation. However, we should highlight that BNDES's agenda has expanded steadily through the accumulation of new sectors, customers, products and challenges. As development frontiers are in constant motion, the Bank has continuously added new industries to its portfolio over time, without getting rid of the old ones. The result is that it widened the operational range in the second decade of existence, despite being born as a financier of infrastructure projects and heavy industry. This diversification led to the current large portfolio of financial tools and clients, ranging from credit card for micro and small enterprises to financing mega hydropower projects, supporting micro credit, and intangible assets in the field of innovation, among many others.

The changes in investment portfolio, in the portfolio of clients and in the approach to projects forced BNDES to develop new capabilities for its employees. It was no longer enough to master the techniques of industrial projects analysis, or to know how to deal with the private and state companies. It became necessary to understand the dynamics of social policies, learn to negotiate with representatives of unions and civil society interlocutors and adapt credit instruments to new types of projects, many of them more varied than before – the "Bank of infrastructure" has also become the "Bank of garbage collectors."

The ability to develop continually its employees is one of the key elements that have allowed the Bank to cope with its business model evolution and to grow steadily since its foundation, maintaining good profitability, financial strength and social respectability. Training was adequate to the requirements of new tasks, often leading the Bank's officials to prominent positions in formulating and implementing public (state) policies.

The trajectory of BNDES's business is inseparable from the development of its employees. This involves several dimensions: the careful selection of new employees; effective sharing of values; prevalence of the technical approach of the problems (especially the application of the project analysis methodology); leadership by example; training and skills development for supporting activities and business integration (planning, administration, HR, legal controls, auditing, etc.).

At the current stage of development of the country, the challenges related to employees of the Bank merge with the ones Brazilian society faces. There is a growing consensus that development can be sustainable and fair only if there is an increase in labor productivity, and this in turn is a direct function of training, both in terms of values and techniques. Inclusive development is a necessary condition for reducing inequalities in a sustainable manner.

The same applies to the BNDES. To move forward to upgrading to ever-changing socioeconomic needs, the Bank must devote more time and effort to the improvement of its employees. The primary tasks currently facing the Bank is to provide constant opportunities to develop and strengthen the values that gave support to the organization's core competencies in its 60 years of existence.

Pressures facing BNDES

As a state entity, BNDES is under continuous political pressure. Many of these are legitimate demands and priorities of elected governments, others less so. To deal with the political logic and its sometimes contradictory demands, the organization developed an institutional framework with the following main elements.

1　Professional staff (long-term assignment) – BNDES hires employees through a rigorous public selection, granting them competitive pay conditions and attractive benefits. Thus, the turnover rate is very low and the company can invest in human capital formation with a high probability of return. According to Campbell, Coff and Kryscynski, "many strategy scholars have suggested that resources and capabilities may take the form of knowledge and skills that are embedded in people. As such, human capital can be at the core of a resource-based advantage if it is valuable, rare, and can be kept from rivals" (2012, p. 377). This is the case for BNDES.

2　Definition of strict rules and procedures – BNDES has a long tradition of defining explicit norms to rationalize decision-making process, just like any

Weberian bureaucratic organization. In a political and economic environment as unstable as that which Brazil experienced from the 1950s until the mid-1990s, this practice has decisively contributed to reduce the discrepancy between the procedures of the various teams and ensured a minimum degree of coherence and cohesion to the organization.

3 Collegiate decision-making process – from the first step until the approval of a loan, the main decisions are collegiate. There is virtually no room for autocratic decision. This feature almost eliminates the risky behaviors that would lead to the destruction of the organization in a short time.

4 Political appointee headcounts cap – the president of Brazil has the right to nominate the president, vice president and directors, nine positions. The president of BNDES, in turn, can hire a limited number of advisers (currently 56 in a total staff of 2,840 employees). These advisers have no access to any real decision-making position, nor do they participate in deliberative forums. Since they are not part of the hierarchical chain of command, they are not allowed to lead teams, to make decisions or to submit proposals to the Board of Directors. That is, employees of the Bank may progress in their careers up to the executive level just below the Board of Directors.

5 Specialization and autonomy of organizational units (departments) – the operational departments, responsible for project analysis, always have a clearly defined industry focus – department of steel, department of agribusiness, for example. This specialization of the teams allowed the pioneers of project analysis in the first decades of the BNDES to acquire the knowledge required to select relevant projects to receive financial support. At the same time, the depth of industry knowledge gave the organization a great competitive advantage. The Bank has competencies that no other organization has in Brazil, working as a "knowledge bridge" between macroeconomic and business decisions. Among other things, thanks to this kind of knowledge, the Bank's officials frequently participate in governmental major decisions.

Other aspects are worth mentioning. The organizational context also had the goal of creating a long-term career and allowing a minimum degree of autonomy from political stakeholders, elements deemed necessary for the institution to perform effectively its mission. This vision is embedded in features such as the promotion process, where employees are evaluated by their superiors, up to the deputy director level. Deputy directors, unlike all other employees, have automatic progression in their career levels, so that they do not depend on directors' discretion, which are political appointees. Using Mintzberg's approach (2010), managers of BNDES from the early beginning knew they had to negotiate and make connections with external actors. The organizational model would ensure a necessary degree of autonomy and rationality in decision-making and technical issues.

Senior managers always carried out organizational development in a very situational way, responsive to the predicaments of the moment given long-term possibilities, and taking into consideration some rational and bureaucratic guidelines. National and international best practices, such as the Brazil–U.S. Joint

Commission and ECLAC – UN Economic Commission for Latin America and Caribbean – inspired the pioneers. There was also a large dose of pragmatism and intuition. Just as the precise meaning of what is developing in each historical moment is not in the books, "managers in the middle" fostered the organizational development of the Bank, applying their skills, talents and intuition.

The "old school" – no man is an island, but the department is

From its very beginning, BNDES was a professional organization, composed of a small number of highly trained and specialized professionals, proud of their mission and their "product" – Brazilian development. "*Benedenses*" experienced a sense of uniqueness. They felt as if they were different from all other workers of the finance industry. It was the only development bank in Brazil, focused on financing investment in fixed capital, long-term loans, and the pioneer of investment analysis in Brazil and Latin America.

During the first decade, "finance artisans" created work processes not available locally at the time, designing and building many of their own instruments. Professionals were concerned with finding the right credit conditions for each client's needs, almost considering each operation as a unique "sculpture or work of art." An ordinary credit report submitted to the Board of Directors had more than 100 pages, with sections ranging from macroeconomic context, financial projections, to ultra-detailed description and analysis of industrial processes, including comparisons with competitors.

BNDES's structure was quite flat in the early days (Table 3.4). A small number of managers were responsible for supervising the work of large teams, composed of specialists – accountants, economists, lawyers and engineers. Each department,

Table 3.4 BNDES's first organizational chart

Fonte: Arquivo Nacional

| BANCO NACIONAL DE DESENVOLVIMENTO ECONÔMICO |

Ass. Jurídica | DIRETORIAS | Cons. Fiscal

Serviços Especiais | Superintendências | Departamento de Produção

Sec. de Planejamento e Projetos | Assistência Educação e Saúde | Assess. de Obras | Sec. Transporte Marítimo e Logística

Serv. de Manutenção — Serv. (Ilegível)

Pessoal | Material | Comunicações | Orçamento | Contabilidade | Tesouraria

Div. Comercial e Cooperativa | Divisão Industrial | Divisão Agro-Pecuária

Source: BNDES.

the basic organizational unit, specialized in one specific industry, steel, pulp and paper, petrochemical and transportation, for example. The teams had great autonomy. They interacted with the companies, trying to understand their needs and to determine the conditions of the credit.

As mentioned by Mintzberg, one of the clear disadvantages with the professional structure is the lack of control that senior executives can exercise. Power is decentralized, and teams have a lot of autonomy to determine the conditions of the credit. Because of the autonomy of specialized departments, BNDES always faced the risk of operational units practicing divergent procedures simultaneously with different clients and industries. Along with increasing bureaucracy and regulations, one hypothesis is that the Bank dealt with this disadvantage by establishing a series of committees and review procedures to avoid individual control of the product. Collective decision-making processes were set up, making the institution less dependent on the "finance artisan."

The organizational model of BNDES well fitted its business needs. Focused on a limited number of industries and companies, the Bank was almost like an archipelago, with many highly specialized "islands" connected by some shared services. The support units were often considered second class compared to what was seen as the nobler and richer work experience of the project teams.

In the past decade, the social and economic environment for BNDES has changed considerably. Therefore, the Bank is experiencing changes in its organization and its business model.

Since the very beginning, BNDES was a professional organization. The teams responsible for analyzing projects and conceding loans to companies worked with a considerable amount of autonomy, considered a *sine qua non* condition for achieving the desired developmental effectiveness of the Bank. Until today, the vast majority of the operational teams function guided by this principle. The consequence is that every time the Bank decides to enlarge its scope, there is a tendency to establish a new specialized team that will work in the same way as the pioneers designed.

Parallel to the main structure, during the 1960s, the Bank decided to support investment through other instruments. One of the new credit channels was FINAME, a wholly owned subsidiary designed to finance buyers of capital goods. Using the network of commercial and development banks in Brazil, FINAME would work on a more mechanical approach, what Mintzberg calls a "machine

Table 3.5 Operational areas – basic information (2013)

	N. Area (a)	Headcount (b)	N. Depart. (c)	BRL 10^6 (d)	N. Oper. (e)
Professional	10	879	53	75,995	5,055
Machine	1	189	8	66,483	1,009,083
Total	11	1,068	61	142,478	1,014,138

Source: author, based on internal primary data.

Table 3.6 Operational areas – basic information (2013) percentage

	N. Area (a)	Headcount (b)	N. Depart. (c)	BRL 10^6 (d)	N. Oper. (e)
Professional	91%	82%	87%	53%	0.5%
Machine	9%	18%	13%	47%	99.5%

Source: author, based on internal primary data.

Table 3.7 Typical organizational structure of BNDES

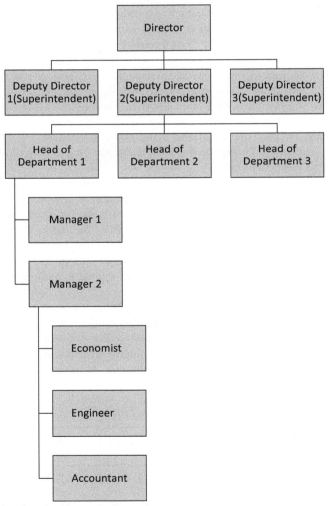

Source: author, based on internal primary data.

organization" or bureaucracy. Its mission was to spread credit throughout the economy, focusing on medium, small and micro companies, which were not in the radar of BNDES, whose efforts were concentrated on large projects with widespread effects over the Brazilian economy.

Nowadays, FINAME has become a paper company and its operations are under the responsibility of AOI, an area of BNDES. The teams at AOI work in a very different way compared to other areas. Since they must deal with a rapidly growing number of financial agents, clients and financial products, IT is critical for achieving its goals. Standard procedures, complex and automated systems are central for AOI. It certainly does fit in the definition of a machine organization.

The tables that follow illustrate the main features of the two groups of areas. Considering the three left columns, there is a clear dominance of traditional areas. The 10 professional units represent 91 percent of the operational areas, and account for 82 percent of headcount and 87 percent of departments. On the other hand, one area alone disburses almost the same amount as the other 10 operational areas (Tables 3.5 and 3.7). Moreover, when it comes to the number of operations and clients, the discrepancy is astonishing – AOI is responsible for 99.5 percent of the total.

Because of the very different approaches to processes, systems and clients, the productivity indicators are very discrepant. In terms of disbursements (millions of BRL), the "machine area" has a multiple of nine times the average amount of a professional area. For disbursement per employee, the multiple is four times, and per department, six times. This means that financial productivity is, and it should be, much higher at AOI.

Taking a "physical" indicator, such as number of operations, a good proxy for number of clients, the difference between the two groups of areas is much wider. AOI accounts for almost 2,000 times more operations than the professional areas altogether.

Brief retrospective – style of management

Conservation and transformation, upgrading and modernizing, without breaking with successful traditions. It is necessary to consider this difficult balance in the journey of renewing human resources policies and people management standards in BNDES. This section tries to answer the question of what was the Bank's style of managing people, which features were favorable to the evolution of the organization and why they are no longer sufficient. Is there a need to make significant changes in the managerial style?

For a long period, the Bank operated on a small scale. A few hundred at its foundation, staff headcount grew slowly, reaching about 1,800 employees at the end of the 1980s, and remaining roughly the same size until the early 2000s. Since the Bank's headquarters are in Rio de Janeiro, 95 percent of its staff is concentrated in the same building. Enjoying stability of employment, *benedenses* (acronyms to BNDES's employees) succeeded in developing a strong and intricate network of relationships, in personal and institutional dimensions, formal and informal. These relationships helped to shape the expected behaviors, often polished by example and interaction with executives and seniors. Moreover, the network functioned as an environment to facilitate consensus and as a mechanism for conflict resolution.

Due to the small number of executive positions and to the very origins of the Bank, a technical career has always been highly valued. Experienced employees, some of them in no managerial position, kept the industry and companies' knowledge. Analysts had large autonomy to do their work and senior management respected this.

In brief, to understand the corporate management style, one must consider the peculiar combination of few employees hired for long-term jobs, a small number of professionals in executive careers and the prevalence of technical decisions.

We could advance the hypothesis that the managers ran the Bank, from its very beginning, with the craft-art-science balance mentioned by Mintzberg. There was science through the application of a formal and rational approach to project analysis. The artisan dimension was always present because of the refusal of mass production methods and the individual commitment to the product. BNDES employees tend to cultivate the self-image of artists, focused on high quality and details. Finally, building a shared vision that inspires all participants in the "noble journey of developing Brazil" was an artistic dimension of management.

In practical terms, these elements provided a management style that set the stage for achieving results and solving problems by means of a system that combined formal tools – forums, as the credit committee – with informal paths, favored by the intimate daily interaction of a small staff, often over a period of decades. The search for consensus has emerged as an unwritten rule, but very effective, to ensure unity of action of the organization.

Notwithstanding the networks, the chain of formal power is basically vertical (see Table 3.7). Directors oversee areas (fundamental units), which are commanded by deputy directors, who, in turn, lead four to seven heads of departments (main administrative units). In the departments, there are a small number of managers, acting as team leaders. This structure has provided the operational areas with considerable autonomy, since negotiation with other units was only necessary on two occasions during the process – in the framing of the initial proposal and the approval by the board. This enabled departments to concentrate energy and focus in the relationship with customers.

It is easy to imagine how difficult it would be to implement and improve support processes, usually located on the lower rungs of the scale of priority. The hierarchical-functional structure did not degenerate into unmanageable fiefdoms due to the consultation and decision-making mechanisms. These mechanisms, both formal and informal, functioned as unifying elements between teams and units. The key factor to establish such unity, mentioned at the outset, was a strong commitment to the four shared values.

In such an environment, it comes as no surprise that the first (2010) and the second (2012) organizational climate research findings reached similar conclusions. The dimensions with the least positive evaluation (favorability index – percentage of strong agreement or agreement answers) were the same: institutional communication, management style, innovative environment and performance evaluation of employees. In a company that favors units' autonomy, communication is not a priority. In an informal setting, styles of management vary a lot from one department to another, from one manager to the other. In an organization focused on selecting projects and clients, trying to discard the bad ones, innovation happens only with conflict. Moreover, in a place where people work together for decades, institutional policies and tools for evaluation were deemed unnecessary ("I know who is a good employee, who is not").

Culture can be defined as shared assumptions, understandings and values exhibited in discourse in stable institutions. In this sense, it is right to say that BNDES has a strong culture, revealed by statements such as "BNDES in this sequence," meaning, from the acronym in Portuguese, that first comes the banking dimension, then national development, economic and, last, social. The statement is brilliant in its concise translation of the spirit that should preside over the actions of each *benedense*. Notwithstanding the need for projects with large social impacts, the institution is a bank and, as such, should never lose sight of the basic truth that a bank lends money and takes it back from the clients.

The convergence had roots in the zeal of many of the employees and executives, not in any explicit concern with consensus. Practice prevailed over speech, and force of example, not institutional programs, was the main medium for communication of values. Decentralized personnel management was one of the characteristics of the Bank, along with being a vertically integrated organization, with primacy of the technical culture, well-established core values, a small number of employees and low turnover. Heads of department interacted with their teams to obtain the expected results, always with great managerial freedom. Formal and explicit standards hardly influenced management style. The various rules and regulations focused on duties and obligations, but almost nothing determined how to deal with people. Leadership evolved over time and with example and compensated for weak human resource policies.

It seems that BNDES developed powerful ways of ensuring sense making, "a way station on the road to a consensually constructed, coordinated system of action" (cited in Weick, Sutcliffe and Obstfeld, 2005, p. 409). The statement "BNDES in this sequence" was an important piece of the cultural web, a story passed along through generations, reminding us that we should be respectful of citizens' money managed by us.

These elements formed the basis for sustaining an organization that spanned six decades of constant turbulence in Brazilian history. Operating amid a national state that had moments of great strength and profound weakness, suffering various political crises and under the constant threat of capture by short-term interests, BNDES adopted a management style that enabled it to remain at the center of the country's decision arena, with good financial records and great technical-ethical respectability.

In the early years of the twenty-first century, it is possible to say that new elements entered this equation and that there is a need to renew, reframe and even discard some traditional elements. Brazil has changed, the Bank is changing rapidly and what worked well for almost 60 years may no longer be enough.

New times, new actions

The practice of financing investment projects has always been the hub of the strategy of BNDES. Many of the strategic priorities and emphases emerged from the interaction between employees of the Bank and its customers, always within a macro view that offers a framework for specific business. "Strategy as a practice" is a good description of the way the institution used to handle strategy. Its classic pragmatism led the Bank's officials to look outward for new needs of companies, clients and government.

The current context presents significant challenges for the institution to continue playing the key role it has played in the Brazilian economy over the past 60 years. In the next paragraphs, I discuss briefly BNDES's main strategic challenges that are framing the change in HR policies.

Scope shift in the Bank's activity

Recent trends in the Brazilian economy have imposed the need to adapt the Bank's policies, personnel, organization and funding. Due to acceleration in investment, both private and public, and because of the 2008 financial crisis, BNDES has experienced significant increase in its scale of operation (annual disbursement grew from US$ 12 billion in 2003, to US$ 190 billion in 2013, an increase of 16 times). Besides that, there was an increase in its scope of action through support to different sectors, internationalization of Brazilian firms became a new frontier, and project analysis is increasing in complexity due to social, innovation and sustainability concerns. The current context requires BNDES and its staff to have a multidimensional look that transcends the assessment of economic and financial aspects, through the incorporation of social, environmental and regional levels. Table 3.8 shows the correlation between the challenges of Brazilian development and the role of BNDES.

Rapid demographic and generational change

In addition to the new socioeconomic context of Brazil, BNDES has been experiencing significant changes in its internal environment. There is currently a major shift in its demographics, caused by the retirement of about 500 professionals from 2007 to 2012, plus a 25 percent increase in total staff.

The organization faces the challenge of maintaining cultural identity, promoting the transfer of knowledge – one of its most valuable assets – and strengthening and spreading its values for the new generation. This challenge becomes even more complex because of the fact that the so-called Generation Y brings a different conception of relationship with work, with implications for the construction of professional identity and expectations regarding career. For Veloso

Table 3.8 The role of BNDES in Brazilian development (2013)

The role of BNDES in Brazilian development 🔊 *BNDES*	
Country Challenges	*Role of BNDES*
Investment growing ahead of GDP	Support for new capacity, especially in high-technology sectors and innovation
Continuity and expansion of investment infrastructure	Credit, project finance and guarantees
Expansion of exports	Financing-supplier's credit
Strengthening labor force skills	Financing
Development of a private, long-term financing industry	Support to bond markets; introduction of new financing instruments, technical support
Improve the governance of public and private organizations	Technical support
Modernization of public institutions	Financing
Promotion of long-term planning	Technical support

Source: author, based on internal primary data.

and colleagues (2008), members of Generation Y, composed of those born after 1978, are influenced by technology, perhaps more concerned with immediate gratification of their desires, questioning, defending their own opinions, and do not conform with the predominance of professional issues over the personal side.

Systems and process management modernization

One of the main guidelines for the Bank's performance was to always support Brazilian development. Despite the success in meeting the challenges of this ambitious business plan, internal systems and processes always played a secondary role, which eventually claimed a high price. This manifests itself through a great deal of effort to match internal procedures and an ever-changing operational frontier.

In 2008, the Bank decided to address the internal challenges and launched the project AGIR – action for integrated resource management. The initiative aimed at modernizing BNDES, based more on processes than on hierarchical-functional requirements. The project included renewal of hardware, such as databases, and implementation of an ERP – enterprise resource planning (SAP), with the support of consulting firms like Accenture.

BNDES has many competencies and a large business scale, but its practices and tools for managing work processes are not fully developed. This can be a source of inefficiency and unsatisfactory productivity, causing unwanted rework. The deployment of new systems and tools will allow a reduction in the time now spent on transactional and operational activities (by technicians and executives), favoring actions of strategic and tactical nature aiming at improving performance.

In an organization whose origins are far from the world of processes, it is easy to grasp the extent of the impacts that AGIR will bring to the BNDES. To inaugurate this new approach without sacrificing the dynamic elements of the original model will be a huge challenge in the coming years.

How the bank's challenges affect HR

More and new demands

The creation of an HR area at the end of 2008 raised people management to a strategic dimension in the organization, which led to the emergence of demands for programs and projects. Staff renewal, beyond the challenges mentioned earlier, also creates operational implications for the human resources area, both in volume and in scope of work. Between 2008 and 2014, the Bank recruited about 1,700 employees, representing almost 60 percent of the total 2,840 jobs currently existing in the organization. The current personnel complement, therefore, is composed of a significant number of new employees and an executive team with relatively short experience. There is a need for a very structured process of integration and training of new employees, transmitting values, transferring knowledge and developing new talent.

Empowering people became the keynote of HR activities. The challenge is to train new staff based on a legacy of knowledge and values historically constructed and to empower managers to act according to an approach that renders them responsible for developing their teams. Managers should change practices, reducing the time spent in technical issues and devoting more attention to team and process aspects.

At the same time, the company needs to develop new approaches to corporate learning. The new agenda must not only focus on providing more training to more people, but also on helping individuals and groups to learn more quickly. The key issue related to learning in a bank relates to solving the problems faced by the organization. The caveat is clear: learning is a way of getting quicker to better results, not an end in itself, noble as it may be.

Corporate HR management is something new to BNDES

Prior to the creation of the HR area, two departments in the administrative area were responsible for providing transactional services and training and development. Therefore, the existence of a unit dedicated to the task of creating and implementing strategic HR solutions is something new, adopting policies and programs aimed at developing the skills needed for BNDES to achieve its goals and objectives.

The company has the great challenge of building an active HR department, recognized as a business partner and a service provider of excellence, adding value to achieve BNDES's strategic objectives. Amid a backdrop of rapid change, it is necessary to spread a new methodology of work, which includes the vision of modern design and process management, aiming to support a solid and sustained transformation of the organization.

Acting as a partner of the business areas of BNDES will not be easy. The tradition of business units that operate with autonomy may hamper the interaction of HR with the other areas. Metaphorically, there is the vision of the organization distributed in silos, with their own life and momentum. In this sense, the deployment of corporate policies of managing people can face resistance, as it questions old ways of doing. Inevitably, HR will touch on various deeply embedded cultural aspects of the organization.

The new agenda to staff management

With so many different challenges, human resources management in BNDES requires modernization. Some of the issues yet to be developed are as follows.

1   Encourage commitment – remember the meaning of work (why we work together) by making values part of ordinary life.
2   Try to align incentives and strategy and management style ("put the money where your mouth is").
3   Assist managers in distress – managers need to let go of certain technical content and embrace the development of other skills, which always has implications for professional identity.
4   Facilitate consensus and innovation by promoting appropriate attitudes – this is probably one of the more promising initiatives to help improve quality and productivity. Listening skills have a strong positive impact on the energy of the teams and their ability to work and innovate.

How to deal with an uncertain future?

People management is today one of the most central themes of BNDES's organizational agenda. In a sense, there should be no novelty in it, because the main capital of the Bank is its legitimacy in the market and society, sustained by the way *benedenses* handled the various tasks they received over the decades. Commitment to the country's development, technical excellence and ethics are attributes of the organization and its employees. Nowadays, new internal and external landmarks influence people management at BNDES as in every other organization – increased size and complexity, more demand for transparency, new stakeholders, millennials etc. Thus, the old approach has lost strength and it is necessary to update tradition.

The main HR projects under way point to the introduction of elements previously almost unheard of. The adoption of a competencies management model represents an attempt to further formalize traditional methods. Managers and employees now have explicit reference standards that they should pursue. The example of leaders continues to be fundamental, but is complemented by systems and methods for managing people, among which stand out the use of organized feedback.

At the same time bringing new tools to support management, HR operations effectively reduce the degrees of freedom of managers. Increased formalization of practices and policies will further restrict managerial leeway. The volume of managerial information will increase, putting pressure on managers to take action with less intuition and more method. Formal evaluations should strengthen meritocracy, a pillar of an organization with a solid technical base. Senior management will tend to become more demanding because of the availability of indicators and tools to compare what before stood behind the informality.

The organization wrote down its core values for the first time in 2010. Project and process management are spreading throughout the organization. Modernization of support systems is under way. There is a growing pressure for efficiency. Given this movement, one could ask if there would be space for those characteristics that made the Bank what it is today. Probably one of the biggest challenges of managing people is to find the exact combination of traditional elements and new elements. This is an art and not found in any manual.

The new management methods, more formal, explicit and quantified, should not drown out the positive aspects of tradition, which include the strong convergence around core values, the primacy of political over technical, management by example, among others. There should be continuity in most cultural aspects, deep roots of organizational identity.

Which are the points of intersection between the past, present and future of this organization? What is the bond that cannot be lost? What key elements should be kept, so that the organization does not lose its identity? This chapter advances some clues. The organizational values certainly can serve as glue between generations, a legacy to those who today are joining the Bank. Values, somehow, do influence behaviors, attitudes and skills that are essential to BNDES's professionals.

Trust is an element that seems to have been the keynote of coexistence of *benedenses* in the Bank's history. Here I use the definition of trust as "an early and voluntary acceptance of a risky investment, when one expects that the other party will not act opportunistically" (Zanini 2007). BNDES's professionals managed to build an environment of trust around shared values, the pursuit of technical excellence in their work and shared decision-making processes. All those ingredients should be part of the Bank's recipe in the future.

The relation between trust and cooperation is not simple. For many, like Zanini (2007), trust is the basis for cooperation. One trusts the other, and then both cooperate to achieve better results. Some authors, including classics like Machiavelli and Hobbes, point to the fact that other means could foster cooperation, like coercion, for instance. Cooperation could also be the basis for trust, reversing the more usual understanding.

After reviewing various interpretations, Gambetta concludes that it is almost impossible to prove that trust is the natural basis for human behavior. Nevertheless, "it may be rational to trust trust and distrust distrust" (2000, p. 235). There are two main reasons to do so. First, by acting as if one trusted, it is possible to gather information about others and set the right attitudes and behaviors. Second, the more trust is used; the more there is likely to be. The combined reasons, even being weaker than common sense would expect, are "enough to motivate the search for social arrangements that may provide incentives for people to take risks" (p. 235).

As a tentative conclusion, I advance the hypothesis that many generations of employees and managers at BNDES have established a framework of norms and behaviors to maximize trust and cooperation. This does not mean that there is no competition or coercion. So far, it seems that the dose of cooperation has been enough to allow the Bank to take the right decisions. In the future, I think that more cooperation, inside and outside the organization, will be needed due to the increasing complexity of the business environment. This is the subject for a future chapter.

The dual nature of BNDES and its impact on the innovation journey

Banks and innovation do not walk hand to hand as a rule. A banker would never have come up with such a disruptive innovation as an iPad. Banks' business essence is quite simple: lend money to someone with many collaterals and take it back with interest in due time. The clear majority of bankers will engage in riskier deals only when competition and declining profits force them to do so. Bankers tend to be very conservative and insist on the successful formulas of the past.

Unlike a commercial bank, a development bank should be innovative to tackle the challenges posed by this specific "business," that is, development of a country. The boundaries of development are in constant change, always moving. Evidence from BNDES suggests that innovation is strategically necessary in this kind of organization, but the costs tend to be high and conflict is almost an inevitable side effect.

In Portuguese, the "b" of BNDES signifies Bank. Development ("d") comes in third place and social ("s") is the last one. The banker mindset comes first not only in the acronym. The main processes and tools of the organization embody the discipline associated with being part of the financial industry. Even when seduced by a project with many positive social and environmental externalities, a BNDES employee always must investigate its financial sustainability and repayment capacity. The answer is "no" if the proponent does not prove that it will be able to repay the loan. No positive cash flow, no collaterals, no loans.

From the very beginning, the major output of the credit concession process is to classify projects as viable and unviable. Credit analysis always takes into consideration macroeconomic, social, technological and environmental dimensions of the projects. However, at the end of the day, financial indicators have a "go – no go" nature. The aim is to preserve the banking dimension of the organization. As one former deputy director of the industrial area put it just after retiring from BNDES, "looking backwards, I am sometimes more proud of the bad projects that I did not approve, than of the good ones that I supported."

The right mindset to respond to business requirements is sometimes at odds with innovation. Selection is typical of the second phase of innovation, as mentioned previously. In the first phase, searching for new ideas and opportunities requires that participants do not judge very soon, do not select right from the start. "Defer judgment" is one of the most important rules for having a productive search. On the other hand, at BNDES, quick and effective judgment is one of the most valuable attributes of an employee. The promotion of many of the managers happened exactly because of this characteristic. The consequence is that they judge every time, frequently suffocating new ideas and draining energy from less bold colleagues.

Another way of looking at this two-sided coin is to consider the "let's do it" approach. BNDES has a strong commitment to do what is required by each context and development phase. It means that access to managerial positions is contingent on execution. The more one can execute, the more likely one is to enter a managerial career. This adds another difficulty for the innovation journey: managers not only tend to judge all the time, but they also prefer to jump to execution. The first and third phases of innovation – search and commitment – are frequently too short, not allowing for a balanced process. Some dimensions are forgotten or barely considered, imposing a burden on the execution phase, when all the hidden topics tend to reappear.

Besides these mindset biases, other elements bring difficulties to the innovation processes of the Bank. Organizational structure is very traditional, vertical and function oriented. As a state-owned company, the Bank has many internal and external regulations, increasing inertia and a "stick to what worked well in the past" mentality. Due to the collaborative nature of work and the decision-making process, it takes a long time to evaluate new ideas.

The main HR challenges in BNDES relate exactly to the complexity of pushing innovative decision making in a very conservative organization. The difficulties posed to some of the main projects are a case of a more general situation, where "managers see change and innovation as highly ambiguous and react to it in terms of their interpretation of how it will affect their own jobs, status and ambitions" (Mumford and Ward, 1968, p. 101, cited in Pettigrew, 2009, p. 35).

As Pettigrew states, "the content of strategic change is thus ultimately a product of a legitimation process shaped by political/cultural considerations, though often expressed in rational/analytical terms" (1987, p. 659). If he is right, the HR journey in search of management innovation is still in its first steps.

Change and continuity in BNDES

> [During the first conversation between the two, in February 1972,] Nixon complimented Mao for transforming an ancient civilization. [. . .] Mao answered: "I haven't been able to change it. I've only been able to change a few places in the vicinity of Beijing."
>
> (Henry Kissinger, *On China*, 2011, p. 120)

Management literature usually does not use the concept of power as an analytical tool. Power has become illegitimate within management. Interestingly, legitimacy seems more acceptable to the mainstream way of thinking, and perhaps this explains why the concept of soft power has not gained currency within management studies (although it is obviously important in management practices). As Courpasson suggests, "organizations should be seen as 'soft bureaucracies,' in which centralization and entrepreneurial forms of governance are combined" (2000, p. 141). Based on a Weberian approach and analyzing organizational forms and patterns in France, the author defines organization as a combination of "structures of domination" and "structures of legitimacy." His conclusion is that "in spite of the success of the network form utopia, the re-emergence of bureaucracies is a sign that organizations are more and more politically centralized and governed" (p. 141). In Nye's terms, the balance between hard and soft power dimensions might have changed, but hard power is the ultimate driver of governance.

The emergence of organizations based on "structures of games" is recent, at least for the specialized literature. During the 1970s, scholars noticed that the traditional concept of "structures of domination" was no longer enough to understand the dynamics of organizations. Crozier and Friedberg, cited by Courpasson, concluded, "The major stake for people in organizations is to control uncertainty, and uncertainty is a source of power and opportunity for hidden struggles" (1997, p. 144). They define people as actors capable of acting on their wills, not only responding to rules centrally defined. In this context, "the system of organizational governance is produced by a set of local games, and not by a political centralization capable of ruling and imposing people's stakes and people's strategies" (Courpasson, 2000, p. 145). Soft power would have become more important than hard power in organizational life.

Based on case studies, Courpasson concludes "that in this political structure (soft bureaucracies), domination and legitimacy are intertwined, precisely because domination cannot be based only on coercion and violence" (p. 155). The typical soft governing tools, such as strategic planning, are not per se evidence of the predominance of a new form of organization. Courpasson argues, "Legitimacy is necessary to justify that organizations need to be governed from the centre, even if they are apparently more entrepreneurial and decentralized" (p. 155).

"We should admit that the expansion of a liberal management based on decentralization and the 'marketization' of organizations and autonomy goes hand in hand with the development of a highly centralized and authoritarian form of government – a combination we have called 'soft bureaucracies'" (Courpasson, 2000, p. 159).

It is not clear for me that Courpasson's interpretation is a general theory of organizations, if such a thing exists. The point I would like to make is that his approach seems to describe quite adequately BNDES's governance in the past five years. During this period, senior management has launched a series of initiatives aiming at increasing managerial effectiveness and control. Among the main projects already in place we should mention: strategic planning based on balanced scorecards; a contribution and development plan for all employees; conformity analysis tools; redesign of processes and implementation of SAP systems; and performance evaluations based on objective indicators (mostly in operational areas).

Traditionally, BNDES has been an organization where employees and organizational units enjoyed a remarkable degree of freedom concerning centralized governance systems. Even without sliding to an uncoordinated mass of conflicting agendas, there has been a growing concern that the autonomy of different units became a threat to the Bank's effectiveness and efficiency. The initiatives mentioned in the previous paragraph have the common feature of reducing the degree of autonomy of units and employees. New standards and controls were implemented in order to allow senior managers to have a close evaluation of performance and disincentive unintended deviations.

If this interpretation were correct, BNDES would fit very well into Courpasson's framework. One could interpret the new organizational processes and projects as a change in the "structures of domination" with simultaneous introduction of new "structures of legitimacy." Emergent elite members have legitimated their position with "modernization projects" aiming at efficiency and rationalization of working processes. It comes as no surprise that the more normative projects have been struggling with fewer resources and less attention than others do. For instance, the challenge of evaluating social and environmental effectiveness of projects funded by BNDES has not taken off so far, even with growing demands from civil society organizations and supervision bodies.

Since its very beginning, the Bank has insulated itself against "aggressions" coming from disordering events. Managing a large amount of fiscal or quasi-fiscal money just like a federal government, BNDES's officers developed a culture of ethics and technical excellence nurturing and protecting the organization against the risks of the political and economic context. While many state and private institutions have sunk during the past six decades because of economic crisis, mismanagement and corruption, the Bank accumulated a large social capital based on public reconnaissance of its excellence.

A sharp observer and participant of the history of the organization once said, "BNDES is the largest family company in the world." His point was that insulation left its mark on the Bank's culture and internal politics. Negotiation based on interpersonal interactions among elite members inside the Bank was always the norm. The rule of reciprocity and even quasi-familial ties explained the formation and long life of group alliances. Sometimes different interest groups within the Bank had different political and ideological views, but this was never the most important driver in group formation. Once a group was established, it behaved very much as a "circle of friends" in Chinese *guanxi* style. The members tended to move together within the organization, support each other's projects and use the reciprocity rule, especially in protecting and helping someone who lost his executive position.

Unfortunately, I cannot explore this point in full depth because this is part of the untold history of the Bank and there is no literature on the subject. However, if this analogy is true, domination schemes are deeply rooted in BNDES's culture and in its members' behaviors. The formal decision-making processes live together, side by side, with informal processes. The consequence is that formal and informal arenas become spaces to negotiate major changes in operational policies, priorities or organizational design and practices. Innovations must obtain the "blessing" of the most influential circles through a complex set of shadow conversations and bargains, in order to have "everybody (that counts) on board."

References

Campbell, B., Coff, R. and Kryscynski, D. "Rethinking sustained competitive advantage from human capital," *Academy of Management Review*, Vol. 37, No. 3, July 2012, pp. 376–395.

Courpasson, D. "Managerial strategies of domination: power in soft bureaucracies," *Organization Studies*, Vol. 21, No. 1, Egos, 2000, pp. 141–161.

Crozier, M. and Friedberg, E. *L'acteur et le système*. Paris: Seuil, 1977.

Gambetta, D. "Can we trust trust?" in Gambetta, D. (ed.), *Trust: Making and Breaking Cooperative Relations*, electronic edition. Oxford: Department of Sociology, University of Oxford, chapter 13, 2000, pp. 213–237, www.sociology.ox.ac.uk/papers/gambetta213-237.pdf.

Luna-Martínez, J. de and Vicente, C. L. "Global survey of development banks." *Policy Research Working Paper*, 5969, Washington, DC: World Bank, February 2012.

Mintzberg, H. *Managing – desvendando o dia a dia da gestão*. Porto Alegre: Bookman, 2010.

Mintzberg, H. "Organization design options." PowerPoint presentation.

Nye, Jr., J. S. "Soft power," *Foreign Policy*, 1990, pp. 153–171.

Pettigrew, A. M. "Context and action in the transformation of the firm," *Journal of Managerial Studies*, Vol. 24, No. 6, November 1987, pp. 649–670.

Pettigrew, A. M. *The Politics of Organizational Decision-Making*, kindle edition. London: Tavistoky, 2009.

Thompson, L., Wang, J., and Gunia, B. "Negotiation," *The Annual Review of Psychology*, Vol. 61, 2010, pp. 491–515.

Weick, K., Sutcliffe, K, and Obstfeld, D. "Organizing and the process of sensemaking," *Organization Science*, Vol. 16, No 4, July–August 2005, pp. 409–421.

Zanini, M. T. *Confiança: o principal ativo intangível de uma empresa – pessoas, motivação e construção de valor*. Rio de Janeiro: Elsevier, 2007.

4 Knowledge of organizational behavior and consultancy projects

A critical examination

Rajiv Kumar

Introduction

Many years ago, Kurt Lewin suggested that human behavior could be a product of two things: (a) the state, or personal characteristics, of a person, and (b) the environment in which the person operates (1936). I want to invoke this framework to articulate why consultants frequently end up rendering bad, incomplete, short-sighted, impractical, and sometimes scandalous advice (Craig, 2005; Fincham, 1999; Sturdy, 1997). Existing commentaries (e.g., Craig, 2005; Sturdy, 1997) on this issue seem to overemphasize the role consultants play in this sad state of affairs, echoing fundamental attribution error (Ross, 1977). Although such an approach does have a grain of truth, it is also important to realize that the context or environment plays an important role in ensuring that consultants and consultancies rarely remain effective. In other words, context ensures that success of a consultancy is left more to chance than to thoughtful, careful, and heedful consultants.

I have deliberately taken an extreme position in this chapter, assuming that taking such a position is going to be helpful in *highlighting* some key reasons consultancies fail to deliver. As I mentioned earlier, this failure is also due to the context in which consultants operate and consultancies occur. In this chapter, I draw on my experience of providing consulting services to a state police department in India in order to dwell on the following interrelated features of context: (a) the nature of knowledge that forms the basis of such endeavors, (b) the nature of the process through which such services are provided, and finally, (c) the nature of organizational and social milieu within which consultancies take place rather ineffectively.

This analysis is important because it has the potential to highlight some problems in an endeavor wherein popular concepts (such as organizational culture in my specific case, and competencies, employee engagement, and so forth in general) are borrowed to pack perceived problems in them, and an outsider, a perceived "expert," uses further borrowed knowledge – concepts, theories, and methods – to solve the perceived problems. I argue that this endeavor is fraught with problems such as (a) muting the voices of people who routinely experience the problems but get overwhelmed by alien and yet glittering terminology, (b) imprecise inclusion of phenomenon (Strauss and Corbin, 1998) in a conceptual domain by people who hurry to use a borrowed concept without sufficiently critiquing it, (c) inaccurate and incomplete elicitation of real issues due to limitation of methods and theories, and (d) articulation of "solutions" that, therefore, seem "scientific" but end up doing considerable violence to the bewitched majority, ably supported by the existing hierarchical structure of knowledge inside and outside an organization. The help provider, i.e., consultants, and the help seeker, i.e., clients, both are *helpless* before these larger and subtle forces, as I attempt to show in this chapter. The upshot of these contextual forces and ensuing problems is that consultancies leave a lot to be desired for both the consultants and the clients. Considering the theme of this book – governance – I visualize that the contextual elements I discuss in this chapter render the governance of a consulting relationship or service provision suboptimal.

The issues that I tackle in this chapter can be sensed at two levels. One is a mundane level where one routinely finds an organization stuck with a myriad of disappointments, instances of lack of cooperation (Barnard, 1938), shirking, corruption, lack of justice (Cohen-Charash and Spector, 2001), and so forth. I am assuming that all organizations experience this and seek help. The seeking, and provision of help from an outsider, an expert, brings me to the second and deeper level at which the issues exist. This is the level where I sense the inadequacy of concepts, theories, and methods playing a bigger role. To make matters worse, there is always a hierarchy of stakeholders involved, and hence knowledge (in which I include concepts, theories, and methods) ends up becoming a tool that partly solves the problem, but also oversimplifies, befuddles, obfuscates, and suppresses dissent. I elaborate on these interrelated issues in the remaining sections of this chapter.

I begin by providing a brief background of a study that I co-conducted. Next, I describe the contextual problems I have mentioned in this introduction. I describe the way consulting relationships are decided and how the assignments are carried out, in order to highlight how they adversely impact the outcomes. Then I discuss the deficiencies in organizational behavior (OB) knowledge that do not permit the discovery of a quality solution. I end by discussing the implications of my arguments.

Background of the study

The background of this chapter is mainly in an extended period of consultancy I provided (with two other colleagues) for the police department of a state in India. This department had expressed its intention to commission a study to assess its culture with a view to get an accurate insight into the internal work culture. Along with this, it had asked for a possible roadmap for improvements in the potential areas that need specific interventions for improved stakeholders' satisfaction. Stakeholders included not only internal employees, but also external parties such as the general public.

Policing in India is organized mostly at the state level. Law and order is primarily the responsibility of state governments in India. However, the central government, through the Ministry of Home Affairs, also plays an important role. The police force in each state is headed by a senior officer of the Indian Police Service. Police forces in India have a long history, dating back to the pre-independence era. This history is noteworthy, as it had led to the expansion of the organization in size (e.g., having several types of setups looking after training, recruitment, administration, intelligence gathering, and so forth), activity, and geographical reach. Therefore, rendering advice to such an important and large organization was a daunting task to begin with.

As the concepts, theories, and methods (labeled as *knowledge* in this chapter) form an important part of my commentary on the context of consulting, I briefly elaborate on the background leading to the concepts, theories, and methods used in this study. Organizational culture emerged as the natural choice for the main concept to employ in this consultancy, given the explicit request from the client. Moreover, subsequent discussions with the client convinced us of the suitability of the concept. Once the concept to focus on became clear, the theories of organizational culture (e.g., Cook and Szumal, 1993; Hofstede, Neuijen, Ohayv, and Sanders, 1990; Pareek, 1998; Pettigrew, 1979; Schein, 2004) naturally emerged as candidates for consideration. But the exposure to literature and theory around organizational culture could only do so much, as my team and I had to decide which of these works to ultimately follow. A few considerations drove our choice. First, as the consultancy demanded identification of areas for improvement, we had to focus on a theory that had an empirical basis. In other words, we had to rely on something that could be measured, either quantitatively or qualitatively (and ideally through both these approaches). Next, we had to have some comparative norm data available so that we could compare the findings of this organization with the other organizations. And last, we had to be sensitive about the Indian context. Considering all this, we decided to use the organizational culture framework given by Pareek (1998).

The next piece of knowledge we used in this project pertained to methods employed for data elicitation, collection, and analysis. The following section on research design describes this.

Research design

There were two phases of the study, as outlined here. First, we had a qualitative phase in which we interviewed officers, inspectors, and other lower-level staff. These were semi-structured interviews. Following snowball sampling, we asked the respondents to suggest more potential respondents who could provide interesting data considering the study purposes. We also took into account the suggestions of the main contacts in the client organization in this regard, i.e., we interviewed the police officials suggested by the main contact persons in the headquarters.

This was followed by a quantitative phase in which we conducted a questionnaire-based survey. The questions were chosen based on the interviews and literature. Apart from the questions tapping different aspects of organizational culture, we also included questions on job satisfaction and leadership, as these had emerged as important variables to study during interviews. The English questionnaire was translated into the local language using back-translation (Brislin, 1986). The questionnaire also had a section for open-ended responses.

The questionnaires were sent to different districts by the contact people in the police headquarters. In most of these districts, the managers of police units there took the responsibility of getting their subordinates to respond. We had to follow up in a few districts, but mostly the hierarchical architecture ensured that filled-in questionnaires were returned to us on time. Respondents were given the option of anonymity. We gave our contact details (phone numbers, postal address, and email IDs) in case someone wanted to contact us directly. We did get some phone calls seeking clarifications regarding some questions.

One noteworthy aspect of hierarchy, power layers and ensuing helplessness of lower-level employees, emerged during the process of data collection. As this consultancy was commissioned by upper levels of the hierarchy without much, or any, consultation with employees at lower levels, the decision makers were probably oblivious to the problems of the lower rungs. Additionally, as historically the police organization has been a centralized, command-and-control organization, we got to discover that it was the first such exercise – of seeking even lower-level employees' opinions – in this department. And hence, some lower-level police personnel (constables and inspectors) were so happy with the data collection itself that they called us, or sometimes sent text messages, to thank us.

Problems of context

How do consultancies come about?

It is important to understand how the need for outside help arises in organizations. To the outsiders who routinely provide such help (e.g., consultants or trainers), this question may seem meaningless precisely because it is so routine. Sometimes people miss noticing things because they are too small, infrequent, and insignificant to notice, and sometimes people fail to notice things because they are everywhere and hence quite commonplace. But to understand how the practice of medicine disappoints the doctor as well as the patient, perhaps understanding the etiology of the ailment is useful.[1] I turn next to this question.

As stated earlier, some level of imperfection is pretty natural in organizations. Organized activities that rest on human contributions are destined to be less than perfect. There are several reasons for believing so. People are bounded rational, people exhibit a variety of cognitive biases and errors; people have mild to intense differences among themselves (Robbins, Judge, and Vohra, 2013), and what people want as results by involvement in the organization is always much more than what any formal organization can offer. However, not every imperfection, big or small, requires outside help. In fact, sometimes bigger ailments may not receive outside help, but smaller problems do. Hence it is interesting to examine the factors driving the decision of hiring paid outside help. I sense two broad categories of these factors. One is obviously a powerful enough collation of internal voices that could drive such a decision. This is what happened in this specific case too.

A high-ranking official drove the decision to hire outside experts to study the felt problem. However, it would be a mistake to assume that decisions like these, particularly in highly formalized bureaucracies (it was a government department, after all), are entirely driven by one person. What are essential for these decisions to materialize are (a) an absence of strong resistance, and (b) an indifference of other powerful actors. This is what I also sensed, as by the time we could start the data collection exercise, the incumbent who had championed the initiative got transferred. The next person *had to* implement this project already decided; naturally, his involvement was lower. This is not to say that the next person did not cooperate; in fact, he provided excellent support. But what became clear in due course was that for other stakeholders, this project was just a routine part of their job, involving meeting outside experts for interviews, facilitating collection of data, arranging the logistics for visits, and so forth. The understanding and intellectual involvement of a person who moots and champions an idea would always be different from someone who subsequently has no option but to implement the idea. If the key actors disappear from the stage, the play or the act is seldom able to follow the script. This is not to say that the entire interaction was a bland one; we did come across people who were excited, involved, and engaged with us intellectually. But there were other kinds of interactions too. Given all this, I infer that consulting projects begin in a political context wherein (a) someone powerful enough champions the initiative and (b) other powerful actors do not resist or remain indifferent about it. This assumption also relates to the next contextual problem that envelops consultancies.

Apart from the role of internal politics (i.e., emergence of a conducive enough coalition around a consultancy decision), there are some external factors too that impinge on this decision. To illustrate, the project that I carried out was also motivated by a similar study conducted in a different state of India. That study had received some positive coverage in the media, and the central government had encouraged other states to replicate it. These are also occasions for people to show initiative and get recognition. The power structure in large bureaucracies is such that it is much more difficult to penalize lack of initiative or even noncompliance; it is much easier to reward citizenship behavior (Organ, 1988). And that creates enough motivational space for people to combine noble intentions (of solving problems) with careerist intentions. I do not have data to support this, and hence this is a conjecture on my part. But given that organizations are political places, I suspect this conjecture deserves to be considered rather than ignored.

Another related factor is that consultants could get hired because powerful people desire to be seen as doing something about the myriad of problems that afflict organized activities. After all, there are prizes to be won for being seen as having a bias for action (Bruch and Ghoshal, 2004). Additionally, organizations seek legitimacy in order to derive resources from the environment. In the case of government departments in general, and police department in particular, the popular perception is that they are overstaffed, inefficient, and corrupt. And therefore, being seen as an organization that is concerned to receive advice from the more efficient sectors of society adds to the legitimacy of these organizations. Studies like these are useful from a branding and public relations standpoint, as they create an image of these organizations modernizing through incorporating the latest management thoughts.

Consultants are sometimes also hired because the upper echelon wants to give business to its friends and other people in its network. After all, the old boys' network does seem to work (McDonald, 2011). And last, consultants are sometimes hired to legitimize a decision that the upper echelon wants to foist upon the organization. Although organizations are hierarchies, if the usage of reward and coercive power to achieve some end could also be legitimized (French and Raven, 1959), it gives an extra moral cushion to the exercise of reward and coercion.

What these two broad categories of factors (internal or problem driven, and external or prestige and benefits driven) ensure is that powerful people in the client organization feel either impelled or compelled to articulate a credible reason to hire external consultants. But if the second category of reasons plays a bigger role, the chances of some real benefit accruing to the silent majority in the hiring organizations are subverted from the beginning itself. It does not really matter how noble the intentions of consultants are, or how truthful and sophisticated are the tools employed by the consultants; the project is doomed because there is very little space for a genuine inquiry and development of solutions. This is not to assert that such not-so-noble reasons always fail both clients and consultants; but if some real benefit does emerge from such consultancies, they are byproducts, or unintended yet noble consequences of not-so-noble actions (Merton, 1936). Powerful actors in the client organizations end up co-creating a situation in which the provision of genuine help gets stifled.

How are consultancies carried out?

Even after deciding to engage a consultant, the initial framing of the problem is quite important. One cannot afford to look like a novice. Unlike in the medical model, where a patient frequently describes the symptoms, here the patient has the compulsion to come across as knowledgeable enough to be able to label the problem. To a less trained eye, fads often look enticing enough to pack the symptoms in them. The charm of management knowledge is too strong to resist because such knowledge is typically packaged and branded as a powerful panacea, duly supported by tools such as books, business press, consulting firms, seminars, workshops, and so forth. Consultants are privileged because of their background, tools, and language they use. And that runs the risk of affected people in the client organization getting mesmerized with the form as opposed to the content. To illustrate, routine infractions of rules or norms become a pain for employees. But whether this is a problem of culture or something else, that remains a nebulous and imprecise exercise. Yet another illustration of this could be seen in the fact that work–life balance emerged as a major problem quite late in the study. Initial interviews were dominated by senior officers, who for some reason did not talk about this as an issue.[2] But subsequent data (qualitative as well as quantitative) highlighted this as a major issue for lower-level staff. Hence the problems or infractions that most likely had their origin in lack of adequate time for oneself and one's family *appeared* as problems of culture. Similarly, initial interviews highlighted that dealing with media scrutiny and pressure from human rights groups was a major challenge. I do not believe that these challenges in the workplace would be meaningfully dealt with by studying organizational culture. These instances make me claim that to a spell-bound student of management (i.e., high-ranking officials in this case), the latest fad may look persuasively charming. Possibly this happens also because the less trained eye is a colonized mind, and has taken the received knowledge as granted (Mignolo, 2009). If desired results are not coming, or problems recur, the collective mindset, or culture, needs rectification; resource constraints and daily problems of the unprivileged minority – as reported later – get overlooked while defining the problems to solve. And then a consultancy project tends to get misaligned right from the beginning.

I want to highlight another remaining issue. As mentioned earlier, organizations are hierarchies and political places. And hence, the process through which felt problems are captured and articulated is imperfect. First, not all stakeholders feel the same problem, or feel the problems in the same way. For example, when living conditions in a barrack are poor, it is a felt problem for people who are living there. But even then, police officers who could get leave to spend time with their families in nearby places would feel the problems differently than the police officers who had to spend months altogether in the dingy barracks. But the same problem is not felt by officers who do not have to live in barracks. So not only are the same problems experienced differently, but in a large organization, different people have different problems. And it is a political process that determines which problems are accorded enough importance to seek paid external help. I do not subscribe to the viewpoint that people at the top know what is more important; many times, these people at the upper echelons do not have much clue about the problems of the hoi-polloi. So in case the upper echelon does hire paid external help to solve a problem, the problem may not be the most important one, or the most pressing one.

The process of consultation relies heavily on the reported account of employees. There are at least three reasons why this heavy reliance on what people tell (qualitatively or quantitatively) is unhealthy. Not everyone is equally informed about what ails an organization. Next, organizations are political places and hence some reporters of the accounts might be driven by political agendas. And last, access to employees is filtered by the gatekeepers in the client organization, and hence not everyone gets an equal opportunity to convey whatever he or she wants to convey.

As I explain later in this chapter, the concepts of organizational behavior (perhaps of management also) are imprecise, and in the complex hierarchy of relationship between a client and a consultant, ruling an imprecise concept out becomes more than an exercise in logic and adducing forward evidence. The client is more powerful because it is paying the consultant, and the consultant is more powerful because s/he is credited with expertise and knowledge. However, the client is unlikely to accept a wholesale modification in the initial framing of the problem, because it is expensive to do so. And hence, although the evidence from the field or data collected may indicate – tentatively or firmly – that employee engagement is not an issue, if the client has framed the problem to be one of disengaged employees, it gets sticky and leaves its imprint on the subsequent actions of the consultant.

Another factor that ensures suboptimal results is the time-bound nature of solution making. Because the underlying assumption of solution search by an expert is that the expert possesses the necessary wherewithal for search, it naturally follows that the search should be expected to get over in a time-bound manner. Some other factors create a milieu in which the time-bound search evolves into a rush for both the solution seeker and solution provider. These factors include the monetary compensation entailing an unequal relationship – the organization paying for the consultation gains legitimacy to demand delivery, or even to change the content and schedule of delivery – and multifarious activities that go on in parallel at both the client and consultant's end. A consultant seldom works on only one problem commissioned by a client. Consultants have multiple accounts, and hence their attention is divided. Similarly, it is rare to find people from the client organization fully occupied with the problem. Moreover, the activities planned as building blocks of a solution – their imperfection notwithstanding – seldom go as per the plan. And the upshot of all this is a rush to complete a delivery.

Speaking more generally, yet another limiting feature of the consulting process is that once the initial decision to hire is finalized, the next set of players who step in is (a) less powerful, and (b) less invested in the solution search. And that creates its own set of problems. To illustrate, there is always something lost in translation; the people from both the consultant and client side are unlikely to have the same quality of understanding that the original people involved had or had developed before the hiring decision was finalized. Moreover, the person championing the idea from client side could help the consultants get better-quality data. But as s/he is no longer actively involved, it becomes more difficult for the consultants to get the same quality of data.

I contend that these reasons – initial framing of the problem, non-availability of the project initiators, the project being just one of the activities for people both from the client and consultant side, and demands of time-bound delivery – degrade the output quality. These conditions nibble away at the initial zeal and good intentions and the final delivery becomes a compromised version of what was initially envisaged.

Inadequacies of OB knowledge

In this section, I critique the OB knowledge that forms the basis for consultancies. OB as a discipline (I want to avoid commenting on management in general as it involves other disciplines such as marketing, finance, and so forth) is in a state of crisis even in the places where it has enjoyed considerable longevity. Its knowledge production process is questioned, its knowledge dissemination practices are questioned, and its usefulness for practitioners is also questioned. With this as background, it does not have much promise to offer solutions in societies where it did not even arise *ab initio*.

OB knowledge is not perfect even for classroom teaching (Pawar, 2015). And yet it is used as the basis for rendering advice. As mentioned earlier, for this chapter, I am considering concepts, theories, and methods as OB knowledge. Each of these elements has its own limitations that impinge upon the consultancy process. I highlight these limitations one by one.

Concepts

Concepts contain a family of meanings. Concepts are the building blocks of organizational behavior (Osigweh, 1989). However, despite having such an important role to play in the building and development of the discipline, OB concepts are loosely specified and measured (Schwab, 1980). According to Kaplan (1964), as the science progresses, concepts should become more and more precise, and ideally it should be possible to declare with abundant confidence what a concept is and what it is not (Osigweh, 1989). But that is not the case with OB (Locke, 2003). The reason behind this sad state of affairs is that researchers have not paid enough attention to conceptualization and measurement practices, while they have been galloping to build theories. The production of knowledge, i.e., published research, privileges theory development over concept clarification and stronger measurement. I have nothing against theory development, but the problem is that theory development and theoretical contributions cannot be avowed ends in themselves unless the building blocks are given their due importance. To illustrate, the concept of organizational culture itself has been specified in multiple ways (Pareek, 1998). And to illustrate the problems further, organizational culture has typically been conceptualized as a multidimensional construct. And multidimensional constructs have to be specified and measured carefully (Law, Wong, and Mobley, 1998). But the research on organizational culture has not paid heed to these advices. The same situation is seen in the measurement of other OB concepts too, as Hinkin (1995) pointed out. Construct validity (Nunnally and Bernstein, 1994) is seldom reported for several measures of OB concepts (Hinkin, 1995). As mentioned earlier, this imprecision makes it difficult to define the problem sharply as a consultancy begins. If the problems articulated by the client seem like they are falling in multiple conceptual domains – each of which has its own theoretical superstructure surrounding it – it further muddies the process of problem definition.

In this specific case, I illustrate the problems that imprecise conceptualization entail for consultancies, by elaborating on two dimensions of the organizational culture we measured. As per Pareek (1998) organizational culture has eight dimensions, two of which are authenticity and trust. Authenticity is a cultural dimension that refers to the value employees place in general on congruence between feelings and behaviors, owning up to mistakes, and the extent to which manipulation and deception are avoided. Trust as a dimension of organizational culture refers to the extent to which employees maintain the confidentiality of information, honor mutual obligations, help others in crisis, confide in superiors and make oneself vulnerable without any fear of exploitation, and so forth. Of themselves, these two dimensions seem alright for measuring, comparing the scores obtained with norms, and thereby finding areas for improvement. As the reader would recall, this all gels nicely with the mandate the police department gave us. But the problems of conceptual imprecision hit us when we realize that authenticity is a feature of leadership (George, 2003), and trust is a feature of interpersonal relationship (Schoorman, Mayer, and Davis, 2007) as well. Even if I ignore the concomitant questions about measurement – that is, at which level should one measure authenticity and trust, at the level of individuals' leadership and interpersonal relationships, or as organizational features – other vexing issues arise. If trust and authenticity have multiple meanings, which items should ultimately be used in measuring them? And if comparison norms are available for some, but not for others, how does one reconcile the scores to recommend some action? All these dilemmas leave a consultancy project grappling with both deficient and spurious measurement of concepts.

Theories

Miner (2003) found that only a small percentage of OB theories were rated as highly useful by OB scholars. This is a telling piece of evidence; OB scholars themselves do not feel confident about the usefulness of a large majority of OB theories for application! What can a consultant do in such a situation? Assuming that academic theories occupy the upper echelon of evidence-based knowledge, it just conveys that the state of the discipline is not healthy enough to offer advice.[3]

Methods

Consultants typically adopt primary data collection as the vehicle to understand problems before they solve them. This approach assumes that organizational respondents (employees, managers, customers, and so forth) are obedient servants of the inquiry that a consultant initiates. That may or may not be true. Problems of social desirability (Crowne and Marlow, 1964) and other politically motivated responses apart, the methods and techniques themselves are not perfect enough to yield pure enough data. I highlight this problem by describing two issues.

First, the measurement instruments in OB are rarely examined for construct validity (Hinkin, 1995). And hence, their application in a consultancy becomes suspect. Next, as Hakel (1968) points out, anchor descriptors such as usually, often, frequently, and so forth do not evoke a precise response from all people who respond. And hence collating the responses of people becomes a difficult exercise.

Borrowing a phrase from Prasad, Prasad, Mills, and Mills (2015), the spread of OB knowledge has been obviously less coercive but insidiously hegemonic. Isn't it too much of a coincidence that the employee attitudes in India and everywhere else where the textbook of Robbins, Judge, and Vohra (2013) sells are taught to fall in the precise categories that the American scholars have so assiduously found over the years? It is quite another matter that by their own yardsticks, the knowledge is scandalously short of validity (Miner, 2003; Pawar, 2015).

It takes a special type of fortitude in scholarship to withstand or ignore the pressure of internal contradictions in OB, as highlighted earlier. On one hand, the repeated calls for construct clarity and purer measurement seem to have fallen on deaf ears, and on the other, there has been an oversupply of advice on what theory is (Whetten, 1989), what theory is not (Sutton and Staw, 1995), what theorizing is (Weick, 1995), how imagination can be disciplined to yield better theory (Weick, 1989), and so forth. It seems like a ritual after every few years (with increasing frequency) that the established *pundits* in the field would bemoan the state of knowledge, issue some sage advice in a measured tone as to how to build more theory[4] and then crave more of the same, i.e., theory, albeit of a stronger variety (whatever that means). But it takes an even stronger variety of naivety, or a bigger dose of arrogance, to assume that the surfeit of not-so-useful concepts and theories would be the perfect lenses through which to view the organizational life thousands of miles away from them. It is one thing that the pantheon of OB scholars has no food to nourish its own malnourished theories or medicine to resuscitate those who are gasping for breath. But it is quite another to export them across the globe assuming that organizations would otherwise atrophy to death.

Discussion and implications

The worst form of colonialism is probably colonizing the mind (Mignolo, 2009). This is what is seen in the application of OB knowledge in societies like India. The *fait accompli* here in OB is that first we borrowed Western concepts, tools, and theories, and then we asked the question: how can we accommodate cross-cultural differences, or how can we accommodate the contextual idiosyncrasies? We should have done this the other way around, first developing indigenous concepts and theories, and then borrowing content after examining its relevance. So the fledgling societies, rather than building their own strengths, borrowed content, and the results seem to be almost a fiasco.

The irony is that this colonialism was not only brought about by the conqueror (Alatas, 2000); the conquered actively sought it. The collective efficacy of the conquered societies was at such a low that they lapped up the "superior knowledge" of the West in social sciences too. There was no need to do so. But the leaders of these societies were themselves more Westernized than the Westerns. And hence they invited Harvards and MITs to come and foist their knowledge on India. There was very little attempt to learn how natives organized their work. In case the irony still does not hit you, just imagine which Western theory would have invented the unique philosophy and methods of Gandhi, which guided the mass freedom movement in India. But despite having achieved such stupendous success, we did not begin any attempt to develop a Gandhian theory of organized human behavior; we borrowed how to manage human behavior at work from the United States. And hence my problem is not so much with the arrogance of OB knowledge as discussed previously; my problem is with the ready acceptance of OB knowledge by people within India (maybe elsewhere too). It is not so much the colonizers, but the desire of the colonized to mimic the colonizers that forms my worry.

Over the years, different stakeholders in India have emphasized the indigenous development of OB concepts and theories. Some scholars, including Pareek (1998), whose work formed the basis of this consultancy, have even attempted to develop such indigenous knowledge (Prasad, 2017). But the results seem far from sufficient. Even the recent wisdom of adopting qualitative methods to improve the state of concepts and theories does not seem to have done much good for developing societies. Very few studies have attempted to find out the extent to which Western concepts and theories fit the local context in Eastern societies. To illustrate, Chuang, Hsu, Wang, and Judge (2015) found that the Chinese people interpret the Western concept of person–environment fit with noteworthy newness. We need more studies of this kind.

Returning to the original topic of consultants and consultancies, there are contextual reasons driving the suboptimal performance of consultants. The consultation process suffers from an overreliance on the medical model of diagnosis and prescription. To make matters worse, the doctor, the patient, and the knowledge of treatment all have their limitations. The alternatives (such as appreciative inquiry or action research) have not taken root to the extent that creates natural demand for them. The articulation of "solutions" from such a process, therefore, seem "scientific," but end up doing considerable violence to the bewitched majority, ably supported by the existing hierarchical structure of knowledge inside and outside an organization.

In the specific context of government departments and public-sector organizations from where I have drawn data and ideas, I sense that the contextual impediments discussed earlier get further accentuated. These organizations are more centralized, and considering the charm of employment in these kinds of organizations, employee attrition is very low here. The career systems in these organizations are such that people get recruited at either managerial level or junior levels, and then remain there for the rest of their lives. It is highly unlikely for lower-level staff to progress through the hierarchy and head these organizations. And therefore, the factors driving suboptimal consultancies may inflict more harm here. For example, as the officers and managers progress to reach the senior levels of hierarchy, they may get further distanced and removed from the challenges of lower-level employees. And hence problem definition is even more likely to get faulty. And because the private sector is considered more efficient and public organizations carry the stigma of being bloated and unproductive, the glitzy "knowledge" seems like a ripe fruit to cure the ailments of these organizations.

But given the state of this knowledge, I am not sure what good would it bring to these organizations having a vital developmental and social role. Probably it is not surprising that a lot of big consulting firms earn a huge portion of their revenue by providing consulting services to these kind of organizations. That is singularly unfortunate, given the debilitating contextual features of consultancy I have attempted to show in this chapter.

Perhaps all these also indicate that we need a deep examination of the assumption that an outsider can divine more than a reflective insider can. Additionally, the clients also frequently assume that an outsider will be able to bring best practices. Both these are short-sighted assumptions. Any outsider is highly unlikely to be able to develop enough tacit knowledge (Polanyi, 1966/1997) through consultancy and data collection to be able to provide effective solutions. Perhaps the best that an outsider can do is to make a large number of people inside the client organizations – people across hierarchies, and not only the usual suspects in the upper echelon – aware of their own realities through data elicitation and heedful dialogue. Solutions most likely would then naturally emerge to them (Rogers, 1951). Going with the assumption that one can do anything more seems like folly at best and misplaced arrogance at worst.

Notes

1 Although I am against the medical model of consultancy, I have invoked this imagery to convey that an in-depth inquiry could shed some light on the reasons behind the repeated failures and disappointments seen in consultancy.
2 I can only speculate as to why it happened. Possibly the senior officers did not have that much of a workload, or they had better support system, commensurate with their workload. Or, they felt like highlighting more important issues, according to their own perspectives, as opposed to this intractable and perennial problem.
3 And to make matters worse, the knowledge production is hemmed in by an inordinate belief in existing theories (Hambrick, 2007). Research submissions are routinely rejected because they do not look theoretical. Had theories been useful, one could have understood this. But without much usefulness, gatekeepers of knowledge seem to guard the honor of theories with religious fervor.
4 It is a mystery how they view the existing state of theories, which only the theorizing scholars found worth anything.

References

Alatas, S. H. (2000). Intellectual imperialism: definition, traits, and problems. *Asian Journal of Social Science, 28*(1), 23–45.
Barnard, C. I. (1938). *The functions of the executive.* Cambridge, MA: Harvard University Press.
Brislin, R. W. (1986). Research instruments: field methods in cross-cultural research. *Cross-Cultural Research and Methodology Series, 8,* 137–164.
Bruch, H. and Ghoshal, S. (2004). *A bias for action: how effective managers harness their willpower, achieve results, and stop wasting time.* Cambridge, MA: Harvard Business Press.

Chuang, A., Hsu, R. S., Wang, A. C., and Judge, T. A. (2015). Does West "fit" with East? In search of a Chinese model of person–environment fit. *Academy of Management Journal*, 58(2), 480–510.

Cohen-Charash, Y. and Spector, P. E. (2001). The role of justice in organizations: a meta-analysis. *Organizational Behavior and Human Decision Processes*, 86, 278–321.

Cook, R. A. and Szumal, J. L. (1993). Measuring normative beliefs and shared behavioral expectations in organizations: the reliability and validity of the organizational culture inventory. *Psychological Reports*, 72, 1299–1330.

Craig, D. (2005). *Rip-off! The scandalous inside story of the management consulting money machine*. London: Original Book Company.

Crowne, D. P. and Marlowe, D. (1964). *The approval motive: studies in evaluative dependence*. New York: Wiley.

Fincham, R. (1999). The consultant–client relationship: critical perspectives on the management of organizational change. *Journal of Management Studies*, 36(3), 335–351.

French, Jr., J. R. P., and Raven, B. (1959). The bases of social power. In D. Cartwright (Ed.), *Studies in social power*. Ann Arbor, MI: Institute for Social Research.

George, B. (2003). *Authentic leadership: rediscovering the secrets to creating lasting value*. San Francisco, CA: Jossey-Bass.

Hakel, M. D. (1968). How often is often? *American Psychologist*, 23(7), 533.

Hambrick, D. C. (2007). The field of management's devotion to theory: too much of a good thing? *Academy of Management Journal*, 50(6), 1346–1352.

Hinkin, T. R. (1995). A review of scale development practices in the study of organizations. *Journal of Management*, 21(5), 967–988.

Hofstede, G., Neuijen, B., Ohayv, D. D., and Sanders, G. (1990). Measuring organizational cultures: a qualitative and quantitative study across twenty cases. *Administrative Science Quarterly*, 35, 286–316.

Kaplan, A. (1964). *The conduct of inquiry*. San Francisco, CA: Chandler.

Law, K. S., Wong, C. S., and Mobley, W. M. (1998). Toward a taxonomy of multidimensional constructs. *Academy of Management Review*, 23(4), 741–755.

Lewin, K. (1936). *Principles of topological psychology*. New York & London. McGraw-Hill Book Company.

Locke, E. A. (2003). Good definitions: the epistemological foundation of scientific progress. In J. Greenberg (Ed.), *Organizational behavior: the state of the science* (pp. 415–444). Mahwah, NJ: Lawrence Erlbaum Associates.

McDonald, S. (2011). What's in the "old boys" network? Accessing social capital in gendered and racialized networks. *Social Networks*, 33(4), 317–330.

Merton, R. K. (1936). The unanticipated consequences of purposive social action. *American Sociological Review*, 1(6), 894–904.

Mignolo, W. D. (2009). Epistemic disobedience, independent thought and decolonial freedom. *Theory, Culture & Society*, 26(7–8), 159–181.

Miner, J. B. (2003). The rated importance, scientific validity, and practical usefulness of organizational behavior theories: a quantitative review. *Academy of Management Learning & Education*, 2(3), 250–268.

Nunnally, J. C. and Bernstein, I. H. (1994). *Psychometric theory*. New York: McGraw-Hill.

Organ, D. W. (1988). *Organizational citizenship behavior: the good soldier syndrome*. Lexington, MA: Lexington Books.

Osigweh, C. A. Y. (1989). Concept fallibility in organizational science. *Academy of Management Review, 14*(4), 579–594.

Pareek, U. (1998). Studying organizational ethos: the OCTAPACE profile. In J. E. Jones (Ed.), *The Pfeiffer library* (Vol. 15, 2nd ed., pp. 167–173). Misenheimer: Jossey-Bass/Pfeiffer.

Pawar, B. S. (2015). Some features of organizational behavior knowledge and the resulting issues in teaching organizational behavior. *The International Journal of Management Education, 13*(3), 289–301.

Pettigrew, A. M. (1979). On studying organizational cultures. *Administrative Science Quarterly, 24*, 570–581.

Polanyi, M. (1966/1997). The tacit dimension. In L. Prusak (Ed.), *Knowledge in organizations* (pp. 135–146). Newton, MA: Butterworth-Heinemann.

Prasad, A., Prasad, P., Mills, A. J., and Mills, J. H. (2015). *The Routledge companion to critical management studies*. Oxon & NY: Routledge.

Prasad, N. J. (2017). A postcolonial critique of India's management education scene. In Manish Thakur and Rajesh R. Babu (Eds.) *Management education in India* (pp. 23–42). Singapore: Springer.

Robbins, S. P., Judge, T. A., and Vohra, N. (2013). *Organizational behavior*. New Delhi: Pearson.

Rogers, C. R. (1951). *Client-centered therapy*. Boston, MA: Houghton Mifflin.

Ross, L. (1977). The intuitive psychologist and his shortcomings: distortions in the attribution process. In L. Berkowitz (Ed.), *Advances in experimental social psychology* (Vol. 10, pp. 173–220). New York: Academic Press

Schein, E. H. (2004). *Organizational culture & leadership*. San Francisco, CA: Jossey Bass.

Schoorman, F. D., Mayer, R. C., and Davis, J. H. (2007). An integrative model of organizational trust: past, present, and future. *Academy of Management Review, 32*(2), 344–354.

Schwab, D. P. (1980). Construct validity in organizational behavior. In B. M. Staw and L. L. Cummings (Eds.), *Research in organizational behavior* (Vol. 2, pp. 321–348). Greenwich, CT: JAI Press.

Strauss, A. and Corbin, J. (1998). *Basics of qualitative research: techniques and procedures for developing grounded theory* (2nd ed.). Thousand Oaks, CA: Sage.

Sturdy, A. (1997). The consultancy process – an insecure business? *Journal of Management Studies, 34*(3), 389–413.

Sutton, R. I. and Staw, B. M. (1995). What theory is not. *Administrative Science Quarterly, 40*(3), 371–384.

Weick, K. E. (1989). Theory construction as disciplined imagination. *Academy of Management Review, 14*(4), 516–531.

Weick, K. E. (1995). What theory is not, theorizing is. *Administrative Science Quarterly, 40*(3), 385–390.

Whetten, D. A. (1989). What constitutes a theoretical contribution? *Academy of Management Review, 14*(4), 490–495.

Part II
Legitimacy challenges

5 Urban environmental governance and legitimacy of state claim for global climate justice

Dilemma and debates in Bangladesh

Md Khalid Hossain[1]

Introduction

Equality and fairness as state principles are imitated in the constitutions of many countries, just as are environmental protection and equality and fairness linked to resource conservation. The Argentine constitution, for example, states that "all residents enjoy the right to a healthy, balanced environment" and the Portuguese constitution states that "everyone shall have the right to a healthy and ecologically balanced human environment and the duty to defend it" (Boyce, 2002: 13). More than 50 constitutions around the world include a safe environment – whether national or global – as a citizen right (Shelton, 1991).

The seminal book *Limits to Growth* (Meadows et al., 1972), an outcome of a report by the Club of Rome to analyze the future of the world vis-à-vis economic and planning systems of that time, argued that excessive resource use and environmental pollution would limit future economic growth. Its consequences would force future generations to divert capital and manpower generated by short-term economic growth to minimize unmanageable ecological constraints. Moreover, associated exponential increases in "population, food production, industrialization, pollution, and consumption of nonrenewable natural resources" would hinder predicted economic growth (Meadows et al., 1972: 25). This view echoed Polanyi's (1944) analysis that business running in capitalist mode and focusing heavily on factors of production would not help society. Polanyi challenged the arguments favoring a market-based economy and observed economic prosperity and a high standard of living coming from market-based growth as short-term achievements on the path to long-term suffering. Such suffering would manifest as both social disorders and environmental disorders. In the current context, these predictions have been widely accepted. Environmental destruction is linked with the capitalist mode of economic activities and its associated activities, where capital generation and its use are considered more important than other concerns, including the environment (Clark and York, 2005; Makhijani, 1992; Meadows et al., 2004).

Consequently, demand for ensuring environmental justice has become stronger by the day, with governments and concerned citizens around the world deciding to take precautionary measures, following the "Precautionary Principle." In 1990, during his opening speech at the conference on "Action for a Common Future," Prime Minister Jan P. Syse of Norway reflected on this principle: "We have scientific evidence to state that action is required. And where uncertainty still exists we must give the environment the benefit of the doubt" (Cameron and Abouchar, 1991: 1). In 1990, the Intergovernmental Panel on Climate Change (IPCC) produced its first assessment report, which formed the basis of global climate change negotiations (IPCC, 1996). In 1992, during the Earth Summit in Brazil, 178 governments from around the world signed the United Nations Framework Convention on Climate Change (UNFCCC), acknowledging the need to address environmental concerns (Jefferson, 1998). Since the early 1990s, influenced by environmental movements as well as scientific evidence, a change has occurred in relation to climate change and the role of governments and other key actors.

Whereas in the global arena, developing countries sought climate justice due to the historical violation of their environmental rights by industrialized countries' capitalist economic system on a global scale, inside the domestic arena, environmental justice was a fraught issue with citizens' rights being violated in pursuit of similar development models, often pursued even more aggressively. The question has arisen whether a developing state seeking climate justice from other countries is obligated to ensure environmental justice for its own citizens. This chapter focuses on this question, examining the failure in urban environmental governance in Bangladesh, a country highly vulnerable to climate change and thereby seeking climate justice in global negotiations. Bangladesh, as an exemplar, represents other developing countries facing similar dilemmas. This chapter attempts to unfold the debate around the dilemma and presents a governance framework to move forward in mitigating conflict between claiming climate justice and ensuring climate or environmental justice.

The fissures between climate justice and environmental justice

The Environmental Protection Agency (EPA) of the United States defines environmental justice as "the fair treatment and meaningful involvement of all people regardless of race, color, national origin, or income with respect to the development, implementation and enforcement of environmental laws, regulations and policies" (EPA, 2016). This suggests that climate change is a global environmental issue, and that climate justice is a branch of environmental justice. However, this is not unequivocally reflected in the thoughts and actions of groups and states around the world.

While it has been observed that the government of the United States is concerned about environmental justice, such concern has largely been related to domestic environmental issues. In 2001, the United States decided to pull out from the Kyoto Protocol, the first global legally binding agreement to ensure global climate justice. Such a stance of the United States and other developed countries like Canada and Australia established the fact that a country's perception and action related to environmental justice and climate justice may not be uniform. Distinguishing climate justice from the traditional notion of environmental justice as stipulated by the EPA (2016), Meyer and Roser indicate that climate justice is a "historical injustice involving a complex intersection of global and intergenerational justice" (2010: 229). They argue that developing countries did not emit much and would need to emit more in order to achieve economic growth. Climate justice provides them the right to pollute, whereas industrial countries have to reduce emissions. In addition, continued climate change caused by industrialized countries would further victimize vulnerable developing countries through natural disasters. Hence to ensure global climate justice, industrialized countries also need to provide compensation to developing countries (Meyer and Roser, 2010). Such arguments differentiate climate justice from environmental justice to some degree by establishing the former as a geopolitical issue. Others such as Schlosberg and Collins (2014: 361) suggest that environmental justice has focused on "inequitable distribution of environmental risks and governmental protection" within a country, i.e., poor and vulnerable communities have been marginalized by richer communities gaining more from destruction of the natural environment and leaving the risks of downsides of such destruction to the poor. Similarly, when climate justice is in question, it is about unequal gain from destruction of the global environment by industrialized countries compared to developing countries.

As some industrialized countries differed in their approach to domestic environmental justice and global climate justice, both academic and nonacademic discussions have so far focused on such discrepant behavior of industrialized countries. However, discrepant behavior has been emerging in another form in developing countries.

Environmental justice and urban environmental governance in developing countries

Following Schlosberg and Collins (2014), it could be argued that ensuring environmental justice within a country's boundary is a prerequisite for ensuring climate justice globally. To do that, good environmental governance needs to be ensured at different levels. Rhodes suggests that governance means "authoritatively allocating resources and exercising control and co-ordination" (1996: 653). As such environmental governance also implies authoritative allocation of natural resources by government and establishing control and coordination for proper utilization of those resources and protecting those resources.

It has been observed that environmental governance is a serious concern in urban growth centers. In their study, Fragkias and colleagues (2013) mentioned that to offer economic benefits, globally 60 percent to 80 percent of final energy usage happens in urban areas and in that process more than 70 percent of global greenhouse gas emissions are from urban areas. Since the current trend of urbanization is significantly contributing to environmental pollution, Creutzig and colleagues (2015) also indicated a high-level potential of energy use reduction from urban areas in their analysis, as much as 25 percent in a business-as-usual scenario through energy-efficient urbanization in Asia. Along with the scenario of energy usage and greenhouse gas emission, the World Health Organization (WHO) recently reported that more than 80 percent of people living in urban areas are exposed to poor air quality levels and the situation is worse in the cities in low- and middle-income countries, as 98 percent of those cities do not meet WHO air quality guidelines (2016). However, in high-income countries, that percentage decreases to 56 percent.

In his study, Satterthwaite opposed the traditional perception that a significant number of poor people coming to and living in urban areas of developing countries are causing environmental pollution and destroying natural resources. He argued that environmental degradation happening in urban areas is due "to the consumption patterns of non-poor groups (especially high-income groups) and the urban-based production and distribution systems that serve them" (2003: 74). He also claimed that "low levels of consumption, resource use, and waste generation" by the urban poor have actually helped to keep down environmental degradation in urban areas (74). Satterthwaite's arguments therefore indicate that environmental justice has not been ensured in urban areas and environmental governance in urban areas faces the challenge of dealing with the powerful and non-poor groups of society. Since urban development as well as industrial activities contributes to significant environmental pollution in comparison to rural areas and rural population, good urban environmental governance is highly important to ensure environmental justice domestically and climate justice globally.

However, as mentioned, scholars have repeatedly indicated urban poverty as a cause behind environmental degradation in urban areas and argued that the poverty issue needs to be tackled in the process of urban environmental governance. Baud and Dhanalakshmi (2007) pointed out the mixed urban environmental governance challenges in developing countries, where around half of the urban population lives in absolute and relative poverty. Environmental challenges created by the poor are topped up with a demand for resources from middle- and high-income groups in urban areas. The latter groups influence the ever-increasing price of resources and services due to their rising income while creating traffic congestion and environmental pollution in the city. Consequently, it is argued that for more accountable and better-performed services, urban environmental governance should have multi-stakeholder arrangements between providers and users of environmental services, including arrangements between the government and private-sector companies, between communities and the private sector, as well as between community-based organizations (CBOs), NGOs and local government (Baud and Dhanalakshmi, 2007).

In this connection, Mol (2009) also underlined that non-state actors like private companies and NGOs should be given more responsibilities and these actors should be involved in more activities for better urban environmental governance. Simultaneously, the state should emphasize establishing the rule of law and decentralize environmental policy making and implementation for improved urban environmental governance (Mol, 2009). Considering climate change impacts in urban areas and the need for building resilience, Tanner and colleagues (2009) presented an urban environmental governance framework that they termed as a "climate resilient urban governance assessment framework." Close to the works of other scholars, their framework also argues that decentralization and autonomy, accountability and transparency, responsiveness and flexibility, participation and inclusion and finally experience and support should be the characteristics of the urban environmental governance framework in relation to climate resilience.

Urban environmental governance in Bangladesh: the experiences

Bangladesh is vulnerable due to numerous physical impacts of climate change. But as a least developed country (LDC) with very scarce natural resources to exploit, it has low capability to adapt to climate change impacts. Besides, Bangladesh has a fast-growing economy as well as a number of rapidly growing urban centers. Bangladesh therefore offers a different perspective on climate justice, environmental justice and urban environmental governance.

While there is much literature on urban environmental governance in Bangladesh (e.g., Bhuiyan, 2010; Rana, 2011; Sujauddin et al., 2008), it is from the perspectives of urban governance or environmental management. The issue has not been linked to the debate of making legitimate claims for climate justice by the government through scrutinizing its roles. For example, the study of Bhuiyan (2010) indicated the negative impact of the lack of good governance of urban solid waste management in some Bangladeshi city governments. He emphasized a well-built public–private partnership to ensure good urban environmental governance. Similarly, Sujauddin and colleagues place importance on the "initiation and enhancement of community-based solid waste management practices at each and every location in the municipalities with close collaboration of government, as well as of other national and international organizations" to reduce environmental pollution in urban areas of Bangladesh (2008: 1695). While both studies offer solutions to pressing urban problems, the justice dimension is missing. This present study draws on secondary data to examine three urban governance initiatives around the city of Dhaka from a justice perspective.

Dhaka, Bangladesh's capital city, is already a problematic city in relation to urban environmental governance, with its 20 million population cramped in a relatively small area. While the city is also growing vertically like many other urban growth centers around the world, with horizontal expansion, major water bodies and agricultural lands have been transformed into housing and commercial areas. Most of the real estate agents in Dhaka are well known for their anti-environmental actions. While more than 2,500 real estate agents operate in the city, fewer than half of them are member of recognized formal associations. An estimate suggests that nearly 90 percent of real estate companies in Dhaka do not have the government's mandatory registration, but are still operating through corrupt means (Hasan, 2016). While Dhaka already experiences a hot, humid and wet tropical climate, rapid urbanization has further transformed the city into an urban heat island where there is a serious lack of vegetation and water bodies. Dhaka experiences heavy downpour during rainy seasons, and waterlogging is a common feature of the city due to the absence of soil and water bodies. Climate change is predicted to worsen Dhaka's situation as it would further increase flooding and drainage congestion along with heat stress (Monsur, 2011).

The Hatirjheel Development Project

As indicated, lack of wetland has long been a problem in Dhaka. This is due to the rapid and uncontrolled urbanization happening in the city over the years as land developers with minimum or no interest in the protection of the natural environment took control of urban development. Traditional Dhaka city water bodies have been grabbed and transformed one after another by land developers. As a result of this, the impervious area has substantially increased in Dhaka, obstructing natural drainage patterns and reducing detention basins. Consequently, the runoff concentration time has shortened and peak flow has increased. Despite having a flood protection dam around the city, inhabitants of Dhaka experience regular flooding due to rainfall during the monsoon period in Bangladesh every year. Drainage congestion and extensive waterlogging adversely affect all spheres of life by creating economic, social and environmental problems (Mowla and Islam, 2013). Dhaka's urbanization, related destruction of wetlands and suffering due to waterlogging has thus been viewed as a failure of urban environmental governance.

If the current rate of loss of wetland continues, scholars have predicted, there will not be any temporary wetland in Dhaka within the next 15 years. This is a highly alarming situation for a city like Dhaka, which had around 50 percent of its areas as wetlands around 70 years back (Mowla and Islam, 2013). To address this situation, the government enacted the Water Body Conservation Act of 2000 by prohibiting any kind of development in wetlands. Some studies have argued that Dhaka still has around 20 percent of wetland and there is scope for wetland conservation (Obayadullah, 2015). But due to the enormity of the situation, the practical scope is largely dependent on the actions of the government, which in recent years has promoted the mega-project approach. The Hatirjheel Development Project was initiated as one such project for wetland conservation and regeneration in Dhaka.

The Hatirjheel and Begunbari canals have been considered the largest water retention basins of Dhaka, but were subjected to illegal grabbing like many other water basins of the city. Initially, in the late 1990s, the Hatirjheel Development Project was proposed to build an elevated road above Hatirjheel and to develop the area as a commercial one with a lake. However, the idea of developing Hatirjheel as a commercial area has not been welcomed by environmentalists as it was found contrary to wetland conservation. The project idea was consolidated in

2007 when the government discussed building a circular road around the lake at Hatirjheel rather than only building an elevated road. Accordingly, in 2009, the Dhaka City Development Authority (widely known as "RAJUK"), in association with the Dhaka Water and Sewerage Authority (WASA) and the Local Government Engineering Department (LGED), initiated the Hatirjheel Development Project to recover 304 acres of land and water retention basins. While the Bangladesh University of Engineering and Technology (BUET) designed the project, the Bangladesh Army took the lead in construction works to assure the speedy implementation of the project (Mazid, 2013; Nabil, 2013).

The initial phase of the Hatirjheel Development Project was completed in 2012 and the roads planned were opened to the public. While many structures were demolished and a considerable amount of land was recovered to implement the project, it was not possible to demolish one 15-story building within the lake. Termed as the "cancer" of the Hatirjheel Development Project by Bangladesh's High Court, the building is the headquarters of the Bangladesh Garment Manufacturers and Exporters Association (BGMEA). The BGMEA is viewed as the most powerful business association in Bangladesh since readymade garments (RMG) are Bangladesh's most important export product. The sector earns more than 75 percent of Bangladesh's export earnings and employs more than 4 million Bangladeshis. A considerable number of businessmen involved in the RMG sector are also lawmakers in the national parliament of Bangladesh. Although the BGMEA building was against the spirit of the environmental project as well as detrimental for the project, it was not part of the government's plan for the Hatirjheel Development Project to demolish the building. It was the High Court of Bangladesh that issued a *suo-moto* rule (a judge acting without being requested) in October 2010 following the publication of a newspaper report indicating that the BGMEA building was constructed without the approval of RAJUK. The BGMEA acquired the land through forgery and filled up the water body illegally (*The Daily Star*, 2016a; Niloy, 2013; Shaon, 2016).

The High Court appointed several *amicus curies* to get their opinions about demolishing the BGMEA building, all of whom argued in favor of demolition. In April 2011, the High Court ordered the building demolished as it found the building had been built not only by violating the wetland protection act, but also through corrupt and nontransparent actions by the BGMEA. The High Court observed that the land where the BGMEA building was built was owned by the government's Bangladesh Railway until 2006. The Bangladesh Railway handed over the land to the government's Export Promotion Bureau (EPB) for constructing a world trade center in 2006. However, the BGMEA claimed that it had bought the land from the EPB in 2001, which the High Court found as false. After the High Court verdict, the BGMEA appealed at the country's Supreme Court. However, in June 2016, the Supreme Court upheld the verdict of the High Court, which implies that the government has to demolish the BGMEA building (*The Daily Star*, 2016a; Niloy, 2013; Shaon, 2016). The case of the Hatirjheel Development Project as an environmental project of the government and the anti-environmental existence of the BGMEA building with the patronage of the same government show the weak status of urban environmental govern-ance compared with the interests of certain elite groups in Bangladeshi society.

The Purbachal New Town Project

To accommodate the rising population in Dhaka, where around half a million new migrants come each year (*The Daily Star*, 2016b), the Purbachal New Town Project was initiated in 1994 to develop and allocate around 25,000 residential and 2,000 non-residential plots. The project is around 16 kilometers away from the center of Dhaka and spreads over 6,150 acres of land between the Balu and Sitalakhya Rivers (Hasan, 2014). It is expected that around 10 million people would be accommodated in this new town near Dhaka. Expectations are that this new town would reduce the pressure on the natural environment that has resulted from Dhaka's rapid urbanization. The Dhaka City Development Author-ity or RAJUK is the focal government organization to implement the project, and RAJUK (2016) claims that the project would "maintain the balance of [the] environment by proper urbanization" and it would "create [an] environment friendly and sustainable atmosphere."

While more than two decades have passed, the project is still continuing and expected to complete by 2019. From the very beginning, the project was marked by the slow progress of development works due to frequent changes in project design and other procedures to serve the interest of different people aiming to get undue benefits from the project (Hasan, 2014). Many other people who aspired to stay at Purbachal after receiving plots have lost hope and are utterly frustrated. However, RAJUK officials argue that the delay in implementing the project is due to the lengthy land acquisition process, problems created by local influential people around the project area and legal challenges presented by the environmentalist groups questioning the environmental soundness of the project. These delays in implementing the project have resulted in a more than 125 per-cent increase in initial project cost (Hasan, 2014).

While RAJUK presented the project from the beginning as environment-friendly, some actions of the project were against the spirit of protecting the natural envi-ronment, raising concerns among environmentalists. As mentioned, one of the reasons behind the delay in project implementation was legal challenges brought against RAJUK for violating the environmental laws of the country. RAJUK was alleged to have designed the project site mainly to develop more plots for the powerful people of society, creating negative impacts on the environment (Hasan, 2014). RAJUK claims that it has emphasized preserving the entire forest area in the project location since there were 148.5 acres of core forest area and around 43 acres of scattered forest pockets in 20 locations of the project site. However, Roy (2012) presented some evidence against the claims of RAJUK. He mentioned that around 1,300 acres of forest would be lost to implement the Purbachal New Town Project. Sixteen hundred acres of land have been acquired by the govern-ment in five villages to implement the project where around 10,000 villagers living on farming and fishing have been preserving *sal* trees on their land over the years. It was argued that the project did not get an environmental clearance from the Department of the Environment (DoE), as a report of the DoE produced in 2010 mentioned that land acquired for the project would affect the rich biodiversity of the area by destroying *sal* forest with notable tree coverage (Roy, 2012).

Due to the DoE report, the Prime Minister's Office (PMO) sought an explanation from the housing and public works ministry (with which RAJUK is affiliated) about the project and related environmental clearance. However, the ministry claimed that no forest or arable land had been acquired to implement the Purbachal New Town Project. The ministry's claim was found to be misleading since RAJUK itself had documents indicating that around 42 percent of the area was covered by forest and around 40 percent by cultivable land. It was found that some influential people in the villages were highly compensated by RAJUK to create division among villagers and to provide extra benefits to the rich people in the area (Roy, 2012). There were delays in acquisition of land due to the intervention of the prime minister in 2000, which was later revoked and a reacquisition notice was issued in 2009 after a long delay (Roy, 2012). Along with this environmental violation, the Purbachal New Town Project was also accused of filling up the Sitalakhya River to implement the project. The Centre for Environmental and Geographic Information Systems (CEGIS) produced satellite images to indicate the impact of RAJUK's earth-filling activity on the flow of the Sitalakhya River in 2005 and 2006. The images showed that the width of the river was reduced in 2006 in comparison to the previous year due to RAJUK's action related to the Purbachal New Town Project. Although RAJUK was challenged both by the Water Development Board of the government and by environmentalists on the ground of violating environmental law, no visible remedial action was taken (Roy, 2009).

In 2013, the Bangladesh Environmental Lawyers' Association and six other rights groups jointly filed a writ petition to stop the activities of the Purbachal New Town Project for violating environmental laws by the government and not having an environmental clearance. The High Court then directed RAJUK to stop project activities until it received an environmental clearance for the project and asked the government to explain its role in protecting and conserving the forest, wetland and cultivable land of the project area (*Dhaka Mirror*, 2013). However, the project works have slowly been going on after the Supreme Court directed RAJUK to continue the development work through protecting the natural environment in the project area (Mahmud, 2014).

Similar to the case of the Hatirjheel Development Project, the case of the Purbachal New Town Project of the government as a so-called environment-friendly and sustainable project shows that government departments are violating environmental laws even if those laws are made by the government. The patronage of the government to ensure housing for well-off urban populations through the Purbachal New Town Project demonstrates again the weakness of urban environmental governance in Bangladesh.

The Hazaribagh Tannery Relocation Project

The Hazaribagh area is situated in the western part of Dhaka and adjacent to one of the very important rivers of Dhaka, the Turag River. From 1947 to 1971, when Bangladesh was part of Pakistan and known as East Pakistan, businessmen from West Pakistan started to set up factories in Hazaribagh through procuring raw materials. While political power was concentrated in West Pakistan, such development of Hazaribagh went on without any planning and through neglecting environmental concerns (Strasser, 2015). Over the past six decades, more than 200 tanneries (where skins are processed) were set up in Hazaribagh. As mentioned, no significant environmental concerns were raised by related government agencies and ministries when these considerable numbers of tanneries were developing in Hazaribagh. A lot of people live around these tanneries in Hazaribagh, where rawhide and skins are not only processed in factories, but also in open areas. These activities have rendered the entire Hazaribagh area uninhabitable from an environmental contamination perspective as the chemical contamination is very significantly above the dangerous level. However, since Dhaka is densely populated, many people have been living in Hazaribagh and adjacent areas with high health risks, including the workers working in the tanneries (*Prothom Alo*, 2016a; Sarker and Siddique, 2013).

The tanneries in Hazaribagh once again make a mockery of urban environmental governance in Bangladesh. Since leather and leather goods are increasingly earning foreign currency and the industry employs more than half a million people, the government has a priority to develop the sector. While many factories in Hazaribagh are export-oriented, a number of them have dangerous ratings but have been operating over the years through overlooking all environmental laws. Almost all the factories in Hazaribagh have been operating without effluent treatment plants (ETP), and highly toxic water is released without any treatment. As in many other cases, the government's role in addressing the situation has never been proactive. By contrast, environmental groups along with the High Court have been proactive and concerned in this regard, as in the Hatirjheel Development Project and the Purbachal New Town Project. The High Court directed the government to shift tanneries from Hazaribagh in 2003, which was also a strong demand of environmental groups. However, there was no significant progress in this regard over the years despite spontaneous initiatives by the government (*Business Outlook*, 2016; *Prothom Alo*, 2016a; Sarker and Siddique, 2013).

In the early 1990s, policy makers in Bangladesh initially discussed relocating the tanneries of Hazaribagh because of their adverse impacts on the natural environment of Dhaka. The major river flowing along Dhaka, the Buriganga River, has to absorb most of the untreated waste of the city, and it was found that 70 percent of that waste comes from the tanneries. Although the government had several meetings to relocate tanneries from Hazaribagh and acquired land near Dhaka to relocate tanneries and building a central effluent treatment plant (CETP) for treating toxic waste, the government failed to relocate the tanneries due to the resistance of tannery owners. The government's initial efforts were not wholehearted in insisting on relocating tanneries, and even after the directives of the High Court, the government did not make major efforts for relocation. Finally, the government set up a committee in 2008 to relocate tanneries to Savar from Hazaribagh by February 2010. Unfortunately, this deadline was not respected and the tanneries have still not been relocated (*Prothom Alo*, 2016a; Sarker and Siddique, 2013).

A similar directive was also given by the High Court to the government, but tannery owners as well as the government continued to request extension of the deadline. The government was asked by the Court to negotiate compensation packages with tannery owners and to intervene in transferring bank liabilities of tannery owners. While the Hazaribagh Tannery Relocation Project was initiated in January 2003 with a completion date in December 2005, the construction schedule was later extended to June 2010. The initial plan was to shift around 150 tannery units by building infrastructure on 200 acres of land in Savar (a nearby sub-district of Dhaka). To follow the Court directives, the Ministry of Industries took over the role of implementation agency and a related committee fixed a compensation amount to address the loss to be incurred by tannery owners. However, the tannery owners claimed a much higher amount for compensation due to high relocation costs. The government also refused to bear the cost of setting up the central effluent treatment plant and asked tannery owners to set it up. These discussions between the government and the tannery owners pushed the price of the treatment plant up by six times. Environmental groups are also unhappy about the new area chosen for relocation in Savar due to its proximity to another river (*Business Outlook*, 2016; *Reportsbd*, 2014; Sarker and Siddique, 2013). The apathetic approach of both the government and the tannery owners is behind the additional concerns raised by the environmental groups.

In early 2016, the Ministry of Industries provided an ultimatum to tannery owners in Hazaribagh to relocate within three days. The ultimatum was unrealistic, as most of the tannery units could not finish building up new units in Savar and the central effluent treatment plant was not fully ready for operation (*Prothom Alo*, 2016a). While tanneries in Hazaribagh continued to destroy the natural environment, in June 2016, the High Court again intervened and ordered tannery owners to pay around 600 U.S. dollars per day as compensation for damaging the environment. The Court asked the government to assess the environmental losses and damages caused by tanneries in Hazaribagh (*The Independent*, 2016). Environmentalists also urged the government to stop providing any utility services to tanneries in Hazaribagh and to cancel their land allocations (*Prothom Alo*, 2016b). However, influential tannery owners continued to subvert the entire process by claiming that leather goods are earning foreign currency for the country. The government has been found to be greatly influenced by tannery owners, overlooking the environmental costs that are far beyond the economic gains the tanneries bring to Bangladesh (*Reportsbd*, 2014). The Hazaribagh Tannery Relocation Project, which was supposed to finish in two years, has therefore been under way for around 13 years, and it is not clear when the project will be completed. The project is another example of failed urban environmental governance in which environmental losses and damages caused by influential businesspeople have gone unaddressed by the government, while the Court and environmentalists had to show their concerns on the basis of laws originally developed by the government itself.

Failure of urban environmental governance: dilemmas and debates

From the cases presented in this chapter from Bangladesh, it can be argued that urban environmental governance is seriously flawed and has failed in Bangladesh, at least in the context of its capital city, Dhaka. In the Hatirjheel Development Project, environmental governance largely failed in favor of serving the most powerful business association in Bangladesh. The Purbachal New Town Project benefits urban middle-class and influential people while being a failure of environmental governance. Finally, the Hazaribagh Tannery Relocation Project has not yet been completed because of failure to challenge the interests of tannery owners, with long-lasting damages to the natural environment of the city.

One of the arguments behind poor urban environmental governance in Bangladesh is the favorable consideration of industrial development (providing incentives to garment factory owners or tannery owners), with environmental degradation that seems justified on the basis of existing theories on economic development and consequential environmental degradation. In relation to this trade-off, there is a pessimistic view that argues that environmental damages and losses become so high in pursuit of economic development that neither environmental nor economic collapse can be avoided in the long run. However, there is also an optimistic view that likes to argue that environmental degradation is a natural consequence of economic development and after achieving a certain level of economic growth or income threshold (becoming an advanced or developed economy), addressing the environmental problems will be an automatic process (Shafik, 1994; Stern et al., 1996).

In this regard, development partners, including international financial institutions like the World Bank, did not influence the Bangladesh government in a timely manner, as they were also primarily in favor of economic development without considering environmental concerns. The World Bank and the International Monetary Fund (IMF) influenced developing countries like Bangladesh to pursue export-led growth through trade liberalization as a condition of providing financial assistance (Palley, 2011). Focus on the export growth of RMG and leather products with little concern for the natural environment occurred as a result of the neoliberal doctrine of international financial institutions.

In this regard, based on her longitudinal econometric analysis of the relationship between economic development and environmental quality for a large sample of countries, Shafik (1994) argued that environmental indicators do not improve with rising income. She found that while indicators like water and sanitation improve over time due to rising income, some indicators like dissolved oxygen in rivers, municipal solid wastes and carbon emissions steadily worsen despite rising income. It has been found that when poor people within society or less advanced countries have to bear the costs of environmental degradation, rich or influential people do not have much incentive to change their behavior, and they continue their activities that are detrimental for the natural environment (Shafik, 1994). In each of the cases presented in this chapter, it was the poorer people of society who have borne the costs of environmental degradation. Land was acquired from ordinary people to develop the Hatirjheel project, but could not be acquired from the BGMEA. Villagers and farmers lost their agricultural land during the course of the Purbachal project development. Slum dwellers and people dependent on rivers have been suffering due to the Hazaribagh tanneries. Consequently, it could be argued that in Bangladesh, the situation of urban environmental governance tends to worsen since current environmental costs are borne by powerless and poor people in urban areas while rich and influential people are protected. The scenario of rising inequality in society does not offer much scope for a changing scenario in the future. This argument could also get support from the analysis of Boyce. He argued that "the extent of an environmentally degrading activity depends on the balance of power between the winners, who derive net benefits from the activity, and the losers, who bear net costs" (1994: 177). According to Boyce (1994) and evident in Bangladesh, more environmental degradation is happening since winners are powerful relative to losers.

However, the government faces a dilemma in this regard since so-called winners of the process are contributing to the economic development of Bangladesh, which is also the primary agenda of the government. Moreover, the cases of urban environmental governance in Bangladesh are regular stories repeated in many other developing countries around the world. Yhdego (1991) presented the example of Dar es Salaam in Tanzania, where polluting industries were not controlled, initially due to the absence of urban and environmental planning. El Araby (2002) explored the case of Cairo in Egypt, where the government could not show a long-term vision to ensure improved urban environmental governance as urbanization is occurring rapidly and the government is largely unprepared to plan for urban growth and development. This is another dilemma for governments in countries like Bangladesh since past practices of government seem incapable of addressing the contemporary challenges of urban environmental governance.

In this regard, Button indicated the challenges faced by government from a policy perspective as he found that "the interactions between changing economic, environmental and social parameters make it difficult to track issues and to develop both short-term reactive initiatives or longer-term strategic plans" (2002: 17). While discussing the case of Afghanistan, Amanullah (1995) mentioned that some of the policies or governance philosophies of the government undermine its environmental policies and often influence the government's decision to not have strong environmental policies. He pointed out the common belief in many developing countries that if industries are regulated by environmental regulations, future industrial growth and economic activity are negatively affected. As long as such beliefs inform the government's policies, it will always face a dilemma in ensuring better urban environmental governance by prioritizing the natural environment over any other issue.

Conclusion

Mahatma Gandhi, unofficially regarded as India's father of the nation, provided a popular suggestion to all of his followers – "*You must be the change you wish to see in the world.*" The argument of this chapter is rooted in a similar premise, as it is argued that a state's claim for global climate justice cannot be mutually exclusive of that state's responsibility to ensure environmental justice within its own boundaries. To substantiate this argument, this chapter presents the failures of urban environment governance and the violation of environmental justice in Bangladesh as similar to what happens on a global scale, where developed and powerful countries violate climate justice, and the global environmental justice system fails due to the actions and inactions of powerful countries.

All three cases presented in this chapter regarding the failure of urban environmental governance further justify the arguments of Satterthwaite (2003) discussed earlier. He blamed high-income groups in urban areas for urban environmental degradation and argued that urban environmental governance can be ensured through dealing with powerful and non-poor groups. In this chapter, it is evident that while government tried to take environment-friendly projects in Dhaka, the desired achievements of the projects could not be ensured due to the interference of rich and powerful groups. At least in the current urban setting, the government could not act in the interests of the poor and has undertaken projects with an environmental lens primarily to serve the urban elites and the middle class. Consequently, environmental justice has not been upheld within the country and the government has been losing its moral ground to claim global climate justice through compensation and lowering of greenhouse gases from rich and powerful countries.

This chapter argues that while the government represents Bangladesh at global forums and negotiations, it is the responsibility of the government to ensure environmental justice at the national level so as to legitimately represent Bangladesh at the global level in claiming climate justice. It should be a parallel process, and it is not valid to claim that Bangladesh will only ensure national-level environmental justice after achieving a certain level of economic growth or national income. Such claim are weak as the process of achieving that growth and income currently largely serves the rich and powerful people of society, marginalizes poor people and, above all, degrades the environment to an extent where recovery would not at all be possible.

As the way forward, this chapter presents an assorted but balanced governance framework to proceed in mitigating the conflict between claiming climate justice at the global level and ensuring environmental justice at the national level. The framework is based on the arguments of Lemos and Agrawal (2006), Baud and Dhanalakshmi (2007), Mol (2009) and Tanner and colleagues (2009) discussed earlier in this chapter. They emphasized not only the government's regulatory role, but also the participation of non-state actors including communities, businesses and NGOs through a multi-stakeholder arrangement process. In Bangladesh, it is evident that environmental groups, the justice delivery system (e.g., the High Court) and communities are already involved in the process of offering their perspectives on environmental problems and ensuring environmental justice at the national level. Although businesses have often been seen as the cause behind environmental degradation, any arrangement without business engagement would not be sustainable in the long run.

In the framework presented earlier, it is argued that political government would not only formulate regulation and focus on enforcing regulation, but also would create space for participation so that a multi-stakeholder arrangement (MSA) process is materialized. Community and civil society organizations (CSOs) would generate evidence for justifying the needs of environmental protection and, rather than blocking any initiative, would try to offer a balanced solution. Since the situation does not always remain favorable, community and CSOs need to be able to raise their voices when there are cases of environmental degradation. Participation in the MSA process would best serve the interests of the community and CSOs, as well as of businesses. Business organizations need to create value, while protecting the natural environment is also needed to attain sustainable business (SB) in the long run, since environmental destruction may badly affect consumers and markets. In following the value, it is expected that the business organizations would proactively engage in conducting environmental impact assessments of their business ventures, as well as abide by environmental law. As already seen in Bangladesh, the justice system, the High Court and the

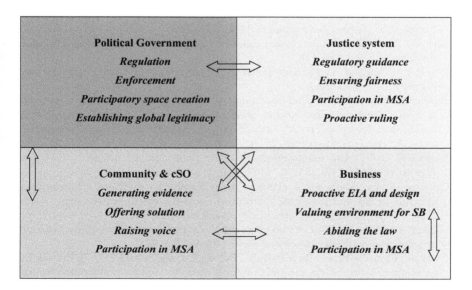

Figure 5.1 Proposed multi-stakeholder arrangement

Supreme Court, are a significant part of the MSA process, although they cannot be formally included in the process due to their neutral status. Their regulatory guidance is of crucial importance for the political government, and proactive environmental rulings are supportive of the community and CSOs. However, the justice system should ensure fairness among all stakeholders with different interests. If everyone engages in this manner, the government would be able to establish global legitimacy to effectively insist on global climate justice, while ensuring environmental justice at the national level.

In the light of the proposed governance framework, it could be said that the arguments presented in this chapter may create an opportunity for countries with similar development status as Bangladesh to further improve their urban environment governance, strengthen their national-level environmental justice system and acquire stronger legitimacy to claim climate justice from advanced economies.

Note

1 The views expressed are of the author and not of his organization.

References

Amanullah, N. (1995). Environmental management dilemma in Afghanistan. *Journal of Environmental Health*, 58(4), 28–30.

Baud, I. S. A. and Dhanalakshmi, R. (2007). Governance in urban environmental management: comparing accountability and performance in multi-stakeholder arrangements in South India. *Cities*, 24(2), 133–147.

Bhuiyan, S. H. (2010). A crisis in governance: urban solid waste management in Bangladesh. *Habitat International*, 34(1), 125–133.

Boyce, J. K. (1994). Inequality as a cause of environmental degradation. *Ecological Economics*, 11(3), 169–178.

Boyce, J. K. (2002). *The Political Economy of the Environment*. Cheltenham: Edward Elgar Publishing Limited.

Business Outlook (2016). No let up in tannery relocation from Hazaribagh. Available at: http://businessoutlookbd.com/index.php?option=com_content&view=article& id=1618:no-let-up-in-tannery-relocation-from-hazaribagh&catid=43:magazine-news. Accessed on: August 23, 2016.

Button, K. (2002). City management and urban environmental indicators. *Ecological Economics*, 40(2), 217–233.

Cameron, J. and Abouchar, J. (1991). The precautionary principle: a fundamental principle of law and policy for the protection of the global environment. *Boston College International and Comparative Law Review*, 14, 1–27.

Clark, B. and York, R. (2005). Carbon metabolism: global capitalism, climate change, and the biospheric rift. *Theory and Society*, 34(4), 391–428.

Creutzig, F., Baiocchi, G., Bierkandt, R., Pichler, P. P. and Seto, K. C. (2015). Global typology of urban energy use and potentials for an urbanization mitigation wedge. *Proceedings of the National Academy of Sciences*, 112(20), 6283–6288.

The Daily Star (2016a). BGMEA building must come down. Available at: www.the dailystar.net/backpage/bgmea-building-has-be-demolished-1233724. Accessed on: August 30, 2016.

The Daily Star (2016b). Unbridled urbanization: how long is it sustainable? Available at: www.thedailystar.net/editorial/unbridled-urbanisation-1301806. Accessed on: November 2, 2016.

Dhaka Mirror (2013). HC asks RAJUK to stop Purbachal project work. Available at: www.dhakamirror.com/other-headlines/hc-asks-rajuk-to-stop-purbachal-project-work. Accessed on: August 27, 2016.

El Araby, M. (2002). Urban growth and environmental degradation: the case of Cairo, Egypt. *Cities*, 19(6), 389–400.

Environmental Protection Agency (EPA) (2016). *Learn about environmental justice.* Available at: www.epa.gov/environmentaljustice/learn-about-environmental-jus tice. Accessed on: June 6, 2016.

Fragkias, M., Lobo, J., Strumsky, D. and Seto, K. C. (2013). Does size matter? Scaling of CO_2 emissions and U.S. urban areas. *PLoS ONE*, 8(6), e64727.

Hasan, J. (2014). *Purbachal township to take 5 more years to complete.* Available at: http://print.thefinancialexpressbd.com/2014/06/24/41120/print. Accessed on: August 25, 2016.

Hasan, J. (2016). *Majority of realtors operate in Dhaka sans RAJUK registration.* Available at: www.thefinancialexpress-bd.com/2016/10/14/49430/Majority-of-realtors-operate-in-Dhaka-sans-Rajuk-registration. Accessed on: November 1, 2016.

The Independent (2016). Relocation of Hazaribagh tanneries: HC releases fine order. Available at: www.theindependentbd.com/post/48968. Accessed on: August 8, 2016.

Intergovernmental Panel on Climate Change (IPCC) (1996). *Climate Change 1995: Economic and Social Dimensions of Climate Change.* New York: Cambridge University Press.

Jefferson, M. (1998). International frameworks for controlling sulphur and carbon emissions: political and institutional developments. *International Journal of Global Energy Issues*, 10(2–4), 93–106.

Lemos, M. C. and Agrawal, A. (2006). Environmental governance. *Annual Review of Environment and Resources*, 31(1), 297–325.

Mahmud, A. H. (2014). *Legal issues delay development at Purbachal project.* Available at: http://archive.dhakatribune.com/law-rights/2014/aug/05/legal-issues-delay-development-purbachal-project. Accessed on: August 5, 2016.

Makhijani, A. (1992). *From Global Capitalism to Economic Justice: An Inquiry into the Elimination of Systemic Poverty, Violence and Environmental Destruction in the World Economy.* New York: Apex Press.

Mazid, M. A. (2013). *Hatirjheel project: how it came into being.* Available at: www. thedailystar.net/news-detail-263437. Accessed on: July 9, 2016.

Meadows, D. H., Meadows, D. L., Randers, J. and Behrens III, W. W. (1972). *The Limits to Growth.* New York: Universe Press.

Meadows, D. H., Randers, J. and Meadows, D. L. (2004). *Limits to Growth: The 30-Year Update.* Vermont: Chelsea Green Publishing Company.

Meyer, L. H. and Roser, D. (2010). Climate justice and historical emissions. *Critical Review of International Social and Political Philosophy*, 13(1), 229–253.

Mol, A. P. (2009). Urban environmental governance innovations in China. *Current Opinion in Environmental Sustainability*, 1(1), 96–100.

Monsur, S. K. (2011). *Dhaka's vulnerability to climate change*. Available at: www.thedailystar.net/news-detail-194224. Accessed on: November 1, 2016.

Mowla, Q. A. and Islam, M. S. (2013). Natural drainage system and water logging in Dhaka: measures to address the problems. *Journal of Bangladesh Institute of Planners*, 6, 23–33.

Nabil, Z. H. (2013). *Where elephants once tread*. Available at: http://archive.thedaily star.net/magazine/2013/01/02/cover.htm. Accessed on: August 5, 2016.

Niloy, S. (2013). *BGMEA Bhaban is cancer in Hatirjheel project*. Available at: http://bdnews24.com/business/2013/03/19/bgmea-bhaban-is-cancer-in-hatirjheel-project. Accessed on: August 10, 2016.

Obayadullah, A. Z. M. (2015). *Saving the wetlands around Dhaka*. Available at: www.theindependentbd.com/printversion/details/4187. Accessed on: August 8, 2016.

Palley, T. I. (2011). *The rise and fall of export-led growth*. Available at: www.levyinsti tute.org/pubs/wp_675.pdf. Accessed on: November 30, 2016.

Polanyi, K. (1944). The self-regulating market and the fictitious commodities: land, labor, and money. In G. Dalton (Ed.), *Primitive, Archaic, and Modern Economies: Essays of Karl Polanyi* (pp. 26–37). Boston, MA: Beacon Press.

Prothom Alo (2016a). Tannery relocation looks "impossible" within deadline. Available at: http://en.prothom-alo.com/bangladesh/news/91783/Tannery-reloca tion-looks-%E2%80%9Cimpossible%E2%80%9D-within. Accessed on: August 30, 2016.

Prothom Alo (2016b). Green activists demand plot cancellation of Hazaribagh tanners. Available at: http://en.prothom-alo.com/bangladesh/news/120083/Green-activists-demand-plot-cancellation-of. Accessed on: September 10, 2016.

RAJUK (2016). *Purbachal new town at Yousufgonj and Rupgonj*. Available at: www.rajukdhaka.gov.bd/rajuk/projectsHome?type=purbachal. Accessed on: August 30, 2016.

Rana, M. M. P. (2011). Urbanization and sustainability: challenges and strategies for sustainable urban development in Bangladesh. *Environment, Development and Sustainability*, 13(1), 237–256.

Reportsbd (2014). *Hazaribagh tanneries: an urban nightmare beyond imagination*. Available at: www.reportsbd.com/g-nfg-j-tukytumsdgswdgqdhgetyjryuktuil-tykr yjert-wrthwerhweh-w. Accessed on: August 23, 2016.

Rhodes, R. A. W. (1996). The new governance: governing without government. *Political Studies*, 44(4), 652–667.

Roy, P. (2009). *RAJUK fills up Sitalakhya bank for housing scheme: ignores WDB's objection; river width shrinks at Purbachal project point as govt itself violates rules*. Available at: http://archive.thedailystar.net/newDesign/cache/cachednewsde tails106172.html. Accessed on: August 24, 2016.

Roy, P. (2012). *RAJUK to raze forests for housing: Trees, farmland in 1,600 acres area to vanish for Purbachal project*. Available at: www.thedailystar.net/newsde tail246936. Accessed on: August 23, 2016.

Sarker, P. K. and Siddique, A. B. (2013). *Hazardous Hazaribagh*. Available at: http://archive.dhakatribune.com/environment/2013/jun/05/hazardous-hazaribagh. Accessed on: August 3, 2016.

Satterthwaite, D. (2003). The links between poverty and the environment in urban areas of Africa, Asia, and Latin America. *The Annals of the American Academy of Political and Social Science*, 590(1), 73–92.

Schlosberg, D. and Collins, L. B. (2014). From environmental to climate justice: climate change and the discourse of environmental justice. *Wiley Interdisciplinary Reviews: Climate Change*, 5(3), 359–374.

Shafik, N. (1994). Economic development and environmental quality: an econometric analysis. *Oxford Economic Papers*, 46, 757–773.

Shaon, A. I. (2016). *No bar to demolishing BGMEA building*. Available at: http://archive.dhakatribune.com/bangladesh/2016/jun/03/no-bar-demolishing-bgmea-building. Accessed on: August 10, 2016.

Shelton, D. (1991). Human rights, environmental rights, and the right to environment. *Stanford Journal of International Law*, 28, 103–138.

Stern, D. I., Common, M. S. and Barbier, E. B. (1996). Economic growth and environmental degradation: the environmental Kuznets curve and sustainable development. *World Development*, 24(7), 1151–1160.

Strasser, J. (2015). *Bangladesh's Leather Industry: Local Production Networks in the Global Economy*. New York: Springer.

Sujauddin, M., Huda, S. M. S. and Hoque, A. R. (2008). Household solid waste characteristics and management in Chittagong, Bangladesh. *Waste Management*, 28(9), 1688–1695.

Tanner, T. M., Mitchell, T., Polack, E. and Guenther, B. (2009). Urban governance for adaptation: assessing climate change resilience in ten Asian cities. *IDS Working Paper 315*, Brighton: IDS.

World Health Organization (WHO) (2016). *Air pollution levels rising in many of the world's poorest cities: news release*. Available at: www.who.int/mediacentre/news/releases/2016/air-pollution-rising/en. Accessed on: August 30, 2016.

Yhdego, M. (1991). Urban environmental degradation in Tanzania. *Environment and Urbanization*, 3(1), 147–152.

6 'A class war has begun in South Africa'

An analysis of COSATU's framing of the 'Marikana massacre'

Teke Ngomba

Introduction

On 16 August 2012, South African police forces killed 34 miners who were striking at the Lonmin platinum mine in Marikana. Prior to these killings, 10 other people had already died at the site – including non-striking miners, security guards and two police officers (BBC News, 25 June 2015). Few events in post-apartheid South Africa have led to deep national soul searching and international scrutiny like the killings in Marikana – especially the 16 August shootings, which constituted the 'worse single act of police brutality since South Africa became a democracy in 1994' (SABC, 15 August 2016).

The passionate political debates and academic analyses within and beyond South Africa about the Marikana killings have revolved around attempts to respond to these key questions: What went wrong? How did we get to this situation and what needs to be done to prevent another Marikana? While many perspectives on these issues from key actors such as mine workers, the media and police have been examined by scholars, the views of the Congress of South African Trade Unions (COSATU), which is one of the central actors in the South African political and socioeconomic scene, have not been systematically analyzed within the budding prominence of 'Marikana scholarship'.[1]

COSATU is indubitably a 'significant player in South African civil society and politics' (Hlatshwayo, 2011, p. 169), and it tends to have a 'loud voice' which at times 'can be louder than that of political opposition parties on a variety of issues' (Gordon, 2015, p. 326). This chapter aims to scrutinize COSATU's 'voice' in relation to the Marikana killings by empirically responding to this central question: how did COSATU frame the Marikana killings? This chapter examines this issue through an analysis of official statements from COSATU about the Marikana killings.

As an important member of the governing tripartite alliance in South Africa, Marikana served as a significant test of COSATU's (often conflicting) loyalties to its members and the government. This, as well as the underlying context of the Marikana killings and COSATU's avowed anti-neoliberal stance, permeate its discourses about the Marikana killings. This chapter shows the ways in which these discourses exemplify the contentious debates at the heart of the orientation of the post-apartheid South African state. This chapter also shows how COSATU's discourses point to and raise questions about the nature of political and economic governance in South Africa and in particular, the orthodoxy of neoliberalism as well as the extent of its contestation by ordinary citizens and civil society in poor and marginalized contexts.

Broadly speaking, the Marikana killings happened in a context characterized by the following: the rise of neoliberal logic in South Africa's macroeconomic orientation; the contestation of this logic and its socioeconomic fallouts; the increasing crisis of governance at the level of the government in particular and tensions and fissures within the trade union sector. Following this introduction, this chapter proceeds by concisely unpacking each of these contextual aspects. Thereafter, the methodology and data used here will be presented followed by the findings and a conclusion.

Development strides and challenges in post-apartheid South Africa

The official fall of apartheid in South Africa in 1994 ushered in an era of enormous hope and expectations regarding the socioeconomic development of the country. Undeniably, the enormity of the expectations grew out of the poor living conditions of the black majority population during apartheid. Conscious of all these hopes, successive post-apartheid governments have struggled to define socioeconomic policy options that can address the legacies of apartheid and lift millions out of precarious livelihoods while navigating the intricacies of the global economic system.

Charting this course has been fraught by personal confrontations notably amongst the leadership of the governing African National Congress (ANC) as well as ideological debates/battles regarding the macroeconomic orientation of the country. The cause of disagreement has been the adoption of neoliberal policies in post-apartheid South Africa. Beginning from 1996 in particular, the South African government has adopted a predominantly neoliberal orientation (see, for instance, Bond, 2011, p. 355) which has led to a further integration of the country into the global financial system, amongst others.

Of particular interest for the purposes of the discussions in this chapter is the extent to which this neoliberal logic permeates the mining sector in South Africa. With its large reserves of minerals, mining is 'very central to the South African economy', and this is reflected in the fact that about '60% of South African exports are mining-sector related' (AFP, 13 June 2013). The combination of a state-sanctioned neoliberal approach and available large reserves of minerals has specifically led to the 'ascendancy of capitalist interests' in the mining sector in post-apartheid South Africa (Chinguno, 2013, p. 640; Segatti and Pons-Vignon, 2013, p. 541).

It is important, however, to point out that while neoliberal logics have clearly been dominant as the broad macroeconomic orientation in post-apartheid South Africa, this is far from being a settled ideological orientation, as evidenced, for instance, in the contentious debates within and between the ruling ANC and its governing alliance partners, the South African Communist Party (SACP) and COSATU. As a result, the official socioeconomic development framework of successive post-apartheid governments has oscillated between versions of neo-liberalism, social democracy and developmental statism. The high level of fluidity and contention regarding the developmental approach of the post-apartheid state within its first two decades is reflected in the fact that since the 1990s, at least nine different socioeconomic policy frameworks have been adopted by the government (Segatti and Pons-Vignon, 2013; see also Karriem and Hoskins, 2016, p. 5).

Considered in their different levels of implementations, this range of documents, which reveals a mixture of ascendant neoliberalism and some doses of social democracy and developmental state logics, has produced a rather mixed picture when it comes to the status of socioeconomic development in South Africa. In the years immediately after the end of apartheid, for instance, South Africa 'basked in a glow of national reconciliation, early growth and optimism' (Southall, 2014, p. 48). Across the past two decades, the South African state has moved decisively to tackle the racially based socioeconomic legacies of apartheid. This has involved initiatives such as furthering the provision of housing, electricity and potable water to black communities; instituting a black economic empowerment programme and the establishment of a social grants welfare system for the poor, which, by continental standards, is indeed impressive and unique (see Karriem and Hoskins, 2016, pp. 7–8; Segatti and Pons-Vignon, 2013, p. 538).

This positive scorecard notwithstanding, as Bernstein noted, 'twenty years into democracy, South Africa is in trouble' (2014, p. 20). Often, scholars exemplify this perception of 'South Africa in trouble' by pointing to two issues: the still dire socioeconomic situation of millions of South Africans and the worrying levels of bad governance. As concerns the first issue, the stark assessment is that South Africa is 'still characterized by high levels of inequality and poverty' (Davids and Gaibie, 2011, p. 232). Almost 50 per cent of the population of about 54.5 million lives below the poverty line of $2 a day (Karriem and Hoskins, 2016, pp. 7–8). In 2011, South Africa overtook Brazil as 'the most unequal society – with the gap between the poorest and richest individuals the highest in the world' (Gumede, 2015, p. 331). The striking thing with the inequality in South Africa is its persistent racial dimension with 'the white population continuing to enjoy dramatically better living conditions than the black African population' (Davids and Gaibie, 2011, p. 232). The situation is worsened by the high level of unemployment, which is now close to 27 per cent of the population – about 5.8 million people (Reuters, 9 May 2016).

For several analysts, one of the central reasons for South Africa's current dismal socioeconomic situation is the country's decision to 'commit itself' to the neo-liberal policies of 'economic liberalization' which have contributed to 'increasing unemployment, the privatization of state assets, the informalisation of labour, greater levels of private debt and rising inequality (Curless, 2016, p. 11; see also Bond, 2011).

As concerns the second issue – worrying levels of bad governance – the current frame of analyses amongst observers of South Africa is that the 'Zuma-led ANC has become increasingly statist with alarming signs of social conservatism and authoritarianism' (Pillay, 2013, p. 11). There has been no shortage of high-profile corruption scandals or accusations of abuse of office and due process during the reign of President Zuma. While it is true that corruption and other manifestations of bad governance in post-apartheid South Africa did not start under President Zuma, these have definitely taken a new dimension during his reign, not least because President Zuma has been personally accused of a range of corrupt practices.

The increasing frustration of ordinary South Africans with the current state of socioeconomic development and the almost constant revelations of corruption at the level of the ruling ANC elites clearly contributed to the ANC's declining electoral performance across the years. The most recent is its poor performance during the 2016 local elections, in which it lost control of the capital for the first time since the end of apartheid (BBC News, 6 August 2016). The political and socioeconomic travails of the country as well as the internal problems of the ANC have logically put to test the relationship between the ANC and its governing alliance partners, the SACP and COSATU. Next, I briefly examine the historical and contemporary role of COSATU in South Africa and highlight the fissures in trade unionism in the lead-up to the Marikana shootings.

COSATU and the fissures in South African trade unionism

The South African organized labour movement, epitomized contemporarily in COSATU, is seen by several scholars as 'one of the most powerful on the African continent' (Gordon, 2015, p. 325). COSATU is the largest trade union federation in South Africa. It has 21 affiliated trade unions with an overall membership of 'more than two million workers of whom at least 1.8 million are paid up' (COSATU, 2016).

Since its formation in 1985, COSATU has been at the centre of political developments in South Africa. COSATU has embraced 'social movement trade unionism', which refers to the tendency for trade unions to combine 'workplace and community struggle' (Webster and Buhlungu, 2004, p. 229). COSATU has used this strategy historically to successfully fight against apartheid, and this particular legacy has imparted COSATU with valuable 'political legitimacy' (Dibben et al., 2015, p. 477; Pillay, 2013, p. 11).

With the end of apartheid and in furtherance of its 'social movement unionism', COSATU joined what it describes as a 'strategic political alliance' with the ANC and the SACP. Through this alliance, COSATU aims for the 'establishment of a democratic and non-racial South Africa, economic transformation and continued process of political and economic democratization' (COSATU, 2016).

Popularly known as the 'tripartite alliance', this has essentially been the governing coalition in South Africa since the 1994 democratic transition. As a result of this alliance, COSATU has tended to consistently lend its 'mobilization power' to the ANC during election campaigns in particular, and many ex-COSATU officials have moved on to hold 'crucial positions in the cabinet, parliament and civil service' (Masiya, 2014, p. 455; Webster, 1998, p. 42). While this set up gives COSATU. in principle, some 'influence over the formulation and implementation of policies' (Webster, 1998, p. 42), in reality, there are indications that COSATU is less influential in determining the government's socioeconomic policies. There have been recurrent strains in the alliance, not least because of the ideological schism between COSATU and successive ANC governments as far as macroeconomic policies are concerned. As indicated earlier, while the post-apartheid state has tilted towards neoliberalism with some doses of 'social democratic-type politics' (Gall, 1997, p. 215), COSATU propounds a different ideology: socialism. In a 2006 speech, COSATU's general secretary emphasized that:

> COSATU believes in the radical transformation of society and ultimately the building of a socialist society as an alternative to the exploitative and unfair capitalist system that now reigns in our country. In that respect, our vision only starts by our demands for improved conditions for workers in the capitalist society. Ultimately, we also work to build a new society to replace capitalism, one where the needs of our people shape our economy and not the drive of a few to make more profits. This militant and radical approach to politics and society distinguishes COSATU from many unions in South Africa and in the world. It provides the standpoint from which COSATU engages with the state and capital and broader mass democratic movement.
>
> (Zwelinzima Vavi, 7 December 2006)

With this chasm in ideological orientation, it is no surprise that COSATU has tended to openly challenge some government policies deemed too neoliberal, such as the 1996 Growth, Employment and Redistribution macroeconomic strategy (Webster, 1998); the government's privatization plans in 2001 (Webster and Buhlungu, 2004, p. 233) and more recently its E-Tolls plans (Ruiters, 2014, p. 422). In a recent rebuff of the government's National Development Plan, COSATU's general secretary contended that:

> The underlying reason for South Africa's ongoing crisis of unemployment, poverty and inequality is that government has been undermined and corrupted by forces of global capitalism, its local allies and elements within our revolutionary movement itself. Despite the January 8th Statement's clear recognition that 'monopoly capital still has an unhealthy effect on our economy,' the cabinet has allowed the very same monopoly capitalists to persuade them to go along with the National Development Plan's neoliberal economic policies which are anti-poor, anti-working class, anticommunist and anti-ANC.
>
> (Zwelinzima Vavi, 2015; Editorial in *The Shopsteward*,
> Vol. 23, No. 6, of December/January 2015, page 5)

To COSATU apologists, these challenges to the government are indicative of its independence from the ANC. To critics, however, they simply confirm that COSATU has 'not been able to win its struggle against the ANC over fundamental macroeconomic policies' (Masiya, 2014, p. 454). Worse, these challenges and COSATU's active involvement in internal ANC leadership struggles (especially during the 2007 Mbeki–Zuma transition) leave the impression that COSATU is now more of a political union than a classical trade union federation (Gordon, 2015, p. 328; Masiya, 2014, p. 455). In a summary of this recurrent critique against COSATU, Botiveau indicated that even though COSATU still maintains 'key elements of social movement unionism', it has:

> to some extent, drifted towards a form of political unionism whereby it has narrowed internal democratic space and shown signs of creeping oligarchy, uncritically mobilizing support for the ANC during elections and refusing to work with groups that argue for an end to the Alliance.
>
> (2014, p. 137)

Given this, there has been widespread frustration with COSATU and some of its affiliated unions. One group of frustrated workers with relevance to this chapter has been miners. Some miners have criticized COSATU and its affiliated trade union in COSATU, the National Union of Mineworkers (NUM), of being corrupt, too close to management and not doing enough to fight for better working and living conditions for miners, especially the protesting rock drill operators. This category of miners, who were at the forefront of the Marikana strike, are often poorly paid and tend to live 'precariously in informal settlements without running water, toilets, electricity and roads' (Chinguno, 2013, p. 641; Swart and Rodny-Gumede, 2015, p. 325). As several reports indicate, when miners protested in Marikana and beyond in 2012, they rejected NUM and 'put together worker committees to negotiate their demands on their behalf, circumventing the official bargaining processes' (Gumede, 2015, p. 335).

Eventually, the Association of Mineworkers and Construction Union (ACMU), which is not affiliated to COSATU and is headed by former NUM members, emerged as the striking miners' union of choice (Chinguno, 2015, p. 579; Gordon, 2015, p. 339). This struggle for union members and allegiance within these mining unions has ushered in an unprecedented spate of bloody inter-union rivalry within the mining sector and within COSATU (Botiveau, 2014, p. 128; Chinguno, 2013).

While ACMU and NUM bickered in 2012, the crisis within COSATU and fissures of trade unionism in South Africa moved one level higher in 2014 following the request from one of COSATU's affiliate unions, the National Union of Metalworkers of South Africa (NUMSA), for the dissolution of the tripartite alliance. Ahead of the 2014 general elections and contrary to COSATU's official view that the tripartite alliance is 'the only vehicle capable of bringing about fundamental transformation in South Africa' (COSATU, 2016) NUMSA, in a dramatic move, refused to endorse the ANC, pointing out that the ANC and the tripartite alliance 'had failed workers' (Hunter, 2014). NUMSA was subsequently expelled from COSATU for violating its constitution. As a sign of solidarity with NUMSA, seven other COSATU-affiliated unions voluntarily suspended their participation in COSATU. Shortly after NUMSA's expulsion, COSATU controversially dismissed its general secretary, Zwelinzima Vavi, who is an open critic of the ANC and the decision to expel NUMSA (Marrian, 2014).

Given all this, it is clear that the blend of the enduring socioeconomic legacies of apartheid, the contested neoliberal inclinations of the post-apartheid state and the crises of public governance and fissures in trade unionism created a potentially explosive situation. So while shocking, the incidents in Marikana in 2012 were not entirely surprising to many observers – including COSATU. In fact, as Swart and Rodny-Gumede noted, the Marikana killings were truly 'indicative of [the] underlying crises in government and the fabric of society' in South Africa (2015, p. 323).

Even though the Marikana strikes and fallouts were not entirely surprising even to COSATU, the events put COSATU in the limelight and in a bind. Because of the tripartite alliance, when things like the Marikana strikes and killings happen, COSATU and its leaders are often:

> caught in an uncomfortable and unresolved contradiction. While the union leaders are under pressure to represent members' interests and meet their high expectations, they are also politically and organically linked to the ANC which imposes significant restraining influences.
>
> (Gall, 1997, p. 215; see also Webster, 1998, p. 59)

How COSATU navigated this contradiction discursively as concerns the Marikana killings is the focus of the empirical angle of this chapter. As mentioned in the introduction, scholars have analyzed the Marikana killings from several angles, but COSATU's reaction is yet to receive systematic empirical scrutiny. COSATU's official reaction often receives just a passing mention such as the statement from Ruiters that COSATU has been 'self-critical about its role in the Marikana events' (2014, p. 422) and the argument from Alexander that COSATU's response to Marikana was 'limp' (2013, p. 615).

While these views hint at COSATU's reactions, they are just that – hints. In this chapter, I undertake a systematic analysis of official statements from COSATU regarding the Marikana killings with the aim to respond to this central question: how did COSATU frame the Marikana killings? Next, I present the methodology and data used to respond to this central question.

Methodology and data

To examine how COSATU framed the Marikana killings, I analyze relevant official statements from COSATU about the Marikana strikes and killings. As Paret argues, while official statements from organizations like COSATU are 'limited in what they reveal about the inner workings of unions, they nonetheless provide a useful window' into how unions interpret events around them (2015, p. 345).

The official statements from COSATU come from two key sources – press statements published on COSATU's website[2] and relevant reports published in *The Shopsteward*, COSATU's bimonthly magazine[3]. To select the press statements analyzed, I collected all statements published from January 2012 to 10 September 2016. The key criteria used in selecting press statements included the following:

- It is focused on the August 2012 strike in the Lonmin platinum mine in Marikana and subsequent events directly connected to this strike.
- The statement is issued as a COSATU statement or co-issued as a statement by COSATU and an affiliated union(s) or members of the tripartite alliance. This means that if statements about the strike are issued by NUM, for instance, they have not been selected since the key interest is not to examine the reaction of COSATU's affiliates, but rather COSATU itself.

I followed similar criteria to select articles from *The Shopsteward*. I downloaded the PDF versions of all 22 issues of *The Shopsteward* published between February 2012 and August 2016 from the COSATU website. Only relevant reports written by COSATU officials or *The Shopsteward* staff were selected. So, even though the general secretary of NUM, for instance, wrote a report titled 'Lonmin: the story behind the story' in the June–July 2012 issue of *The Shopsteward*, this article was not selected for the aforementioned reasons.

Following these criteria, 34 press statements and 13 reports from *The Shopsteward* were selected (please see the appendix for the titles of all the statements and reports analyzed). To analyze these 47 documents, I have drawn from Entman's perspectives on frame analyses. According to Entman (1993, p. 52) to frame is to:

> Select some aspects of a perceived reality and make them more salient in a communicating text in such a way as to promote a particular problem definition, causal interpretation, moral evaluation and/or treatment recommendation for the item described.'

This perspective fits well with the key question of this chapter: according to COSATU, what or who caused the strike and killings in Marikana and what are the solutions needed to prevent another Marikana? Which particular interpretations does COSATU emphasize and promote? In examining the ways in which COSATU framed the Marikana killings, a key point of interest is also to examine the ways in which COSATU perceives the role of the state, especially as far as 'treatment recommendations' are concerned.

Next, I present the key findings from a thorough reading of these 47 documents which shows the kinds of interpretations that COSATU emphasized as far as its framing of the Marikana killings is concerned.

Marikana: COSATU plays the blame game

The dramatic killing of the striking miners on 16 August 2012 led to an explosion of commentary and finger pointing within and beyond South Africa. In the midst of all these commentaries, COSATU sought to go above the fray. In a statement published in *The Shopsteward* (which referred to the incidents as a 'massacre'), COSATU's general secretary indicated that COSATU is:

> Refusing to use this tragedy to score points. We won't play the blame-game nor will we use the anger workers and their communities are feeling to drive sentiments against government or anyone. We must await the findings of the commission of inquiry, which we have welcomed, and hope will establish exactly what happened not only on that tragic day but in many months before that day.
>
> (*The Shopsteward*, Vol. 21, No. 3 of June–July 2012, p. 4)

While this suggested a principled approach to restraint in the context of a charged and sorrowful atmosphere, COSATU nevertheless had clear ideas about the causes of the Marikana shooting. In the same statement, COSATU went on to declare that:

> The underlying problems which give rise to incidents like those at Marikana are the stark levels of inequality in South Africa and the super-exploitation of workers by ruthless and rapacious employers.
>
> (*The Shopsteward*, Vol. 21, No. 3 of June–July 2012, p. 4)

Without respecting its own call for restraint, COSATU had already started 'driving sentiments' regarding 'ruthless and rapacious employers'. Taken as a whole, what do the analyzed statements reveal concerning COSATU's framing of the Marikana incidents?

The examined statements show that as per COSATU's analyses, in addition to blaming the government, other systemic factors and particular people/groups of people are responsible for the carnage in Marikana. The identified persons responsible for Marikana as per COSATU are:

* Mine bosses and capitalists
* Former trade union bosses who are creating splinter unions
* Police bosses

The systemic factors responsible for Marikana, according to COSATU, include:

* Capitalism
* Poverty, inequality and unemployment
* The historical legacy of poor pay and working conditions in the mining industry

Although COSATU mentioned all of these issues as bearing some responsibility for Marikana, in line with Entman's (1993) framing perspective, COSATU emphasized and promoted two particular issues as the major causes of Marikana: mining companies/mining bosses and the systemic legacy of apartheid in the mining sector. In this regard, I examine COSATU's discourses legitimizing this responsibility attribution.

COSATU accused mining companies/mining bosses of causing the strike in Marikana through the following strategies:

a.   Corporate greed

As far as COSATU is concerned, the root causes of the events in Marikana are easy to identify. It declared in a statement that in addition to the continuous existence of apartheid-era legislative framework in the mining industry, which 'continues to perpetuate inhumane conditions of exploitation' of miners:

> the underlying causes of what happened on those fateful days can be traced back to the employers' greed which has characterized the mining industry.
>
> (COSATU, 15 August 2014)

In statements published in October 2012, COSATU still pointed to corporate greed as the underlying cause of the upheavals in the mining sector. This corporate greed, according to COSATU, is manifested in the low salaries that miners are paid and in the vast difference between the salaries of mining bosses and miners. In a statement released on 2 October 2012, COSATU indicated, for instance, that:

> It must be said that *the source of all these upheavals is the pathetic levels of pay and working conditions mineworkers are subjected to.* The NUM and COSATU are fully behind all the legitimate demands of the mineworkers for better pay and improved working conditions.
>
> (COSATU, 2 October 2012, emphases added)

In pursuit of this line of argument, on 22 October 2012, COSATU, while condemning the mass retrenchments going on in the mining sector, stated that:

> The crisis that has engulfed the mining industry *is primarily the fault of the employers themselves and they should not attempt to take short-cuts to avoid it.* Had the mining bosses not been *paying workers a pittance,* we would not be having these strikes in the first place.
>
> (COSATU, 22 October 2012, emphases added)

Although as seen later, the problems in the mining sector go beyond salaries, the fact that the August 2012 strike was significantly hinged on demands for pay raise can possibly explain COSATU's 'fronting' of salaries as part of the central underlying causes of the crisis that has 'engulfed the mining industry'.

In describing the salary levels of miners with words such as 'pathetic' and 'pittance', COSATU emotively highlights the dire and unfair situation of miners. This sense of unfairness is heightened in a statement released in August 2014 in which COSATU criticizes the salaries of mining executives. According to the statement, in May 2014, Chris Griffith, CEO of Anglo American Platinum, was paid 'a total R17.6-million, of which R6.7-million was a basic salary', an income which a mineworker will 'have to work 209 years to earn' (COSATU, 15 August 2014).

The specification of the jaw-dropping '209 years' goes a long way to aptly capture COSATU's persistent argument in the analyzed statements that:

> The problems that beset our economy are not caused by the Holy Spirit but *by the greed, selfishness and brutality of capitalist bosses whose ruthlessness continues unabated.*
>
> (COSATU, 23 October 2012, emphases added)

Through such discourses, COSATU, true to its socialist orientations, constructs a classic narrative of 'capitalist bosses' riding roughshod over poor workers. This 'us-versus-them' narration also serves as a vital mobilizing rhetoric given that it personalizes causes and effects at an easy but dramatic level.

b.   Utilization of 'divide-and-rule' tactics in dealing with unions

COSATU faults the mining companies for engaging in what it calls divide-and-rule tactics when it comes to negotiating salaries with the aim of bypassing collective bargaining and weakening unions. According to COSATU, the mining companies' 'tactic' of making 'separate offers to particular groups of workers' rather than engaging in collective bargaining is what 'sparked off the initial protests, which are still spreading throughout the industry and beyond' (COSATU, 8 October 2012).

So on this point, as far as COSATU is concerned:

> *It is the mine employers in general and Impala bosses in particular who must take full responsibility for all the strikes that are spreading in the mining industry.* Impala committed a grave error in offering an 18% increase to one category (miners) to the exclusion of the rest of the workers of Impala and, more seriously, outside the collective bargaining process. [. . .] Expectations have been raised *not by the NUM but by the employers and the recent mine workers strikes are a response to the employers' miscalculation.*
>
> (2 October 2012, emphases added; also
> see COSATU, 8 October 2012)

This statement takes the personalization of the diagnoses of what caused Marikana a step further. COSATU fearlessly apportions responsibility for the chaos to specific actors while offering a clear exoneration of NUM, its affiliated union.

c. Non-respect of mining laws and the role of the state therein

According to COSATU, one of the leading causes of the Marikana incidents was the non-respect of mining regulations:

> Today the *mining bosses continue to openly defy the implementation of the Mining Charter* which has the potential to fundamentally transform the sector. Indeed, a*t the center of these painful events at Marikana was intransigence of the Lonmin Mining bosses* who were refusing to accede to demands for a R12 500 increase in salaries demanded by the workers.
>
> (COSATU, 15 August 2014)

While mining bosses are directly faulted, COSATU also blames the state for enabling this state of affairs through the non-implementation of its own laws. As a result, as one report noted, in order to make sense of Marikana and when describing the tragedy, the 'key phrases which come to mind' include:

> A filthy rich and rapacious industry, controlling 80% of [the] world's platinum, which is a law unto itself [. . .] and a state with mineral rights, but no strategy to leverage these to regulate supply and prices or to build manufacturing capacity. An industry which reproduces the apartheid mining political economy, to serve its selfish interests, and does everything in its power to dodge its commitments under the law, never mind its moral obligations.
>
> (*The Shopsteward*, 2012, Vol. 21, No. 5, pp. 8–9)

Talking about 'moral obligations', the predominant moral evaluations in COSATU's statements about Marikana revolve around the castigation of mine bosses. They are referred to as 'capitalist bosses' whose 'greed, selfishness, brutality and ruthlessness continues unabated' (COSATU, 23 October 2012). Although not clearly specified, it is obvious from the statements that the 'capitalist bosses' that are of prime target are expatriates and not black South African entrepreneurs.

d. Inter-union Conflicts

While COSATU does not directly point at other rival unions such as the ACMU for causing the killings on that fateful 16 August 2012 in Marikana, it nonetheless indicates that members of the ACMU, in collusion with mining companies and police officers, are responsible for the bloodshed in the mining sector – especially the death of NUM officials in Marikana. In addressing these issues, COSATU adopts positively flowery discourses when it talks about itself or the NUM and condescending and disparaging discourses when it talks about the ACMU in particular.

In a statement in August 2012, for instance, which highlighted the intense inter-union rivalries for membership in Marikana between the NUM and the ACMU, COSATU indicated that it wanted to:

> *remind* ACMU that the constitution of our country allows workers a freedom of association and that right has been extended in the labor relations act which gives workers the rights and powers to form their unions and *not to be forced to join some fly-by night unions.* [. . .] We further call our national government to intervene *on these criminals who are busy destroying our 18 years [of] democracy*, which is currently being undermined by some few people both at Impala and Lonmin. [. . .] *Workers must be allowed to choose their union.*
>
> (COSATU, 13 August 2012, emphases added)

In another statement on this directed to its members, COSATU even went the extra mile of associating ACMU with the apartheid past, stating that:

> We are asking our members not to allow fly-by-night so-called unions to take us back *to the old apartheid style of exploiting poor black workers for the individuals leading these unions.* The history of our trade unions and of our federation *is known by everybody in the country* and the role that the federation has been playing to improve the conditions of workers since 1994. That must not be reduced to nothing by new unions that are established through *unruly behavior for personal interests.*
>
> (COSATU, 29 September 2012)

The differences could not be starker: while COSATU has been around for a long time and its legacy is known by 'everybody in the country', the ACMU is just 'some fly-by night union'. Furthermore, while COSATU has been working to 'improve' the conditions of workers since 1994, the ACMU has just been set up through 'unruly behavior for personal interests'. In some ways, this is COSATU acknowledging competition in its 'backyard' while using its 'glorious past' to impose a particular set of narratives on an emerging competitor. Furthermore, it delegitimizes the ACMU not only through assertions about its history and motives, but also through the denigration of its leadership ('criminals') and through the ACMU's potential negative national impact (destruction of 18 years of democracy). All these set the stage for request of its ally – the ANC government, to 'intervene' (without specifying how) to stop these 'criminals'.

While these attacks on the ACMU are delegitimizing discursive strategies, they also serve as re-articulations of a sense of 'team spirit' amongst miners still affiliated with the NUM. This urge for team spirit within a de-legitimization discourse is evidenced in a series of statements in which COSATU called on miners to 'observe maximum discipline and unity in the face of *a political strategy* geared towards dividing them and weakening their position in relation to *mine bosses and capitalists*' (COSATU, 14 August 2012). It described the situation as 'the most serious challenge to workers' unity and strength for many years' (COSATU, 16

August 2012), urging workers 'to remain united and strong and to focus their anger on *their real enemy, the mining bosses'* (COSATU, 11 September 2012a, emphases added).

In these statements, COSATU not only delegitimizes ACMU as nothing but a political project which does not have workers' interests at heart, but it also redirects workers' anger from itself back to the people emphatically identified by COSATU as the cause of the incidents in Marikana: mining bosses. They describe the latter as miners' 'real enemy', conjuring an antagonistic image rather than a collaborative one between employers and employees. This antagonistic imagery is also prevalent in the ways in which COSATU does not shy away from declaring that what it is engaged in and what the Marikana incidents reveal is ongoing class warfare in South Africa between socialists and capitalists. At the height of the tensions following the Marikana incident, COSATU declared on 23 October 2012, for instance, that 'a class war has begun in South Africa' and that 'the capitalists cannot come out victors' (see also COSATU, 9 December 2015).

No more Marikanas: COSATU's suggested solutions

On 28 August 2012, COSATU indicated in a statement that 'everything possible must be done to ensure there will never be any more Marikanas.' What did it suggest? In the analyzed statements, COSATU outlines a series of short, medium and long-term solutions to the mining crises. These include, for instance, calls for the police to carry out more investigations on the attacks against NUM officials; the need for the police force to be trained in crowd management and the need for shop stewards to be trained very well on matters regarding bargaining and procedures to kick-start a legal strike.

When it comes to emphasized 'treatment recommendations' in line with the perspective on framing discussed earlier, three solutions dominate and two of these resonate with a stronger role for the state: strengthening the unity of the federation and its affiliates; nationalization of mines and establishment of a commission of inquiry into the mining sector.

On this first issue regarding unity within COSATU, as indicated earlier, COSATU saw the activities of ACMU and its rapid success in gaining the trust of striking miners and some mining companies literally as an existential threat. In this regard, suggestions for more unity were common in the COSATU statements. In a statement issued in September 2012, for instance, COSATU urged 'all the workers who have left the National Union of Mineworkers to return and help build an even stronger and more united union' (COSATU, 19 September 2012). In an earlier statement, it said the 'old slogan: "united we stand – divided we fall" is not empty rhetoric. It is the key to our success in transforming workers' lives, building a prosperous and peaceful world and preventing any more Marikanas' (COSATU, 24 August 2012).

As concerns the establishment of a commission of inquiry, which arguably is the solution championed most by COSATU, COSATU argues that as far as the mining industry is concerned: 'It is taking far too long for this industry to be transformed and to shake off its legacy from the years of colonialism and apartheid' (COSATU, 15 August 2014). As a result, on the heels of the formation of the Marikana Independent Commission by President Zuma, COSATU called for a:

> Second Independent Commission of Inquiry that will work parallel to the Judicial Commission already appointed by the President. The terms of reference of this second Commission must be to investigate the employment and social conditions of workers in the mining industry, historically and at present.
>
> (COSATU, 4 July 2014; also see COSATU, 8 October 2012)

With regards to nationalization, COSATU argues that given the importance of mining to South Africa's economy, it is regrettable that the mining industry is:

> in the hands of monopoly companies which use [their] mining licenses just to amass profits and not to develop the economy, create jobs and play their part in the radical transformation of our economy.
>
> (COSATU, 15 August 2014)

Given this state of affairs, COSATU believes there is need for a 'decisive state intervention' in such 'strategic sectors of the economy, including through strategic nationalization and state ownership' (*The Shopsteward*, 2012, Vol. 21, No. 5, p. 12).

COSATU's perception of the role of the state with regards to the issues surrounding the Marikana killings is indeed mixed. At one point, it sees the state as the solution – urging intervention to stop ACMU 'criminals' destroying South Africa's democracy – and at another point, it sees the state and its related structures such as its police force as essentially useless if not colluders with COSATU's enemies to fight it. This is prevalent in the statements decrying the attacks against NUM officials. At some point, there are signs of resignation when it comes to dealing with the state. Asked why violence had not ended at the Rustenburg mines, for instance, COSATU's general secretary pointedly responded: 'the state has simply failed us. There has not been a single conviction. Those initially arrested for the Marikana killings are roaming the streets' (*The Shopsteward*, Vol. 22, No. 3 of June–July 2013, p. 13).

But within this resigned or frustrated attitude with the state is a strong recognition by COSATU that the socioeconomic challenges facing South Africa cannot be tackled by a neoliberal state that seeks to allow the market to dictate the pace of development. COSATU envisages a developmental state as the ideal path for South Africa. As it lamented in 2015, 'our government cannot keep on playing the role of a spectator while the persisting global capitalist crisis continues to weigh down heavily on our economy' (COSATU, 9 December 2015).

Conclusion

In a context of the increasing integration of the world through trade and the widespread permeation of neoliberalism across the world, what role should post-colonial states play in local development? What is the ideal relationship between capital, labour and the state in post-colonial societies? The post-apartheid state in South Africa has been grappling with these questions for more than two decades. This chapter has used the Marikana killings and COSATU's framing of these as a kick-off point to exemplify the ideological tensions within governing structures in post-apartheid South Africa as concerns the right balance between capital, labour and the state.

Through these, we see the ways in which local people, through formal and informal collective actions, engage with, appropriate and challenge transnational capital. A lasting legacy of Marikana may not be the establishment of a socialist state in South Africa as COSATU desires. Marikana's lasting legacy will rather be that once more, ordinary South Africans dared forces larger than themselves (the state, unions and corporations) and took a stand to demand to be treated fairly by multinational corporations. As South Africans say – Amandla! Ngawethu! (Power! It Is Ours!)

Table 6.A1 List of press statements analyzed

No.	Title of Press Release or Statement	Date Published Online
1.	COSATU NW condemns the killing of workers at Lonmin	13 August 2012
2.	COSATU condemns the ongoing violence at Lonmin	14 August 2012
3.	COSATU condemns violence at Lonmin and breakaway 'union' NATAWU	16 August 2012
4.	COSATU statement on Malema's attack on the NUM	20 August 2012
5.	COSATU NW calls on workers in Lonmin to mourn	21 August 2012
6.	COSATU message to Marikana memorial services	23 August 2012
7.	COSATU statement on Marikana massacre	24 August 2012
8.	COSATU shocked at 'shot-in-the-back' allegations	28 August 2012
9.	ANC alliance statement on the situation at the Lonmin Marikana platinum mines	7 September 2012
10.	COSATU condemns irresponsible statement by Julius Malema	11 September 2012a
11.	COSATU Eastern Cape Press statement	11 September 2012b
12.	COSATU welcomes end of Lonmin strike	19 September 2012
13.	COSATU NW and the unprotected strikes	29 September 2012
14.	COSATU and NUM statement on the current wildcat strikes in the mining industry	2 October 2012a
15.	COSATU NW condemns the continued attack on NUM shop stewards	2 October 2012b
16.	Statement issued by CoM, NUM and COSATU	4 October 2012
17.	COSATU NW condemns shooting of NUM leaders	7 October 2012
18.	COSATU condemns murders of NUM leaders	8 October 2012
19.	COSATU enraged by mass dismissals and now mobilizing for solidarity actions	22 October 2012
20.	We warned about a ticking time-bomb	23 October 2012
21.	COSATU calls for fair treatment of unions in the mining sector	20 June 2013
22.	COSATU demands that the state should fund Marikana victims' legal costs	3 September 2013
23.	COSATU condemns murder of NUM official	16 October 2013
24.	COSATU statement on Marikana developments	17 October 2013
25.	Killing of workers continues in Marikana	18 October 2013
26.	Still too many deaths in the mines	3 February 2014
27.	COSATU disappointed with Lonmin	21 May 2014
28.	COSATU 11th Congress Declaration on the Lonmin Marikana platinum mine tragedy, the mining industry, and general poverty wages as adopted with amendments 17th September 2012	4 July 2014
29.	The lessons of Marikana: COSATU's 2nd anniversary statement	15 August 2014
30.	COSATU statement on the Marikana Commission Report	9 April 2015
31.	COSATU remembers all workers killed before, during and after the Marikana tragedy	16 August 2015
32.	Coal mining companies should accede to the legitimate and fair demands of workers	7 October 2015
33.	Mining job losses requires bold and visionary action from government	9 December 2015
34.	COSATU NW supports striking workers in the mining sector	NA

Source: www.cosatu.org.za/list.php?type=COSATU%20Press%20Statements

Table 6.A2 List of issues of *The Shopsteward* read

No.	Issue Volume and Number
1.	Vol. 21 No. 1 of February/March 2012
2.	Vol. 21 No. 2 of April/May 2012
3.	Vol. 21. No. 3 of June/July 2012
4.	*The Shopsteward* special bulletin of September 2012
5.	Vol. 21. No. 5 of October/November 2012
6.	Vol. 22. No. 1 of February/March 2013
7.	Vol. 22. No. 2 of April/May 2013
8.	Vol. 22. No. 3 of June/July 2013
9.	Vol. 22. No. 4 of August/September 2013
10.	Vol. 22. No. 5–6 of December 2013/January 2014
11.	Vol. 23. No. 1 of February/March 2014
12.	Vol. 23. No. 2 of April/May 2014
13.	Vol. 23. No. 3 of June/July 2014
14.	Vol. 23. No. 4 of August/September 2014
15.	Vol. 23. No. 5 of October/November 2014
16.	Vol. 23. No. 6 of December 2014/January 2015
17.	Vol. 24. No. 1 May Day Special Edition
18.	Vol. 24. No. 3 of June/July 2015
19.	Vol. 24. No. 4–5 of October/November 2015
20.	Vol. 24. No. 6 of December 2015/January 2016
21.	Vol. 25. No. 1 of February to March 2016
22.	Vol. 25. No. 3 of June/July 2016

Source: www.cosatu.org.za/list.php?type=Shopsteward

Table 6.A3 List of analyzed reports from *The Shopsteward* read

No.	Title and Page of Report Published in The Shopsteward	Volume/Issue Number
1.	NUM members demonstrate against recent retrenchments in mines (p. 61)	Vol. 25. No. 3 June/July 2016
2.	Workers will fight to the bitter end to save their jobs (p. 31)	Vol 24. No. 6 of Dec 2015/Jan 2016
3.	Snippets of the Central Executive Committee (p. 9)	Vol. 23 No. 3 of June–July 2014
4.	Q&A with COSATU SG (p. 13)	Vol. 22 No. 3 June–July 2013
5.	Editorial (p. 4–5)	Vol. 21. No. 5. Oct–Nov 2012
6.	The Marikana moment highlights a lifetime of unanswered needs (p. 8–9)	Vol. 21. No. 5. Oct–Nov 2012
7.	Decision of the COSATU Special Central Executive Committee (p. 10)	Vol. 21. No. 5. Oct–Nov 2012
8.	Statement of the COSATU Central Executive Committee Meeting	Vol. 21. No. 5. Oct–Nov 2012
9.	Marikana diminishing returns: economic activities in the mining sector (p. 32–34)	Vol. 21. No. 5. Oct–Nov 2012
10.	COSATU 11th National Congress Declaration: a call to action (p. 7)	Special Bulletin, September 2012
11.	COSATU 11th Congress Declaration on the Lonmin Marikana platinum mine tragedy, the mining industry, and general poverty wages. As adopted with amendments on the 17th September 2012 (p. 9)	Special Bulletin, September 2012
12.	Editorial (p. 4–5)	Vol. 21 No. 3 June–July 2012
13.	The role of shop stewards in the spotlight after Marikana (p. 9)	Vol. 21 No. 3 June–July 2012

Source: www.cosatu.org.za/list.php?type=Shopsteward

Notes

1 In addition to several individual journal articles and book chapters, for some of this 'Marikana scholarship', see, for instance, the following journal special issues focusing on Marikana: *Social Dynamics: A Journal of African Studies* Vol. 41, Issue 2; *Review of African Political Economy*, Vol. 40, No. 138 and the *Journal of Asian and African Studies* Vol. 51, Issue 2.
2 www.cosatu.org.za/list.php?type=COSATU%20Press%20Statements
3 Press statements accessed at www.cosatu.org.za/list.php?type=Shopsteward. This applies to all further dated COSATU press statements below in this chapter. The list of statements accessed is found at the end of this chapter in Appendix 6.1.

References

AFP (2013). South Africa places high premium on mine stability, says Zuma, 13 June.

Alexander, P. (2013). Marikana, turning point in South African history. *Review of African Political Economy* 40(138) pp. 605–619.

BBC News (2015). South Africa police accused over Marikana mine deaths, 25 June.

BBC News (2016). South Africa local elections: ANC loses in capital Pretoria, 6 August.

Bernstein, A. (2014). South Africa's key challenges: tough choices and new directions. *The ANNALS of the American Academy of Political and Social Science* 652(1) pp. 20–47.

Bond, P. (2011). What is radical in neoliberal-nationalist South Africa? *Review of Radical Political Economics* 43(3) pp. 354–360.

Botiveau, R. (2014). The politics of Marikana and South Africa's changing labour relations. *African Affairs* 113(450) pp. 128–137.

Chinguno, C. (2013). Marikana: fragmentation, precariousness, strike violence and solidarity. *Review of African Political Economy* 40(138) pp. 639–646.

Chinguno, C. (2015). The unmaking and remaking of industrial relations: the case of Impala Platinum and the 2012–2013 platinum strike wave. *Review of African Political Economy* 42(146) pp. 577–590.

COSATU (2016). *About Tripartite Alliance.* www.cosatu.org.za/show.php?ID=2051#sthash.xX1Om6EE.dpuf.

Curless, G. (2016). Introduction: trade unions in the Global South from imperialism to the present day. *Labor History* 57(1) pp. 1–19.

Davids, Y. and Gaibie, F. (2011). Quality of life in post-apartheid South Africa. *Politikon* 38(2) pp. 231–256.

Dibben, P., Klerck, G. and Wood, G. (2015). The ending of southern Africa's tripartite dream: the cases of South Africa, Namibia and Mozambique. *Business History* 57(3) pp. 461–483.

Entman, R. (1993). Framing: toward clarification of a fractured paradigm. *Journal of Communication* 43(4) pp. 51–58.

Gall, G. (1997). Trade unions & the ANC in the 'new' South Africa. *Review of African Political Economy* 24(72) pp. 203–218.

Gordon, S. (2015). Individual trust and distrust in South African trade unions: a quantitative analysis, 2011–2013. *Politikon* 42(3) pp. 325–343.

Gumede, W. (2015). Marikana: a crisis of legitimacy in the institutions that form the foundations of South Africa's 1994 post-apartheid political settlement. *Social Dynamics* 41(2) pp. 327–343.

Hlatshwayo, M. (2011). Is there room for international solidarity within South African borders? COSATU's responses to the xenophobic attacks of May 2008. *Politikon* 38(1) pp. 169–189.

Hunter, Q. (2014). NUMSA expelled from COSATU. *Mail and Guardian*, 8 November.

Karriem, A. and Hoskins, M. (2016). From the RDP to the NDP: a critical appraisal of the developmental state, land reform, and rural development in South Africa. *Politikon* 43(3). DOI:10.1080/02589346.2016.1160858.

Marrian, N. (2014). NUM & ANC: the price of loyalty. *Financial Mail*, 3 July.

Masiya, T. (2014). Social movement trade unionism: case of the Congress of South African Trade Unions. *Politikon* 41(3) pp. 443–460.

Paret, M. (2015). Contested ANC hegemony in the urban townships: evidence from the 2014 South African election. *African Affairs* 115(460) pp. 419–442.

Pillay, D. (2013). Between social movement and political unionism: COSATU and democratic politics in South Africa. *Rethinking Development and Inequality* 2(Special Issue) pp. 10–27.

Reuters (2016). South African unemployment rises to 26.7 percent in first quarter, 9 May.

Ruiters, G. (2014). Spaces of hope: rethinking trade union–community alliances and citizenship in a post-alliance era in South Africa. *Politikon* 41(3) pp. 421–441.

SABC (2016). Four years after police shot dead striking miners, little has changed. 15 August 2016.

Segatti, A. and Pons-Vignon, N. (2013). Stuck in stabilisation? South Africa's post-apartheid macro-economic policy between ideological conversion and technocratic capture. *Review of African Political Economy* 40(138) pp. 537–555.

The Shopsteward, 2012, Vol. 21, No. 5.

The Shopsteward, 2013, Vol. 22, No. 3.

Southall, R. (2014). Democracy at risk? Politics and governance under the ANC. *The ANNALS of the American Academy of Political and Social Science* 652(1) pp. 48–69.

Swart, M. and Rodny-Gumede, Y. (2015). Introduction: considering the aftermath of Marikana. *Social Dynamics* 41(2) pp. 323–326.

Vavi, Z. (2006). *COSATU's 21st Anniversary – 'Tracing the Footsteps of COSATU' – Achievements and Challenges address by Zwelinzima Vavi*, 7 December. www.cosatu. org.za/show.php?ID=1545#sthash.IKo3BJ2t.dpuf.

Vavi, Z. (2015). *Editorial. The Shopsteward*, Vol. 23, No. 6, December/January 2015.

Webster, E. (1998). The politics of economic reform: trade unions and democratization in South Africa. *Journal of Contemporary African Studies*, 16(1) pp. 39–64.

Webster, E. and Buhlungu, S. (2004). Between marginalisation and revitalisation? The state of trade unionism in South Africa. *Review of African Political Economy* 31(100) pp. 229–245.

7 Corruption in local governance as resistance

A post-colonial reading of the Indian state

Arpita Mathur

Introduction

Corruption is a topic of deep interest in Indian politics, media and even everyday discourse of ordinary people. Regulatory mechanisms to combat corruption existed in India even before independence from British rule in 1947. The British government in India passed the Indian Penal Code in 1860, which included sections to deal with 'Offences by Public Servants'. Introducing specialised anti-corruption law in government services, the Prevention of Corruption Act, 1988, the Prevention of Money Laundering Act, 2002 and the Right to Information Act, 2005 were enacted post-independence. India also ratified the UN Convention against Corruption (UNCAC)and the UN Convention against Transnational Organised Crime (UNCTOC)in May 2011. The Central Bureau of Investigation (CBI), the Central Vigilance Commission (CVC) and the Anti-corruption Bureaus of various states are important offices to fight corruption as prescribed by the laws in India.

In spite of having a plethora of anti-corruption measures, the status of corruption in India does not seem to be improving, however. In 2015, India was ranked the seventy-sixth most corrupt out of 168 countries by Transparency International. There is much popular discontent in India about the corruption. India experienced mass protests and political debates around the enactment of the Jan Lokpal Bill, 2013 (Citizens' Ombudsman Bill), which was expected to strengthen anti-corruption law in India. The bill was passed by the upper house of the parliament in 2013.

Corruption-free governance is an essential part of good governance. Since decentralisation of political power is supposed to lead to a government which is more responsive, accountable and participatory, decentralisation should have a positive impact on corruption. This is corroborated through studies highlighting the importance of decentralisation as a good governance initiative in developing countries (Crook and Manor, 1998; Fjeldstad, 2004; Fukasaku and de Mello, 1999; Manor, 1999; Shah, 1998; World Bank, 2000). India undertook decentralisation as a major policy initiative towards good governance by adopting the Constitutional (73rd Amendment) Act 1992. This Act adopted the *panchayati raj* system as the form of decentralised governance for local administration in India. It provided for the constitution of *panchayats* as elected bodies at three levels: village, block and district. The Act provides for *panchayat* elections every five years with some seats reserved for people from scheduled castes and scheduled tribes[1] and for women. But academic research on decentralisation and corruption in India does not reveal a clear relationship between decentralisation and reduction in corruption. Decentralisation's impact on corruption is complex and cannot be stated in simple unconditional statements (Bardhan and Mookherjee, 2006).

In this chapter, the context of *panchayats* as a form of decentralisation in India is used to study corruption in everyday life of the people at the village level. The *panchayat* is the most important arm of the state in a village society. The findings reveal interesting social processes involved in legitimising certain forms of legally corrupt practices. This illegal but legitimated behaviour means that although the behaviour is illegal according to the law of the land, certain forms of that behaviour are considered acceptable by the society and hence gain legitimacy, while the illegal status is still maintained. These processes of gaining 'legitimacy' from the society involve close interaction with the state. This leads us to interrogate whether there is a relationship between legitimising of corruption and notions of state in the minds of the villagers. When people in India have a discourse on corruption, it enables them to construct the state symbolically, but the boundaries between state and society remain blurred (Gupta, 1995). This study attempts at understanding the interaction of the village people with the state. When referring to the state, I am using the modern notion of state in this chapter, although I compare it with the traditional notion of state in the later parts.

The data from this study reveal that corruption is used as a tool of resistance against the state, and this imparts social legitimacy to corruption. The social processes identified in this study inform the notions of the state for the villagers in that particular setting. In this chapter, I analyse how these processes evolved against the backdrop of India's history of being a British colony for more than 200 years. By acknowledging the historico-cultural nature of corruption, our idea is not to embrace a xenophobic perspective of corruption (Hodgkinson, 1997). A xenophobic perspective views corruption as a result of foreign practices which contaminates an otherwise honest native breed. Without terming pre-colonial India as perfectly corruption free, we acknowledge the evolving process of formation of meanings and practices of corruption and notions of state, as informed by a history of British rule and traditional cultural practices.

I begin by describing the methodology used for this study. This is followed by a summary of this study's findings. I use three instances from the findings to depict local corruption becoming an act of resistance against the state. In the subsequent part, this discussion reveals the notions of state at the village level.

Methodology

The data used in this study have been collected as part of a larger study on village-level corruption in India. The methodology used in this study is constructivist grounded theory as developed by Kathy Charmaz (2006). This methodology was chosen as it provided the necessary flexibility and guidelines for doing research on a sensitive issue like corruption. The use of constructivist grounded theory was further backed by a lack of theory on the socially constructed nature of corruption in the context of decentralisation in India.

The sensitive nature of the problem posed challenges even for the selection of the site for data collection as well as establishing a rapport with the villagers. Familiarity with local culture, language and practices was essential. Fieldwork was conducted in villages in the Indore district of Madhya Pradesh, which is my home region. Madhya Pradesh (M.P.) has been one of the pioneers in implementing the *panchayati raj* system. Although the study focused on data collection from a single village, through contacts developed in this village, I visited two more villages to collect information. The demographic details of the village are provided in Table 7.1. The most widely implemented government-sponsored development scheme in this village was the *Indira Awas Yojna*, which is the rural housing scheme for the poor belonging to the below-poverty line (BPL) list. Under this scheme, rural citizens belonging to the BPL list are provided financial assistance for the construction of a dwelling unit. Scheduled castes (SC) and scheduled tribes (ST), as well as non-SC/ST and freed bonded labourers belonging to BPL, are eligible to benefit under the scheme. Since 1995–1996, widows or next of kin of defence personnel and paramilitary forces killed in action irrespective of the income criteria, ex-servicemen and retired members of the paramilitary forces have also become eligible to get benefits under the scheme. A legally defined social stratification exists in India with the entire society divided into broadly four categories in hierarchical order based on their historical socioeconomic dominance, namely, the general category, other backward castes (OBC),[2] scheduled castes and scheduled tribes. The origin of this legal stratification lies in colonial times. When the British started the census system, they created a fixed hierarchy to control a formerly fluid type of social system (Kaviraj, 2009). Hence, constitutionally, India has this hierarchical stratification of the society, but socially, many *jatis* (communities) exist with different status in various parts of the country.

Table 7.1 Village demographics

Total Population	5,000 (680 Families)
General Category	55 families
Other Backward Castes(OBC)	350 families
Scheduled Castes (SC)	125 families
Scheduled Tribes(ST)	20 families
Religion	Hindu and Muslim
Muslim	130 families
Sarpancha	Woman, OBC
Panchayat Secretary	Man, General Category

Data were collected from all 34 BPL families in the village, the *panchayat sarpanch*,[3]other *panchayat* members, the *panchayat* secretary[4] and other people I met during the course of data collection. Data collection was done over a period of six to seven months in two phases from April–June 2013 and August–November 2013. The methods used for data collection included unstructured interviews, informal chats, discussions and observation.

Findings

Types and evidence of corruption

There was clear evidence of the prevalence of corruption. Different types of corruption were found like favouritism and exchange of bribes from the poor as well as the rich. Corruption in disbursement of benefits under *India Awas Yojna* (IAY) and the formation of the BPL list is one such example. The list of below-poverty line (BPL) people was itself flawed, with many non-poor forming part of the list, and many poor missing from the list. Apart from this, there were many poor who had their names on the list but never got any benefits, although they were eligible. There was discrimination on the basis of caste-*jati*, religion and political affiliation. The process for conducting the survey for BPL people was inadequate. It is supposed to be a detailed, door-to-door survey about the assets possessed by every family, but the surveyor did not go to every household. To make the process faster, the surveyor often contacted the village elite and asked them about the poor families in the village. Many times, the surveyor had asked the questions to the neighbours in the absence of the villager. This made the process highly inaccurate because due process was not followed and people were not added to the BPL list by following the legally defined eligibility criteria. Some villagers reported demands for a bribe for getting benefits under the IAY scheme. The *panchayat* secretary himself admitted taking bribes.

Non-reporting and condoning of corruption

Even when it was common knowledge that corruption is prevalent, people condoned corruption. The main reason found for this revealed the importance of social relationships in a village setting. Maintaining these relationships of reciprocity was very important for survival in the village. Reporting corruption could mean spoiling these relationships. The most dominant reason found in this study is the dynamics around these social relationships. In a few instances, there were also other reasons. A second reason was that people were not reporting out of fear of violence or other harm that might be inflicted by the powerful people involved in corruption. Thirdly, there was neglect of corrupt behaviour in the village, although corruption was quite visible and common knowledge. People neglected the misconduct because they were simply inactive in taking a stand against corruption. The fourth reason was ignorance amongst the villagers about the correct method of reporting.

Social relationships

Life in this village, as revealed by the data, was characterised by many types of social relationships, including family and kinship relationships, caste relationships, political affiliations or other socially constructed relationships. These relationships do not have a permanent hierarchy and are context dependent. The degree of closeness of relationships establishes the trust level and reciprocity obligations in social conduct. Access to benefits from the *panchayat* is also determined by the various types of social relationships. Access to social networks determines access to information about one's entitlements in terms of sets of benefits under various developmental schemes. People lacking such access live in a state of deprivation. The degree of closeness and trust level decide the type of corrupt behaviour. When there are very close relations, with high trust, no bribe exchange is required, and work can be done through favouritism only, by use of contacts and networks. When there are close relations, bribe exchange or favouritism both are possible, according to the situation. When there are not so close relationships, then not even an exchange of bribes is possible. Even for giving bribes one needs to have some contacts and relations. The bribe taker would try to know the social background of the bribe giver and try to do some background check, whether he has a past history of reporting about corruption, before accepting a bribe.

Social norms

In this village society, certain social norms evolve from various types of social relationships, which inform the decision to either condone or report corruption. These social norms and contexts inform the legitimacy status of a particular corrupt behaviour. In this study, it was observed that almost all the beneficiaries were related to the *sarpancha* or the *panchayat* secretary or some other member of the *panchayat* through some relationship of reciprocation. However, this network of the *sarpancha* or the *panchayat* secretary is not always fixed and pre-determined. Networks are open and dynamic, moving beyond multiple boundaries of different kinds of relationships. There were many types of social relationships and each had its own boundaries. These social relationships were, however, non-permanent in nature. According to the situation and need, a villager invoked a particular relationship of reciprocity to his advantage. For example, within a family, two brothers may have rivalry for years and may even have daily quarrels involving verbal abuse. But when there is an external threat to the family, they both unite against it.

Bribe exchange was termed as wrong by almost all the respondents, but they still indulged in giving bribes as a matter of survival or last resort. If a person belonging to a highly respectable family indulged in corruption, people may choose to ignore it. But social standing and reputation of a family evolved over time, and it influenced the perception of the people. At the time of elections, personal relationships with the candidates were the deciding factor in voting, rather than political agendas of the candidates. Favouring a *rakhi*[5] sister was considered an act of *dharma*, a duty, which should be abided by in all circumstances, even if it involved some corrupt behaviour. People had a sense of pride in being able to use their networks and contacts towards corrupt ends, without needing to give any kind of bribe. Being able to network with the 'right' kind of people was a source of respect and standing within the community.

When corruption secures social legitimacy, it is condoned. The social norms emerging out of social relationships provide a broad set of guidelines, under the purview of which a villager enjoys a certain degree of freedom to choose whether he should condone corruption, or whether he should himself indulge in corruption. Not all forms of corruption have social legitimacy. All the corrupt acts may fall along a continuum with varied degrees of social legitimacy as per the temporal and spatial dimensions of the subject matter. While harming a really impoverished person through corruption does not have any legitimacy, favouritism towards one's *rakhi* sister enjoys full social legitimacy. In between these two extremes lie various forms of corruption like bribery, favouritism and gift giving. All these have non-permanent legitimacy status, depending on the contextual factors.

Corruption and the state

The data about corruption reveal several instances of citizens' interaction with the state. A significant aspect revealed in data is about citizens' interpretation of the nature and role of the state. The legitimising of corruption by the villagers is closely linked to their notions of the state. I further probe these notions of the state by taking three instances from the findings, representing perspectives of three different stakeholders in the village: a poor villager, the *panchayat* secretary and an elite villager. All three statements include an instance of corruption.

Following is a statement by a poor villager:

> *If someone from my caste gets his name on the BPL list fraudulently, why should I say anything? All governments are corrupt and there is nothing wrong in taking away some money from government. Let my caste brother get some help.*

In this statement, the villager is condoning an act of corruption committed by someone belonging to his own caste. At first, this appears as a way of protecting the social relationships within the caste. When he refuses to report against corruption by a fellow caste member, here violating state laws is a way of establishing solidarity. But the phrase 'all governments are corrupt' speaks about the attitude of the villager toward the state, represented by the government here. Terming all governments as corrupt, irrespective of the political party in power or its actions over time, is an expression of a sense of distrust towards the state. If people have this sense of betrayal, they must have a set of expectations which were left unfulfilled. These expectations are about the governance mechanisms in place through the formal notion of the state. The traditional notions about a governance mechanism have been of a king as the provider, and the villagers as the protected. It was observed in the findings that there was gross ignorance amongst the villagers about their entitlements to benefits under various development schemes of the government. Also, there was ignorance about the correct method of reporting corruption. Despite ignorance about the formal mechanisms, if a villager can comment about corruption in government and feel a sense of betrayal, he definitely has some sense of governance which does not match with the formal structures of governance in place. It is important here to understand the villager's sense of injustice.

He is not able to comprehend his entitlements, but he is able to perceive denial of service by the government. This means that the state here is perceived as a service provider, *panchayat* being the administrative arm through which the state provides. And, as reported in the findings, the functionaries of the *panchayat* are perceived as corrupt because they demand bribes. When the state is perceived as unjust and state functionaries as corrupt, an act against the state (in the example, taking away government's money) becomes an expression of resistance against the unjust and hence socially legitimate. Thus, fraudulent entry into the BPL list by way of corrupt means, although in complete knowledge of the entire village, including the *sarpancha* and the *panchayat* secretary, becomes socially legitimate and hence condoned.

To understand the perspective of the *panchayat* secretary, let us analyse the following statements made by him:

> *The position which we hold is that of a 'daata'.*[6] *I think I am doing a service for the villagers by helping them in exchange for only the minimum money that I have to spend on them.*
>
> *I know that many non-poor are in [the] BPL list but reporting about it would cause a knot in relationships within the community. I am very sad that some poor are not in the list, but I am unable to do anything about it. If I had powers, I would put the entire village in [the] BPL list and let everyone get benefits.*

In this statement, the *panchayat* secretary is accepting that he takes bribes and he is also providing a justification for the amount of the bribes. According to him, he also has to spend money for providing facilities to the villagers under various schemes. This money is spent in going to the district centre, helping in doing paperwork or bribing higher officials. An important word used in this statement is the word *daata*. The *panchayat* secretary has a great sense of self-worth when he calls himself *daata*. This is a highly respectable term in this region. A person is called *daata* out of great reverence and submission. This term connotes the high extent of legitimacy he bestows to his own acts of corruption. He sees himself as the provider to the poor. While the giver is the government, through its various social benefit schemes for the poor, he looks at himself as the sole instrument which links the government and the governed. In this endeavour, he considers it completely just to take some 'fee' for the 'service' he is providing to the villagers; which in reality, is part of his official duty as the *panchayat* secretary. In this community, gaining social respect is an important and desirable aim in itself. And being considered *daata* is an example of gaining high social respect. The position of the *panchayat* secretary is peculiar in the sense that he is a native to the same village and he is also a government functionary. How these two aspects about him relate to each other is a matter which needs analysis.

The *panchayat* secretary looks at himself as not someone 'belonging to the government', but as someone who has 'access to the government'. He shared the sentiment of the villagers that the higher-up officials in the hierarchy of *panchayati raj* system and the members of *panchayat* are inefficient and corrupt. Under those constraints, he tries to gain access to the government and provides services to the villagers. Here the *panchayat* secretary is attempting to protect his own native space when he also condones the fraudulently prepared BPL list by saying that reporting about non-poor would cause a knot in relationships. At the same time, he is expressing discomfort at the non-inclusion of poor in the BPL list. While acknowledging the state as a distant entity for the villagers, the *panchayat* secretary is acting as a mediator between the native world and the modern government by being a provider to the villagers. And while doing this, his own corruption is insignificant for him and justifiable because, according to him, the higher-level state functionaries are themselves corrupt. For him, the state here is represented by the corrupt and inefficient *panchayat* machinery at the higher levels of block and district. When he says that he wishes to let everyone in the village get benefits, he is supporting the same idea of stealing money from the state which occurred during the colonial days, and perceiving it as socially legitimate, as this is his idea of resistance against the unjust state. In this endeavour to act as the respectable provider, the *daata* to the villagers, his own acts of corruption become an act of resistance against the state.

Next let us analyse statements made by an elite in the village:

> *(laughing) I got the pond near my field on lease and also got [a] loan for fishery in the same. I have also attended training on how to do fishery. But I am a Brahmin and everyone knows that I would never do fishery here. I have used that loan money for agricultural purpose. The pond is used by my cattle for drinking water etc.* Panchayat *as well as bank personnel, everyone knows about this but they are very happy with me and know that I have [a] good reputation in the village.*
>
> *When the BPL surveyor comes, I and some of my friends sit with him in the premises of [the] village temple and tell him the names of the poor in the village. Why should he go about roaming in the village when we are there, and we know each and everyone in the village by face and name?*

In these statements, the elite village member went to the extent of bragging about his own acts of corruption. The mere fact that a person can happily share his illegal acts and feel proud about it shows that it enjoys social legitimacy. In this community, if a person can get his work done faster, by sheer networking and contacts with the 'right' people, it is a source of achieving high status and respect within the community. Such use of social relationships and networks towards corrupt ends is seen as a display of 'smartness' in robbing the government for personal gain. The elite, although enjoying more respect and power within the village, share the sense of the government being a distant entity, to be used legitimately as a resource for personal advantage. And hence a corrupt act which is otherwise illegal secures social legitimacy as an act of resistance against the state. In this particular instance, corruption is a means of expressing resistance against the state by robbing it for personal gain and enjoying social legitimacy. Here personal gain also includes gain for the community, caste, religion or village. The statements further show that the village elite assists in preparation of the fraudulent BPL list. This means that he is not only fully aware, but also an accomplice in the formation of a fraudulent BPL list. By including non-poor in the BPL, the village elite is gaining social standing, as helping more people is a source of maintaining status and power differentiation. He ensures that he is needed in the village, and this increases his value within the village society. This is another means of expressing resistance to the state by condoning instances of corruption where non-poor are part of the BPL list, and hence can enjoy benefits by robbing the government of money.

In all the instances discussed in the previous section, there are expressions of resistance against the state. When this is achieved through corruption, then such legally corrupt behaviour becomes socially legitimate. The people here have different ethical standards to measure a particular act as corrupt. If a *panchayat* secretary has the self-image of a 'provider to the needy', he cannot identify himself as doing anything wrong. On the contrary, he looks at himself as doing a great service. This is not a mere justification for accepting a bribe. It is, rather, a demonstration of the internalisation of a corrupt act as acceptable and valuable. The poor villager is acknowledging this and expressing his resistance to the state by condoning corruption perpetrated by a fellow caste member. In his eyes, he is only just in supporting the harm caused to a corrupt government. Similarly, for the member of the *Brahmin* elite who boasts about receiving a benefit to do fishery through corrupt means, this act reinforces his high social status, and he looks upon it in high regard. In all these cases, there is no question of moral or ethical dilemma for the actor at all, as the particular acts are 'legitimised' both socially and culturally. Given that this is legitimised, with no ethical dilemmas, it is seen as a correct way of expressing resistance to the state. Being able to do so is a matter of pride and accomplishment and a source of respect and power within the local community.

The notions of 'state': a void or a conflict?

Observing these treatments of the state by the local people, it appears that the people here are not attuned to the same notion of the state as is meant by the formal structures of the state according to Western notions in largely Weberian terms. This makes it easy to suspect that there is a void, because we are not able to identify a parallel state at the local level with direct counterparts of the formal state. The following discussion probes into this issue whether there is a void or a conflict pertaining to notions of the state at the local level.

From the discussion in previous sections, it may be observed that there are two ways in which people are interpreting the notion of the state. The first interpretation of the state is as governance machinery. The second interpretation of the state is as a service provider. To understand these two notions, we should first understand the historical background of this part of the world, where the present notions of the state are rooted.

Historical background

Governance in ancient and medieval India

In a village, the state is represented by the local government body called the *panchayat*. But even before implementing the policy of decentralisation in India, some form of the *panchayati raj* system was prevalent in various parts of the country, having their localised nuances in terms of administration and powers. This localised form of *panchayats* has been in existence in India since ancient times. The local bodies conformed to a shared understanding of *dharma* and customs and, in matters of internal management, acted as governments of their respective areas even until the year 1800 (Dharampal, 2000b, p. 249). In this society, *dharma* means righteous conduct which is not fixed, but is contingent. It is open to interpretations and changes according to situation, space and time. This is not to be thought of as Hindu religious practice, but was more widely shared within the country as a common value system in this society(Kaviraj, 2009). There was much devolution of powers to the local level, with the king as the head of the state and enjoying a degree of reverence from the people. At the local level, the representatives of the king functioned as direct contacts with the people.

The sphere of local government in ancient India consisted of democratic principles and a strong collectivistic sense (Mookerji, 1919, p. 22). There was a system in which village-level committees were formed for various tasks. Such committees were called by names like *sabha*, *samgha*, *gana* or *sreni*. The functioning of these committees had elaborate procedural mechanisms in which the members would negotiate and resolve issues of relevance to life and living in the village. There were systematic procedures for democratic election of members of these committees (Khanna, 2005, p. 23; Majumdar, 1920, p. 162). The qualifications for the candidates for committee member elections were well laid out. Ownership of land and being well versed in scriptural knowledge also formed part of the qualifications. Concerns for independence, competence, transparency and accountability were taken care of during the election process. There were adequate punishments for violation of rules and inappropriate behaviour. The overall attempt was to reduce fraud and corruption (Majumdar, 1920, p. 167). The local bodies also had judicial powers and imposed fines; inflicting punishments for petty crimes was possible after a decision based on unanimity of opinion (Majumdar, 1920, p. 137). The village assemblies enjoyed considerable autonomy although they were ultimately subject to the state and *dharma*(Majumdar, 1920, p. 172). Inscriptions from southern India reveal that the village corporations exercised practically all the powers of the state within their limited boundaries (Majumdar, 1920, p. 179).

India has had a turbulent history of many wars, attacks from foreigners and changes in political rulers over different parts of the country. But it is interesting that the village communities were little republics, and governance at the local level largely remained unaffected by such changes in the central political authority (Mookerji, 1919, p. 2). Medieval India mainly consisted of Mughal rule, especially in northern parts of the country. Even with the advent of foreign rule under the Mughals, the previous forms of governance continued. While the site of the Mughal emperor's court remained mainly in the walled cities, the rural hinterlands served as a source of revenue and goods. Although Mughals brought about administrative changes in India and had an elaborate system of officials who served this purpose, at the local level, they did not alter the basic mechanisms and value systems of governance. There was non-interference by the state in village matters and respect for boundaries of local governance and administration as *the king was the head of the state, but not of the society* (Mookerji, 1919, p. 4). This stood in sharp contrast with the Western state, where the progressive aspiration has been of state interference and control in practically all walks of life (Mookerji, 1919, p. 4). It was for these reasons that the formation of local self-government in ancient and medieval India has practically been *sui generis* with regional variations, instead of following a national-level decree by the state, like in the West (Mookerji, 1919, p. 6).

The political structures at the village level in ancient and medieval India are evidence of ancient wisdom about handling local matters at the local level itself, with all the necessary checks and balances to prevent corruption. These systems continued to exist for centuries and hence became an integral part of the daily life of the villagers.

The colonial encounter

The next most significant event in the history of India is the advent of British rule. The British first entered India through the East India Company for the purpose of trade. On 11 January 1612, the British received a decree from the Mughal emperor of India granting trade privileges. This was the first establishment of the British on the continent of India (Mill, 1817). The period from 1612 to 1757 was a period of trade only, while the company's political rule in India commenced in the year 1757 and lasted till 1858. During this period, the company acquired its own private armies and took over administrative control in large parts of India. While the Mughal emperors did not attempt to expand the control of the state into domains of local cultures and customs, the colonial government under the British crown was on a civilising mission.

Anti-corruption laws in India were first formulated during the British rule in India. It is important to understand the historical context in which these laws emerged. During the period of company rule, Lord Robert Clive identified corruption as a threat to the operations of the company in India. His definition of corruption included indulgence in bribery by the subordinates in the company, which was detrimental to the British superiors in the company, and to the overall purpose of amassing wealth from the colony. Clive appointed a committee to look into the matter, and the committee decided to restrict the trade in salt, betel-nut and tobacco to superiors only, as Clive believed all the miseries and abuses had grown out of trade in these commodities only (Howitt, 1839).

It was after the revolt of 1857 by Indian soldiers that the Government of India Act, 1858 was passed and the British crown took over direct control of ruling India. After the commencement of British rule in 1858, the Indian Penal Code, 1860 was enacted. This Act remains the main criminal law document in India today, with minor amendments. This code, authored by Lord Macaulay, consists of specific sections (Sec. 161–165) to deal with corruption. According to this law, public servants found indulging in bribery and gaining personal wealth, and thus harming the interests of government, were termed as corrupt. The basic premise of this law was that the government itself is founded on noble principles, for the benefit of the public at large. But this premise is flawed. The 'public' here did not mean the Indian public which was being ruled by the government. Partha Chatterjee comments about the relationship between the state and institutions of public life which constitute the civil society, that 'the "public" which was seen to deserve the recognition due from a properly constituted State was formed exclusively by the European residents of the country. Their opinion counted as public opinion, and the public came to be defined primarily around the freedoms of the British Indian press' (1993, p. 22). The foundation of this government was ruling over a savage colony, a source of abundant wealth, and taking that wealth back to the civilised British crown. The colonial subjects 'were not considered equal members of the civil society and were not fit subjects of responsible government'(p. 24). The British 'wholly subjugated, stratified and legalised the situation which had come into being after their occupation or conquest'(Dharampal, 2000b, p. 255). They themselves contributed to the disruption of a society and then tried to 'save' it with their law and administration.

Before colonisation, India was divided into numerous princely states, each having its own local governance mechanisms. By bringing in uniform laws and a centralised system of governance, the British tried to convert the 'country' of India into a single 'nation-state', for ease of control and administration. India was a country with exemplary cultural, geographical and linguistic diversities, and rich traditional cultural practices. The British had a limited number of white officials to control a country like this. The construction of legal and political systems was a way of systematising this control over India (Birla, 2009).

Within the decentralised local governance tradition of India, centralising state structures also existed during the pre-British period (Stein, 1985). The centralisation which occurred during colonial rule 'possessed roots in the earlier period'(Perlin, 1985). But during the time of colonisation, it reached newer heights at a faster pace as the colonisers used new knowledge and experience. This occurred on a larger scale compared to pre-colonial Indian rulers (Bayly, 1988). This drew on support from a certain section of Indian elite as well. However, most common Indians were not unaware of the oppression such centralisation brought about.

Much resentment against the British government arose amongst the local people. During the British period, any act involving harm to the British government was corrupt by legal definitions. But the social legitimacy of such acts differed. For many Indians, any act harming the British government was part of the struggle for independence. The common perception amongst the population was that government is corrupt. Any person succeeding in harming the government was a hero in the eyes of the people. Thus, the same act may be illegal but socially legitimate.

The Indian freedom movement, mainly guided by the Congress Party, accepted the notion of India as one nation, with the intention of uniting all of India against the British. The nation we have today called India is a result of this British construction.

Independent India

This notion of one nation of India found its way in independent India when the Constitution of India was drafted by modernist political leaders. The independent India 'inherited the British system of government and administration in its original form. The framers of the new Constitution could not think of an altogether new system'(Pylee, 1967). The post-colonial state retained a virtually unaltered form of 'the basic structure of civil service, the police administration, the judicial system, including the codes of civil and criminal law, and the armed forces as they existed in the colonial period' (Chatterjee, 1993, p. 204). This militated against traditional understandings of governance. For a common citizen, the government remained that distant entity with interfaces in the form of officers. The footprints left by British rule are visible in the construction of meanings and practices of corruption in India today both legally and socially.

The present: state as governance machinery

In the previous sections, we observed that historically there were localised nuances about governance in various parts of the country. These local nuances of governance inform the present indigenous notions of the state. The local governance systems which existed in ancient and medieval India continue to exist as informal mechanisms even today. For example, a group of respected elders of the village may sit together at a public place and resolve village matters, without resorting to the modern-day formal or legal structures. These respected elders may not necessarily belong to the financially elite group or higher caste, as people decide respect and trust for a person based on his/her overall conduct throughout life in different situations. Maintaining the obligations of reciprocities is of prime importance in this society as boycott becomes an important penal device. Naming and shaming are utilised as important regulatory tools, because a loss of respect may have serious repercussions for life within a village. Reciprocal obligations are almost essential for survival within a village. Respect and social status within one's own caste and village is a highly desirable aim of life. Any kind of harm to social status and respect has implications in terms of loss of networks and bonding. Village society is characterised by shared reciprocities between all the villagers, across class and caste. Maintaining social status is also an important source of power. These local disciplinary mechanisms may be outside the purview of legal systems, but they are very much in practice.

It can be observed from the data that all the stakeholders are condoning the formation of a fraudulent BPL list. The procedure for formation of the BPL list is the most crucial technical aspect of extending any government support through formal channels. This act of preparing a fraudulent BPL list is an instrument of resistance against the attempted control by the state on deciding who are the needy in the village. People here are resisting this control by defrauding the list and distribution of benefits. Paraphrasing Partha Chatterjee (1993), the act of forming the BPL list is structurally outside the domain of politics, but the formation of this list itself becomes implicated in the modalities of power. Differential power dynamics are at play during the formation of a fraudulent list, to give favours to people deriving social power from social relationships and also to acknowledge different villagers' overall conduct and needs in a particular manner rather than as a standard abstract poverty level. Thereafter, the act of condoning this entire corrupt process is also a tool to reaffirm one's power status within the community, by resisting an important instrument of governmental control in the context of developmental schemes for the poor, i.e., the BPL list.

After independence, the government of India was formulated by replacing British office bearers with Indians (Dharampal, 2000b, p. 255). The new *panchayati raj* system could not replace the traditional systems because the modern *panchayati raj* system is merely an administrative arm of the state, without any substantial powers like law and order, taxation or jurisdiction. As reported in the World Bank report (2000)'Overview of rural decentralisation in India', mechanisms of accountability are not working, criteria for devolution of functions are unclear and fiscal decentralisation is lagging, there is lack of participation in the *panchayati raj* system and there is lack of inclusion from all sections of the society in spite of provisions for reservations for women, scheduled castes and scheduled tribes. There is resistance against the present form of the 'state as governance machinery' because the colonial encounter led to silencing and illegalising of traditional wisdom and methods of governance.

The present: state as service provider

Given the historical fact of India being a post-colonial country, the citizens are facing a unique situation in which they are formally governed by state machinery based on Western notions, but they still abide by the traditional local nuances of governance. As revealed in the data in this study, in such a situation, the villagers can pragmatically interact with the state by interpreting it as a service provider.

In pre-colonial India, for the villagers, the 'face' of the state consisted of the local-level officers of the king and democratically elected members of local governments. The people perceived less distance from the state in this scenario, even when the ruler of the country changed across time. Dharampal (2000a, p. 43) notes that the concept of the ruler–ruled relationship held by the local people before colonisation was one of continued interaction. It denotes that the people did not perceive the state as a distant entity. Passive resistance was used in the Indian tradition to express differences with the ruler. In contrast, the British demanded total submission from the people. The reason for reluctance to get involved with a dialogue with the local people was British officials' own lack of assurance about the legitimacy of their rule in India (Dharampal, 2000a, p. 48). This lack of confidence did not exist in the case of previous rulers in pre-colonial India as they shared the same value system with the local people.

During the colonial time period, this gradually changed, and in independent India, people have a *panchayati raj* system based on notions of governance that do not match with their traditional notions of governance. In the present scenario, people perceive greater distance from the modern state. The data show that the government's policies are far from the ground realities of the village and that there is a sense of distance between the state and the citizen. The state is looked upon as a giver, and the citizens resort to various means to get maximum benefit out of the state. In between the state and the citizen, there are state actors who are perceived as the provider of the benefits coming from the state. The villagers are trying to gain maximum services from the state by interpreting the services as rewards from the distant state.

Basically, two types of ideologies coexist in this society. Since the Indian state was organised on Western understandings of the state, the modern system of governance is present. At the same time, traditional practices and understandings are still alive. These two ideologies appear to be in conflict with each other, but they coexist, without losing their defining characteristics. Here there is a contestation along with an acceptance of existence of differences. Here all the stakeholders within the village are expressing resistance towards the state. When corruption is used as a tool of resistance against the state, then such corruption enjoys social legitimacy. Contestation in the form of resistance against the state denotes a coexistence of power and struggle. There is consciousness about need for autonomy and there is resistance in practice.

This discussion explains the two kinds of different notions about the state in the minds of the local people, which are in conflict with the formal Western notion of the state. Thus there is no void, but a conflict, a conflict between two different notions of the state. Legitimate acts according to the local notions of the 'state as governance machinery' and the 'state as service provider' become in conflict with the legal notions of the formal state, and hence the 'illegal but legitimate' forms of corruption become evident. The processes involved in these illegal but legitimate forms of corruption are deeply embedded in everyday life in the village.

Conclusion

The instances discussed in this chapter of corruption as a form of resistance against the state reveal the specific notions about the state for the people in the village. From the foregoing discussion, it appears that we have resistance as well as conformance to the state. Resistance is related to the first notion of the 'state as governance machinery', as the locals' understanding is not attuned to modern systems and forms of governance. Conformance is about the second notion of the state being a service provider, as all three stakeholders can utilise the services provided by the state, here perceived as a reward. But as revealed in the data, this conformance towards the notion of the 'state as service provider' is being used for the purpose of facilitating corruption, and hence ultimately transforms into resistance; we have already discussed how corruption is used as a tool of resistance against the state. The villagers are looking at the state as a resource from which to extract maximum benefits. Hence this is a superficial conformance and ultimately a resistance.

The forms of resistance observed in the findings in this study highlight the 'everydayness' of resistance as a behaviour. These are not instances denoting a large conflict or revolt. They are instances from how people live their everyday life in this society. Scott (1985) highlights that domination through coercive controls or material power may be influential, but the culture and ideology of the dominated may remain relatively unaffected. It is this aspect of domination which leaves scope for resistance in everyday life. This is evident in the Indian context here; despite many years of colonial rule, the natives can preserve their culture and ideology and use it as an instrument of resistance against the state. Douglas Haynes and Gyan Prakash (1991) argue that revolutionary 'consciousness' may not be essential to the constitution of resistance. Every individual in this village is living life with this everyday resistance and making informed decisions and choices. This informed actor imparts a degree of non-permanency to the closeness of social relationships, to the status of legitimacy of any corrupt act and to the tools of everyday resistance themselves. This also makes it an ongoing process with structures of social and political power constantly shaping and being reshaped by everyday resistance.

Both the local notions of the state discussed here have a common thread in their interpretation. This common thread is of a historical background of colonial encounter. The notions about corruption are rooted in the colonial past. This makes the present circumstances in post-colonial countries peculiar with regards to the existence of corruption, the social legitimacy of corruption and the notions of the state. What remains disturbingly ignored is the fact that all these colonies have had rich indigenous cultures and traditions and governance mechanisms. There are locally understood meanings and practices pertaining to corruption with checks and balances for wrongdoing. In his introduction to the book *The pyramid of corruption*, Kiran Batni (2014) makes an interesting observation that if one takes the world map of the sixteenth and seventeenth centuries and colours all the areas the Europeans labelled as barbaric, and hence colonised, one would essentially find a world map of all the present-day corrupt countries. Corruption, according to the modern definition, encompasses all the former colonies and inevitably remains high when measured according to modern legal regulations and scales.

Notes

1 Scheduled castes and scheduled tribes are socially, economically and educationally backward classes in India as defined under Article 341 and 342 of the Constitution of India.
2 OBCs are 'socially and educationally backward classes' defined under the Constitution of India. The list of castes falling under OBC is maintained by the Ministry of Social Justice and Empowerment and is reviewed from time to time depending on the status of development of these castes on parameters of social, economic and educational development.
3 The *sarpancha* is the elected head of the *sanchayat*.
4 The *panchayat*secretary represents the state at the village level by serving as the bureaucratic arm of the government for local governance.
5 In India, *rakshabandhan* is a popular festival. On this day, every sister ties a thread called *rakhi* on the wrists of her brothers. This thread symbolises the piousness of the relationship. The thread *rakhi* is considered so important and pure that if a girl ties it to any boy who is not her real brother, he becomes her brother from that day onwards. Now he is supposed to fulfil all the duties of a brother towards his sister. In this community, this relationship is given even higher importance than a real brother–sister relationship, because taking care of one's *rakhi* sister is considered an act of very high moral standing. Fulfilling obligations towards *rakhi* sisters is necessary and garners high respect within the community. *Rakhi* relationships exist across religious and caste boundaries.
6 *Daata* in Hindi means provider and protector of the poor and the needy.

References

Bardhan, P. and Mookherjee, D. (2006). Decentralisation, corruption and government accountability. In S. Rose-Ackerman (Ed.), *International Handbook on the Economics of Corruption* (pp. 161–188). Cheltenham: Edward Elgar Publishing Limited.
Batni, K. (2014). *The Pyramid of Corruption*. Chennai: Notion Press.
Bayly, C. (1988). *Indian Society and the Making of the British Empire, the New Cambridge History of India, pt.2* (Vol. 1). Cambridge: Cambridge University Press.
Birla, R. (2009). *Stages of Capital: Law, Culture, and Market Governance in Late Colonial India*.Durham, NC: Duke University Press.
Charmaz, K. (2006). *Constructing Grounded Theory*. London: Sage Publications.
Chatterjee, P. (1993). *The Nation and Its Fragments: Colonial and Postcolonial Histories*.Princeton, NJ: Princeton University Press.
Crook, R. and Manor, J. (1998). *Democracy and Decentralisation in South Asia and West Africa: Participation, Accountability and Performance*. Cambridge: Cambridge University Press.
Dharampal. (2000a). *Civil Disobedience in Indian Tradition*. Mapusa, Goa: Other India Press.
Dharampal. (2000b). *Panchayat Raj and India's Polity*. Mapusa, Goa: Other India Press.

Fjeldstad, O.-H. (2004). *Decentralisation and Corruption: A Review of the Literature. WP.* Bergen, Norway: Chr. Michelsen Institute.

Fukasaku, K. and de Mello, L. (Eds.). (1999). *Fiscal Decentralisation in Emerging Economies.* Paris: OECD, Development Centre.

Gupta, A. (1995). Blurred boundaries: the discourse of corruption, the culture of politics, and the imagined state. *American Ethnologist, 22*(2), 375–402.

Haynes, D. and Prakash, G. (1991). Introduction: the entanglement of power and resistance. In D. Haynes and G. Prakash (Eds.) *Contesting Power: Resistance and Everyday Social Relations in South Asia* (pp. 1–22). New Delhi: Oxford University Press.

Hodgkinson, P. (1997). The sociology of corruption – some themes and issues. *Sociology, 31*(1), 17–35.

Howitt, W. (1839). *The English in India* (2nd ed.). London: Longman, Orme, Brown, Greene, and Longmans.

Kaviraj, S. (2009). The post-colonial state: the special case of India. *Critical Encounters: A Forum of Critical Thought from the Global South.*

Khanna, V. (2005). *The Economic History of the Corporate Form in Ancient India.* Working Paper, University of Michigan Law School. [Online]. Available from: https://pcg.law.harvard.edu/wp-content/uploads/papers/2006sp-Speakers_Paper03_02-21_Khanna.pdf [Accessed 5 April 2017].

Majumdar, R. (1920). *Corporate Life in Ancient India.* Calcutta: Calcutta University.

Manor, J. (1999). *The Political Economy of Democratic Decentralization.* Washington, DC: The World Bank.

Mill, J. (1817). *The History of British India* (Vol. I). London: Routledge & Kegan Paul.

Mookerji, R. K. (1919). *Local Goernment in Ancient India.* Oxford: Oxford University Press.

Perlin, F. (1985). State formation reconsidered. *Modern Asian Studies, 19*(3), 415–480.

Pylee, M. (1967). *Constitutional History of India, 1600–1950.* Bombay: Asia Publishing House.

Scott, J. (1985). *Weapons of the Weak: Everyday Forms of Peasant Resistance.* New Haven, CT: Yale University Press.

Shah, A. (1998). Fostering fiscally responsive and accountable governance: lessons from decentralization. In R. Picciotto and E. Wiesner (Eds.), *Evaluation & Development: The Institutional Dimension* (pp. 83–96). New Brunswick, NJ and London: Transaction Publishers.

Stein, B. (1985). State formation and economy reconsidered. *Modern Asian Studies, 19*(3), 387–413.

World Bank. (2000). *Overview of rural decentralization in India.* Washington, DC: The World Bank.

Part III

Making/unmaking governance

8 Greenpeace and the transnational governance of the Brazilian beef industry

Marcus Vinícius Peinado Gomes
and Mário Aquino Alves

Introduction

Transnational governance is a phenomenon of contemporary capitalism, as it has emerged and consolidated due to neoliberalism and globalisation (i.e., a result of information, capital and labour flow across borders and the establishment of global value chains). Transnational governance is often associated with the weakening capacity of national states to keep market power under control (Djelic and Sahlin-Anderson, 2006; Kristensen and Morgan, 2012; Rasche and Gilbert, 2012). Even though there is a vast literature on transnational governance, such literature often assumes a Eurocentric perspective, leaving aside the challenges represented by governance mechanisms, multinational corporations (MNC), states and transnational NGOs in the context of the Global South (Bartley, 2015; Gomes and Rojas, 2017; Morgan, Gomes and Perez-Aleman, 2016).

Examining transnational governance mechanisms in the context of the Global South is particularly important as the South suffers the consequences of such mechanisms. Considering that one of the main characteristics of transnational governance is a steering form of governance, as the mechanisms developed are an outcome of influence and negotiations (Djelic and Sahlin-Andersson, 2006; Rasche and Gilbert, 2012), they might be used as a method for states and NGOs from the Global North to impose their agenda and worldview over the South. This perspective is even more dangerous when transnational governance mechanisms are advocated as a substitute for a weak regulatory system (especially from the Global South), claiming that these mechanisms are an alternative to building institutions and regulatory mechanisms (Morgan, Gomes and Perez-Aleman, 2016). Furthermore, governance mechanisms could also be a result of how twenty-first-century capitalism encompasses the South, as a supplier of commodities, cheap labour and natural resources that should bear with the negative consequences of MNCs' operations, such as human rights violations and environmental degradation.

It is within this context that this chapter has the objective of examining how Greenpeace has governed the Brazilian beef industry. Since 2009, Greenpeace, JBS[1] and other companies and the Brazilian state have been struggling over the idea of sustainability and its materialisation into practices within this industry. The disputes started after the release of a Greenpeace report denouncing illegal practices in Brazilian slaughterhouses, such as deforestation, invasion of indigenous lands and inhumane labour conditions (Greenpeace, 2009b, 2011, 2012). These denunciations have led to a series of responses, such as the Federal Prosecutors Office's (MPF) civil actions against the companies, multilateral commitments between Greenpeace and the companies and the emergence of new organisations and lawsuits against Greenpeace.

In such a context, this chapter will emphasise the role of Greenpeace as a transnational social movement organisation, acting as a 'bridge' connecting business environmental impacts and the European consumer market by focusing on industries' global supply chain. While doing so, it creates a transnational governance arena that enables political governance regarding environmental issues.

This chapter concludes that Greenpeace's advocacy campaign was successful because the organisation learned how to explore the relationship between North and South by demonstrating to the European consumers (and major Greenpeace donors) that their beef consumption was associated with Amazon deforestation. In order to demonstrate this association, Greenpeace had explored an important characteristic of contemporary capitalism: the beef global supply chain. Such a conclusion emphasises a paradox of governance mechanisms, as Greenpeace is an NGO with roots in the Global North that had to acquire knowledge about the characteristics of Amazon deforestation in Brazil, but was able to denounce environmental degradation and govern an economic sector only by exploring the nature of the North–South relationship within contemporary capitalism.

This chapter is divided into five sections. Firstly, the activity of cattle ranching will be described in terms of its environmental impacts, its association with Brazilian colonial history and its importance as an economic activity that connects Brazil with the international market. Secondly, the methodological procedures of collecting and analysing data will be discussed. Thirdly, 'sustainability' of the Brazilian beef industry will be assessed, highlighting how deforestation becomes a hegemonic topic. Fourthly, Greenpeace as a transnational NGO will be examined, emphasising its campaign strategies and its role as a bridge that could connect different fields (Fligstein and McAdam, 2012) and thus create a governance space. The last section addresses the final remarks and considerations.

Cattle ranching and environmental degradation: from its colonial past to its emergence as an exportation resource

Cattle ranching is an important human activity. Almost every part of the animal – from its meat to its blood and bones – is used as inputs for industries such as fashion, automotive, pharmaceutics and, of course, food. Common sense associates cattle ranching with a rural and nature-friendly activity, making it difficult to link it to environmental impacts. Nevertheless, some research has shown that it is a high-resource-intensive activity, requiring more than 43,000 litres of water to produce 1 kilogram of beef (IFPRI, 2012), and contributing to a great level of carbon emissions (Gerber et al., 2013; Steinfeld et al., 2006), among other impacts (Fearnside, 2005). In the Brazilian context, cattle ranching is also associated with deforestation, having become the greatest deforestation driver of the Brazilian Amazon forest (Barreto, Pereira and Arima, 2008; Fearnside, 2002, 2005; Margulis, 2004).

Although deforestation may occur in the Brazilian Amazon, beef and other products, such as leather, are exported throughout the world – Brazil is the biggest exporter of beef, with the livestock production chain generating an average of US$ 167 billion per year (ABIEC, 2013). At the same time, issues related to the Amazon forest are very sensitive in the transnational arena, especially for European consumers. These characteristics have been contributing to the embeddedness of the Brazilian beef industry in a transnational context.

Nowadays, cattle ranching is the economic activity that occupies the greater portion of area within Brazil (Schlesinger, 2010), supporting a powerful and transnational food-processing industry. It is possible to trace the development of the Brazilian beef industry and cattle ranching back to the Brazilian colonisation period, since this economic activity is closely related to Brazilian history, especially in the consolidation of the Brazilian territory (Schlesinger, 2010; Silva et al., 2012). During the Portuguese colonisation, cattle ranching was employed as a land occupation strategy, so that Portuguese colonisers could claim control of huge areas of natural grazing (i.e., the Pampas region in the south of Brazil) over the Spanish domains in Latin America.

As centuries passed, cattle ranching (and the *charque*[2] industry that supplied food to the inland colonisation towards Brazil) expanded from Rio Grande do Sul – a southern Brazilian state – to the south-east – São Paulo and Minas Gerais states. The reasons for such expansion was to supply the Brazilian market – firstly, to supply the inland expansion and, after 1808, the increasing local market and the Portuguese royal family, which arrived in Brazil due to the Napoleonic War, bringing with it a huge flow of inhabitants (Schlesinger, 2010; Silva et al., 2012).

It is interesting to note that, at the beginning of the twentieth century, the biggest multinational slaughterhouses, mainly North American, arrived in the Brazilian market, among them Wilson & Company, Armour, Swift, Continental and Anglo (Schlesinger, 2010). From 1900 to 1980, such companies dominated the international market of food processing, and they imprinted an export-orientation strategy focusing on the European beef market (Schlesinger, 2010). This export orientation is still present; however, nowadays, the Brazilian multinationals – JBS, Minerva and Marfrig – are the ones controlling the international market of beef and food processing. In recent years, cattle ranching expanded over the mid-west – Mato Grosso – and it is now moving towards the northern region of Brazil – mainly Pará – in the Amazon region (Schlesinger, 2010; Silva et al., 2012; Smeraldi and May, 2008). Obviously, the reason for this current expansion is different from the colonisation period. The cattle ranching expansion towards the northern region can be traced back to the 1970s, when the Brazilian dictatorship regime fostered such activity in the Amazon region as a strategy to occupy the area and to solve land tensions in the north-east and south-west of Brazil (Schlesinger, 2010).

Moreover, during the 1980s, cattle ranching was considered a secure invest-ment due to high inflation rates at that time. Saving money with investments in cattle would prevent inflation wealth corrosion without high costs; thus, such an investment strategy was employed by several wealthy families to secure and increase their fortunes.

Therefore, cattle ranching is not only associated with the history of colonisa-tion in Brazil, but also is a materialisation of the neocolonial insertion of Brazil in global capitalism, as commodity export represents an important connection between Brazil and the world economy. Hence, the rise of Amazon deforesta-tion as a focal issue and the Brazilian beef industry are also embedded in this transnational context. Moreover, it is embedded in the Brazilian political pro-ject of becoming 'the world's barn'. Consequently, Amazon deforestation is not perceived strictly as an environmental problem. It is rather at the centre of the Brazilian development debate, thus joining various strategic questions for the maintenance of this political project.

Without any economic assumptions, the graph that follows illustrates the increase in the exportation of commodities in Brazilian products' exportation profile:

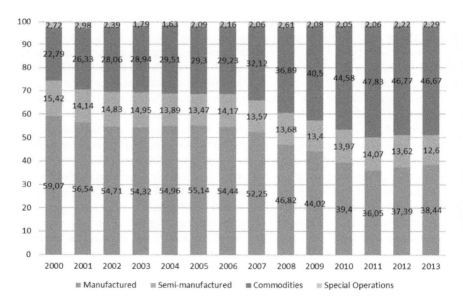

Figure 8.1 Products categories exports

Source: Ministério do Desenvolvimento, Indústria e Comércio 2014.
Elaborated by the author.

Since the 2000s, Brazil has been relying on commodities export as an answer to external economic disequilibrium. Such an answer was favoured by an increase in global commodity prices and weak competitiveness in the service and manufacturing sectors (Delgado, 2010, 2013). Therefore, commodities export has been supporting Brazilian global trade inclusion, and cattle ranching, by beef and other cattle co-products, has been supporting this exportation profile.

Methodology

The main sources of data are documents – such as reports, legislation, media coverage – and interviews with actors involved in the negotiation of sustainability in the Brazilian beef industry. The data were analysed using a critical discourse analysis (CDA) approach (Fairclough, 2010).

Firstly, we collected and analysed public documents aiming to elaborate a historical account of 'sustainability' in the Brazilian beef industry, providing a broader context for analysing the actors' negotiations. During this first moment, the selected documents not only shed light on the main events, consequences and actors' reactions (at least the public statements), but also provided an account of the main conflicts and negotiations, emphasising sensitive topics. The second moment consisted of interviews. Based on the document analysis conducted in the first step, it was possible to identify relevant actors to interview and to elaborate a specific interview schedule for each interviewee, in order to capture his or her perspectives and interactions. Finally, the third step focused on a final round of document collection and analysis. These documents were either searched after the interview in order to gather more information about a topic raised during the interview, or delivered by the interviewees – in this case, they could be either public documents or internal reports and presentations.

In total, 159 documents were consulted, comprising international documents – such as UN documents and international organisations' reports – and Brazilian legislation, being 43 from state-related actors, 50 from civil society organisations, 37 from corporations, six from media coverage and 23 from academic productions. Regarding the interviews, they had the purpose of tracing the steps of actors' negotiations; the starting point for revealing such pathways was Greenpeace's campaigns due to its active participation, which then expanded to corporate and state actors. In total, 28 interviews were conducted, totalling 2,009 minutes, an average of 71 minutes per interview. The interviews were made between 11 July 2013 and 20 February 2014.

Greenpeace and the rise of the problem of deforestation

Although scientific understanding develops over time, leading to improved comprehension of environmental impacts, in the early 2000s, there was already sufficient evidence that the beef industry had environmental implications. Deforestation was an issue of concern, but its environmental impacts were being neglected or, at least, not being tackled. Considering all the different scopes of environmental impacts (e.g., water pollution and consumption, enteric GHG emission, among others), deforestation was the one that emerged as a predominant topic in this industry; the Federal Prosecutors Office (MPF) and

Greenpeace's actions had a crucial role in such a process. In this section, the rise of deforestation as a predominant environmental impact of the Brazilian beef industry will be examined.

As already discussed, deforestation was an emerging concern in the Brazilian beef industry, and, besides, no practice directed to tackle it was being implemented; there was sufficient evidence to sustain an action against such an industry. Supported by such evidence, Pará's[3] headquarters of MPF decided to start an investigation to examine cattle ranching's participation in the Amazon deforestation.

Such investigations started in 2007, and several notifications and information disclosure procedures were taken by MPF to conduct its investigation, thus, it was not a secret investigation. Meanwhile, Greenpeace had also started its secret investigation for its *Slaughtering the Amazon* report (Greenpeace, 2009b). Although both investigations started in the same year, Greenpeace and MPF were not collaborating, and their motives for such investigations also differed. While MPF was focusing on the criminal and illegal aspects of economic activities in the Amazon region, Greenpeace was tracking the Amazon deforestation impact of products commercialised in the European consumer market.

Before examining the consequences of these investigations, it is necessary to further analyse the context in which they were being conducted in order to identify historical patterns brought into play. There were at least three elements providing signals that sooner or later the beef industry would be attacked: (i) MPF and Greenpeace's investigations on cattle ranching, (ii) the vast array of research linking cattle ranching and Amazon deforestation, and (iii) the 2006 Greenpeace campaign against deforestation caused by *soya*. Furthermore, the International Finance Corporation (IFC), the World Bank's financial arm, was concerned with the repercussions of a \$90 million loan approval to Bertin in March 2007 (IFC, 2007), since it had suffered pressure from the Brazilian civil society due to a similar investment in Bertin in 2004 (Drigo, 2013). Hence, players in the Brazilian beef industry were aware that a crisis regarding deforestation could emerge imminently.

A government body, independent from the organisations at stake, could be an efficient strategy to protect the industry's interests, as Barley (2010) has shown in previous studies. Moreover, a roundtable to discuss sustainability could be an interesting organisation, not only to protect the sector, but also to influence sustainability discussions in this context. Therefore, it is not surprising that IFC fostered the establishment of a roundtable to discuss sustainability on livestock: the Grupo de Trabalho da Pecuária Sustentável (GTPS)[4] was created as an informal group in late 2007.

Underneath these initial negotiations around sustainability in the beef industry, it is possible to identify Greenpeace's 2006 campaign building a different context for agency. The campaign was so successful that it not only endowed Greenpeace with knowhow on conducting a forest campaign in Brazil – that draws attention to the correlation of economic activity and deforestation – but the campaign's processes gave Greenpeace the capacity to conduct a campaign targeting an industry with a more complex value chain. It is important to remember, as discussed, that GTPS was created in such a context. Another evidence of the importance of this campaign is that, in 2012, JBS hired Márcio Nappo as its new sustainability director while the company was redesigning its organisational structure that gave sustainability a prominent position. Márcio Nappo was one of ABIOVE's[5] coordinators during Greenpeace's campaign on *soya* and deforestation.

Greenpeace's decision to focus on *soya* and its link with deforestation was a strategic one. Even though research had shown the strong correlation between Amazon deforestation and cattle ranching (Barreto, Pereira and Arima, 2008; Fearnside, 2002; Margulis, 2004; Rivero et al., 2009; Vosti et al., 2003), Greenpeace's decision was to focus on *soya* rather than on the beef industry, starting its investigation in 2004. There were at least two reasons for this decision.

Firstly, at that time, *soya* plantation was engaging intensely in the Amazon region with the association of international capital, bringing strong investments in infrastructure, such as river ports, roads and silos. Such investment was encouraged by foot-and-mouth disease contamination in Europe and the United States, which increased demand for Brazilian *soya*.

Secondly, this was Greenpeace's first campaign linking an economic activity to deforestation, thus the organisation was developing knowledge of how to successfully develop such an association. The *soya* value chain was, and still is, concentrated in a restricted number of multinational companies, while the beef value chain was more widely distributed among a considerable number of slaughterhouses. So, the organisation was learning and testing new approaches.

By focusing on the *soya* value chain Greenpeace was able to link Amazon deforestation to the consumption of *soya* products in the European market (Greenpeace, 2006). However, its success was not restricted to reaching and communicating to Greenpeace's main donation market. A victory was achieved when the major *soya* traders – ADM, Bunge and Cargill – signed the '*Soya* Moratorium' and agreed that none of these companies would buy *soya* from farmers involved in deforestation activities.[6]

Returning to the Brazilian beef industry, Greenpeace published its first report on the matter, *Slaughtering the Amazon* (Greenpeace, 2009b), on 1 June 2009, accusing the biggest beef slaughterhouses, JBS, Bertin, Independência and Minerva,[7] of being the main drivers of deforestation in the Brazilian Amazon forest, through buying cattle from farms practising illegal logging, invading indigenous land and implementing slavery-like forms of work. By tracking the beef chain, Greenpeace was able to identify beef or cattle co-products being shipped to China, the United States of America, the United Kingdom and Italy, associating deforestation with big brands such as Nike, Adidas, Unilever, Kraft, Toyota, Audi, Wal-Mart, Carrefour, Tesco and Timberland, among others (Greenpeace, 2009b). As a consequence, Greenpeace pressured not only the Brazilian slaughterhouses, but several important multinationals, and was thus able to create a direct link between deforestation and consumption in Europe, an incredible achievement for an organisation with donations from European countries as its main source of revenue.

Greenpeace's decision over tracking the value chain was crucial, but it was not the only one that decided to do so in order to reach its goals. MPF has done the same. After starting its investigation in 2007, two years later, in June 2009, MPF filed 20 lawsuits on environmental damages in the State of Pará against producers and slaughterhouses, such as Bertin and JBS, asking for R$ 2 billion of indemnity due to social and environmental impacts in Brazilian society. Furthermore, 69 companies – including Carrefour, Pão de Açúcar and Wal-Mart[8] – were notified that they were buying beef and/or cattle co-products from illegal deforestation areas. After such notification, they were obliged to suspend these purchases, otherwise they would be liable for illegal deforestation (MPF, nd, b; MPF, nd, a). By analysing the beef value chain, MPF was able to track the crime path in the whole value chain, increasing the pressure for change.

The attack on the beef sector's organisational continuity persisted. Firstly, Pão de Açúcar, Carrefour and Walmart suspended for 40 days their purchases from 11 slaughterhouses accused by MPF. Moreover, on 5 October 2009, JBS, Marfrig, Bertin and Minerva signed Greenpeace's Zero Deforestation Commitment (Greenpeace, 2009a). Additionally, GTPS, which was created in 2007 as an informal organisation, became formally constituted on 30 June 2009. Even the Brazilian Development Bank, BNDES, published its Resolution 1854 expanding the socio-environmental obligations for operations in the beef sector, defining new policies for activities involving livestock (BNDES, 2009). Faced with such criticism and attack, the beef sector urged on, presenting more active responses.

Nevertheless, an earthquake was about to come, hitting the heart of the Brazilian beef industry expansion – the IFC decided to withdraw the 2007 loan of $90 million to Bertin, which was granted for expanding its operations while developing new environmental standards for the section, accusing the slaughterhouse of not complying with the contract agreement (Mongabay, 2009). Note that the 2007 financial operation was subject to an environmental improvement in Bertin's operations.

The IFC's decision increased the tension in an already stressed context. In 2014, this was still an extremely sensitive issue. As a consequence, Bertin, which was at that time the biggest Brazilian slaughterhouse, was in a delicate financial situation. BNDES, following its strategy of fostering global players, supported the merger between Bertin and JBS that JBS announced on 29 October 2009. This operation created a worldwide giant. Since then, JBS has become the world leader in production and commercialisation of animal protein (Fleury and Fleury, 2011).

Whereas the context for agency in the first period examined would not encourage the development of 'sustainability' practices, MPF and Greenpeace's actions have transformed such a configuration. By emerging as key actors, both organisations impacted how actors would foresee their future and, therefore, their possibilities for agency altered. There was no more space for stability. Both MPF and Greenpeace use the features of twenty-first-century capitalism (Kristensen and Morgan, 2012) to promote such impacts, as they focus on the value chain rather than on a particular actor, whether companies or governments. This is even more evident in Greenpeace's actions since it is focusing on a global supply chain, tracking inputs produced in Brazil throughout the value chain until their consumption in the European market. Additionally, both organisations aim at drawing companies' attentions to a sensitive matter like 'sustainability' by adding it to the business risks and, therefore, costs.

Greenpeace and the transnational governance of the beef industry

This section aims at examining the role of Greenpeace in acting as a transnational social movement organisation and, by doing so, connecting different fields and contexts, either fostering stability or inducing a context favourable to change and consequently exerting governance by bridging business environmental impacts and the European consumers market by focusing on industries' global supply chain.

As Fligstein and McAdam (2012) argue, fields are interconnected, and what happens in a particular field is likely to spread to proximate fields. Therefore, stability and change could be explained due to this interconnection among different fields (Fligstein and McAdam, 2012). Thus, field proximity is important to comprehend stability and change processes.

It is difficult to analyse whether Greenpeace has interests in the cattle or *soya* industries. The fact that Greenpeace acts in a field does not mean that it has interests in that institutional or organisational field. In fact, it seems that Greenpeace is more concerned with the logic behind the interaction among businesses and their impacts on the environment, rather than with a particular organisational field. Hence, Greenpeace might be informing its actions not only by its understanding on what is happening in a particular field, but by some supra-field elements that cut across different fields, such as how contemporary capitalism works, how capitalism's system of production and distribution impacts nature and the understanding of what sustainable development is. Therefore, Greenpeace is floating around different fields using supra-field elements as guides.

But since Fligstein and McAdam's (2012) work focuses only on fields and their relation to social order, it is partial. It does not provide for a structural continuity such as capitalism that is common to all the different fields. Therefore, it is difficult to differentiate between processes that might impact the whole social order from those restricted to particular fields (Goldstone and Useem, 2012; Morgan, Edwards and Gomes, 2014). Following such discussion, it is possible to reflect on whether the challenges to sustainability, in the context of the Brazilian beef industry, have been delivering changes mainly in this particular field or whether such sectorial discussions have been challenging the prevailing social order.

Before discussing Greenpeace's exertion of transnational governance and its relations with such supra-field elements, it is important to describe Greenpeace as an organisation.

Greenpeace: an organisation

Greenpeace is a leading non-governmental environmental organisation with a transnational approach, with offices in more than 40 countries and an international coordinating body, Greenpeace International, located in Amsterdam. Both in its website and in its last annual report, Greenpeace defines itself as 'an independent global campaigning organisation that acts to change attitudes and behaviour, to protect and conserve the environment and to promote peace' (Greenpeace International, 2012: 56). In 1971, the organisation started as a committee in Vancouver aimed at protesting against nuclear weapons testing in Alaska by the United States. After that, Greenpeace groups spread to other countries and engaged in environmental campaigns, covering issues such as toxic waste and commercial whaling. A few years later, in 1979, Greenpeace International was founded to oversee these groups and their goals and operations under a single worldwide organisation.

The organisation's fundraising strategy is based on donations from individual supporters, independent trust and foundation grants, and it claims not to accept donations from corporations, governments or political parties. In 2012, Greenpeace had achieved a subscriber base of 24 million people worldwide, which generated a gross income of 265 million euros, an increase of 12 per cent in comparison to the previous year (Greenpeace International, 2012: 41–44). The Global North concentrated the highest-giving countries in 2012 (e.g., Germany, the United States, Switzerland, the Netherlands, the Nordic countries and the United Kingdom), but an increase in income and supporters was also seen in East Asian countries, Brazil, Mexico, Argentina and in the Mediterranean.

In order to pursue its goals and respond to the global economic crisis, Greenpeace has a long-term global programme in which climate and forest goals are its priorities, on the basis both of their urgency and their potential impact (Greenpeace International, 2012: 9). This includes campaigns on topics such as renewable energy and energy efficiency, zero deforestation, marine diversity, sustainable agriculture and the end of the release of toxics into water resources.

In terms of its campaign actions, Greenpeace is well known as a fighter organisation. It aims at creating conflicts and combats in order to draw attention to its claims. Greenpeace denunciations are based on serious research with effectively marshalled evidence of the respective environment impacts, as we have seen in the Brazilian cattle campaign.

Regarding Greenpeace's Brazil headquarters, it was created in 1992, the same year as the UN Rio 92 Conference. Its foundation was marked by a protest against the Angra nuclear power plant, in Rio de Janeiro State, through an action that symbolised the number of deaths in the Chernobyl accident. Already in its first year, it started looking at the Brazilian Amazon forest and concentrating its efforts to fight illegal timber, especially mahogany, as it was commercialised in Europe in the furniture industry. In its first expedition to the forest, the illegal timber trade was denounced and the Brazilian Navy expelled the Greenpeace ship with its whole crew. However, due to pressures from civil society and the legal community, the decision was revoked; this is considered the emblematic moment through which Greenpeace Brazil was finally recognised as a Brazilian organisation (Greenpeace, 2010).

Bridging industries' environmental impact and the European consumer market

Reginaldo Magalhães (2010), using Greenpeace's archive of its victorious campaigns (Greenpeace International N.A.), analysed the main campaign targets and issues. The author discovered that it was during the 2000s that the campaigns against the private sector have become more predominant. Examining Greenpeace's systematic record (Greenpeace International N.A.), Magalhães (2010) found out that during the 1970s, Greenpeace had few victories; its targets were exclusively national states and its campaigns focused on nuclear energy and whaling. Over the next decade, Greenpeace continued to focus on national states, mainly on industrialised countries, and began to focus and influence multilateral agreements and organizations (Magalhães, 2010).

It was during the 2000s that Greenpeace campaigns started to emphasise the private sector – victorious campaigns against companies more than tripled when compared to the previous decade (Magalhães, 2010). Such change was not only due to the transnational characteristic of the new international environmental agenda, but, after the Rio 92 conference, a strong feeling among the environmental movement was that national states did not have enough power to promote the desired changes. As to the private sector, it was not only responsible for the environmental impact, but any changes regarding the human impact on the environment should inevitably dialogue with such a sector.

The increasing power of the private sector was as important as the transnational feature of the 'becoming environmental agenda' in encouraging Greenpeace to target private companies in its campaigns. It was this strategic choice of focusing on multinational companies that made Greenpeace's campaigns so successful, increasing substantially its power and reputation. The reason is that Greenpeace, as an organisation, realised that, by using the global and complex supply chains of twenty-first-century capitalism (Kristensen and Morgan, 2012), it could connect an environmental impact in a specific location around the globe to the European consumer market. By taking advantage of the fact that, at that time, most companies did not have complete control of its supply chain – being unable to track all the inputs used in their production – Greenpeace uses another important feature of twenty-first-century capitalism, which is companies' image and reputation, in order to increase pressure on the companies' environmental impact, while building its campaign on supply chain traceability and brand damage.

When discussing the transnational characteristics of social movements, some researchers argue that the globalisation process is a key factor in producing transnational claims that can bring together activists from different localities for supporting it (Ghimire, 2011; Tarrow, 2005). Nevertheless, it is possible to argue that what connects different localities is a global supply chain, thus supporting the development of a transnational claim.

This transition seems to be a learning curve. It was while Greenpeace was campaigning that it realised the potential of focusing on big multinational companies and their supply chain. In its 2007 annual report, Greenpeace International recognises that 'soya and other agricultural products have traditionally been key drivers for deforestation' (Greenpeace International, 2007: 11). This statement was made after the Brazilian '*Soya* Moratorium' in 2006. A landmark of this period was the 'Zero Deforestation' campaign, launched by Greenpeace, together with other non-governmental organisations, aiming at a national agreement to end deforestation in the Amazon. In this report, Greenpeace International also denounces the impact of other global commodity products on forest protection globally, such as the palm oil trade in Indonesia. This seems to operate in a learning curve process that builds on previous experiences, such as the *soya* in the Brazilian Amazon, to make it possible to tackle upcoming issues, such as the palm oil.

Nonetheless, such a process was not an easy one. Even though some Brazilian campaigners had already realised such features of capitalism and how Greenpeace could benefit from them, it was still necessary to convince the organisation to implement such a distinctive campaign. This was one of the reasons why the *soya* campaign in Brazil was 'an experiment' – while campaigning, Greenpeace was developing the necessary knowledge for targeting more complex supply chains.

It is also important to remember that Greenpeace launched its first office in Brazil during the Rio 92 window of opportunity, and its main campaign was on illegal Amazon timber, especially mahogany, that was heavily exported to the European market. So, its initial Brazilian campaign focused on timber legality and depicted the Amazon deforestation under a Eurocentric understanding (i.e., an ideological mentality that understands development and modernity as a European project (Dussel and Ibarra-Colado, 2006), ignoring the needs and the aspirations of the people of the forests.

Such a European perspective does not mean that Greenpeace was defending international interests in Brazil. On the contrary, this was the organisational understanding of the relations between human activities and nature at that period. Greenpeace was – and still is – aiming at protecting the forests and, to do so, its actions are supported by a particular logic that guides such relations. Moreover, as Tarrow (2005) points out, even though transnational social movements fashion transnational claims, activists draw on resources, networks and opportunities of the societies they live in and, by doing so, connect the local and the global. It is in this process that Greenpeace establishes the bridge between environmental impacts in Brazil and the European consumer market, once Greenpeace's main source of revenue was – and still is – donations from Europe (Greenpeace International, 2012).

Final remarks: how Greenpeace regulates the 'slaughtering of the Amazon'

Opinions regarding Greenpeace's actions in the Brazilian beef industry might be diverse. While an industry player might think Greenpeace was too rough on them, others would have a different opinion. However, the context fashioned by Greenpeace, alongside with MPF, enabled the Brazilian beef industry to achieve important advantages in a global capitalist economy.

While organising the beef value chain, Greenpeace also created business opportunities – consultancy and auditing firms are being contracted to evaluate and monitor the slaughterhouses' commitments. New technologies and knowledge, such as geo-referencing and traceability instruments, are being developed for tracking the cattle throughout the entire value chain. AgroTools, one of these companies, is using its expertise to be hired by McDonald's and Wal-Mart worldwide.

Concerning the transnational governance aspects, Greenpeace and MPF had different roles. MPF operated in the Brazilian legal system, forcing the business sector to comply with the legislation and, by putting pressure on key actors of the beef value chain, it played an essential part in haltering deforestation and spreading the state's presence in areas that were not reached before. In contrast, Greenpeace used a guerrilla strategy, aiming at attacking deforestation as an activity cost, mainly by threatening companies and industry reputation, bridging an international arena of sustainability and the environmental impacts on local the level. Furthermore, by doing so, it is reconnecting agricultural activities and commodities consumption in urban areas – such recoupling could increase the awareness of environmental impacts of rampant consumption. Finally, even though Greenpeace focuses on big brands – and their global supply chain – it is still aiming to reach the products in the European market.

In this context, Greenpeace is an important transnational organisation that is fostering transnational governance (Djelic and Sahlin-Andersson, 2006) due to its ability to act both locally and globally and, in the process of linking both levels, it bridges different fields and, ultimately, shapes the industries' practices. It does so by creating an organisational space for negotiation and confrontation, rather than advocating for hard or soft law mechanisms.

While operating through capitalisms' features, Greenpeace is floating around different fields and issues, exerting a different kind of transnational governance. It is precisely because it is exploring features of capitalism to denounce environmental degradation that Greenpeace has enough power to interfere in the flux and processes between private and public spheres, discursively impacting the transnational environmental governance arena. Much attention has been given to the role of soft law schemes and the importance of corporate influence on international environmental politics (Levy and Newell, 2005). However, this chapter has shown that transnational NGOs are also playing this game by exploring capitalism's own features in order to promote corporate behaviour changes. Moreover, although such political governance might lead to the development of soft law schemes and self-regulated standards, it seems to be important to shed light on the role of a transnational negotiation of meanings that ultimately regulates the development of soft law. Therefore, it is important to question what the impacts are of such kind of governance. Which actors are employing it? How is such a governance arrangement influencing corporate behaviour?

Greenpeace enacted this political governance model due to the Brazilian state's relative failure to regulate the beef industry and deforestation, helping to fill an institutional void through soft law schemes. Regardless of whether such soft law schemes will be developed, this political governance exerted by Greenpeace appears to be successful because it is, at the same time, impacting companies' risk perception of not employing 'sustainable' practices, and promoting the development of new technologies, knowledge and businesses (both for private companies and NGOs). By learning how to explore the relationship between North and South within capitalism, Greenpeace was able to demonstrate to the European consumers, from where comes its major source of revenue, that beef consumption was associated with Amazon deforestation. In order to demonstrate this association, Greenpeace had explored an important characteristic of contemporary capitalism: the beef global supply chain. Such a conclusion emphasises a paradox of governance mechanisms, as Greenpeace is an NGO with roots in the Global North that had to acquire knowledge about the characteristics of Amazon deforestation in Brazil, but was only able to denounce the environmental degradation and to govern an economic sector by exploring the qualities of the North–South relationship within contemporary capitalism. It is ironic that Greenpeace exerted governance exactly because it used capitalism's own features to regulate capitalism's environmental degradation.

Notes

1 JBS S.A. is a Brazilian multinational and the world leader in production and commercialisation of beef (Fleury and Fleury, 2011).
2 *Charque* is a Brazilian jerky beef.
3 Pará is a state of Brazil, localised on the north region. Its capital is Belém and it is inside the Amazon Biome.
4 In English: Brazilian Roundtable on Sustainable Livestock. GTPS has the objective to promote sustainable cattle ranching practices by creating collaborations between the beef production chain and disseminating knowledge about sustainable beef.
5 Associação Brasileira das Indústrias de Óleos Vegetais, translating into English: Brazilian Vegetable Oils Industry Association.
6 This agreement was renewed six times, ending in January 2014.
7 When the report was published, JBS and Bertin had not merged yet. Together, these four companies accounted for more than 70 per cent of the market and all of them received public funds from BNDES to expand their operations.
8 The three biggest retailers in the Brazilian market.

References

ABIEC. 2013. *Brazilian Livestock Profile*. São Paulo: Associação Brasileira de Exportadores de Carne (ABIEC).
Barley, S. R. 2010. Building an institutional field to corral a government: a case to set an agenda for organization studies. *Organization Studies* 31(6), pp. 777–805.
Barreto, P., Pereira, R. and Arima, E. 2008. A pecuária e o desmatamento na Amazônia na era das mudanças climáticas. Belém: IMAZON.
BNDES. 2009. *Diretrizes socioambientais para a pecuária bovina* [Online]. Available at: www.bndes.gov.br/SiteBNDES/bndes/bndes_pt/Areas_de_Atuacao/Agropecuaria/diretrizes_pecuaria_bovina.html [Accessed: 8 February 2013].
Delgado, G.C. 2010. Especialização Primária como Limite ao Desenvolvimento. Revista Desenvolvimento em Debate 1(2), pp. 111–125.

Delgado, G. 2013. Reestruturação da Economia do Agronegócio – Anos 2000 In: Stédile, J. P. and Estevam, D. eds. *A Questão Agrária no Brasil: O Debate na Década de 2000.* São Paulo: Editora Expressão Popular, pp. 57–88.

Djelic, M.-L. and Sahlin-Andersson, K. 2006. Introduction: a world of governance: the rise of transnational regulation. In M.-L. Djelic and K. Sahlin-Andersson (Eds.), *Transnational Governance: Institutional Dynamics of Regulation* (pp. 1–29). Cambridge: Cambridge University Press.

Drigo, I. 2013. Rumo à carne sustentável e certificada? As razões e os mecanismos pelos quais os produtores de carne bovina na Amazônia estão iniciando mudanças em suas práticas. São Paulo: Universidade de São Paulo.

Dussel, E. and Ibarra-Colado, E. 2006. Globalization, organization and the ethics of liberation. *Organization* 13(4), pp. 489–508.

Embrapa. 2006. *Boas práticas agropecuárias para bovinos de corte: manual de orientações.* Available at: http://cloud.cnpgc.embrapa.br/bpa/files/2013/02/MANUAL_de-BPA_NACIONAL.pdf [Accessed: 2 December 2012].

Fairclough, N. 2010. *Critical Discourse Analysis: The Critical Study of Language.* Harlow, England; New York: Longman.

Fearnside, P. M. 2002. Can pasture intensification discourage deforestation in the Amazon and Pantanal regions of Brazil? In C. Wood and R. Porro (Eds.), *Deforestation and Land Use in the Amazon* (pp. 283–364). Gainesville, FL: University Press of Florida.

Fearnside, P. M. 2005. Desmatamento na Amazônia brasil história, índices e conseqüências. *Megadiversidade* 1(1), pp. 113–123.

Fleury, A. and Fleury, M. T. L. 2011. *Brazilian Multinationals: Competences for Internationalization.* Cambridge; New York: Cambridge University Press.

Fligstein, N. and McAdam, D. 2012. *A Theory of Fields.* New York: Oxford University Press.

Gerber, P. J., Steinfeld, H., Henderson, B., Mottet, A., Opio, C., Dijkman, J., Falcucci, A. and Tempio, G. 2013. *Tackling Climate Change Through Livestock – A Global Assessment of Emissions and Mitigation Opportunities.* Rome: Food and Agriculture Organization of the United Nations (FAO).

Ghimire, K. 2011. Organization Theory and Transnational Social Movements: Organizational Life and Internal Dynamics of Power Exercise Within the Alternative Globalization Movement. Lanham, MD: Lexington Books.

Goldstone, A. and Useem, B. 2012. Putting values and institutions back into the theory of strategic action fields. *Sociological Theory* 30(1), pp. 37–47.

Gomes, M. V. P. and Rojas, C. 2017. Governança Transnacional: Definições, Abordagens e Agenda de Pesquisa. *Revista de Administração Contemporânea (RAC)*, 21(1), pp. 84–106.

Greenpeace. 2006. *Eating Up the Amazon.* Available at:www.greenpeace.org/usa/Global/usa/report/2010/2/eating-up-the-amazon.pdf [Accessed: 12 January 2014].

Greenpeace. 2009a. *Public Commitment Signed by JBS, Marfrig, Bertin and Minerva Committing to Zero Deforestation.* Available at: www.greenpeace.org/international/en/publications/reports/minimum-criteria-for-industria/ [Accessed: 10 October 2012].

Greenpeace. 2009b. *Slaughtering the Amazon.* Available at: www.greenpeace.org/international/en/publications/reports/slaughtering-the-amazon/ [Accessed: 3 April 2012].

Greenpeace. 2010. *Greenpeace no Brasil.* Greenpeace Brasil [Online]. Available at: www.greenpeace.org/brasil/pt/quemsomos/Greenpeace-no-Brasil/ [Accessed: 20 January 2014].

Greenpeace International. 2007. *Greenpeace Annual Report 2007.* Available at: www.greenpeace.org/international/Global/international/planet-2/report/2009/9/gpi-annual-report-2007.pdf [Accessed: 2 November 2013].

Greenpeace International. 2012. *Greenpeace Annual Report 2012.* Available at: www.greenpeace.org/international/Global/international/publications/greenpeace/2013/GPI-AnnualReport2012.pdf [Accessed: 2 November 2013].

Greenpeace International. N.A. *Greenpeace victories.* Greenpeace International [Online]. Available at: www.greenpeace.org/international/en/about/victories/ [Accessed: 29 December 2013].

IFC. 2007. International Finance Corporation. IFC to Finance Bertin: Project to Set New Benchmark for Environmental and Social Standards in Cattle Ranching and Meat Processing in the Amazon. IFC Home [Online]. Available at: http://ifcext.ifc.org/ifcext/pressroom/ifcpressroom.nsf/1f70cd9a07d692d685256ee1001cdd37/2a71421255949b1d85257298007216a9?OpenDocument [Accessed: 19 January 2014].

International Food Policy Research Institute (IFPRI). 2012. Meat: the good, the bad and the complicated. *INSIGHTS,* 2012, pp. 24–25.

Kristensen, P. H. and Morgan, G. 2012. Theoretical contexts and conceptual frames for the study of twenty-first century capitalisms. In G. Morgan and R. Whitley (Eds.), *Capitalisms and Capitalism in the Twenty-First Century* (pp. 11–43). Oxford: Oxford University Press.

Levy, D. L. and Newell, P. J. 2005. *The Business of Global Environmental Governance.* Cambridge, MA: MIT Press.

Magalhães, R. S. 2010. Lucro e reputação: interações entre bancos e organizações sociais na construção das políticas socioambientais. São Paulo: Universidade de São Paulo.

Margulis, S. 2004. *Causes of Deforestation of the Brazilian Amazon.* Washington, DC: World Bank.

Mongabay. 2009. World Bank revokes loan to Brazilian cattle giant accused of Amazon deforestation. *Mongabay.com* [Online]. Available at: http://news.mongabay.com/2009/0613-bertin_brazil.html [Accessed: 8 December 2013].

Morgan, G., Edwards, T. and Gomes, M. V. P. (2014). Consolidating neo-institutionalism in the field of organizations: recent contributions. *Organization* 21(6), 933–946. Available at: http://doi.org/10.1177/1350508413498956.

Morgan, G., Gomes, M. V. P. and Perez-Aleman, P. (2016). Transnational governance regimes in the Global South: multinationals, states and NGOs as political actors. *Revista de Administração de Empresas* 56(4), 374–379. Available at: http://doi.org/10.1590/S0034-759020160402.

MPF, nd, a. *Bois do Desmatamento.* Ministério Público Federal.

MPF, nd, b. *Histórico da atuação do MPF pela pecuária sustentável.* Available at: http://noticias.pgr.mpf.gov.br/noticias/noticias-do-site/copy_of_pdfs/Historico_regularizacao_pecuaria.pdf [Accessed: 26 March 2013].

Rasche, A. and Gilbert, D. U. 2012. Institutionalizing global governance: the role of the United Nations Global Compact. *Business Ethics: A European Review,* 21(1), pp. 100–114.

Rivero, S., Almeida, O., Ávila, S. and Oliveira, W. 2009. Pecuária e desmatamento: uma análise das principais causas diretas do desmatamento na Amazônia. *Nova Economia* 19(1), pp. 41–66.

Schlesinger, S. 2010. *O gado bovino no Brasil.* Rio de Janeiro, RJ: FASE.

Smeraldi, R. and May, P. H. 2008. *O Reino do Gado: uma nova fase da pecuarização da Amazônia.* São Paulo, Brazil: Amigos da Terra-Amazônia Brasileira.

Silva, M. C. d., Boaventura, V. M. S., and Fioravanti, M.C.S. 2012. História do Povoamento Bovino no Brasil Central. *Revista UFG* XIII(13), pp. 34–41.

Vosti, S. A., Braz, E. M., Carpentier, C. L., d'Oliveira, M. V. and Witcover, J. 2003. Rights to forest products, deforestation and smallholder income: evidence from the western Brazilian Amazon. *World Development* 31(11), pp. 1889–1901.

9 'Donor logic', NGOs, the ruling elite and the decolonisation of education in Bangladesh

Ariful H. Kabir and Raqib Chowdhury

Introduction

In March 2002, the government of Bangladesh permitted BRAC, a non-governmental organisation (NGO), to run a BRAC Education Programme (BEP) initiative titled the 'Primary Initiative of Mainstreaming Education' (PRIME) with state-funded secondary high schools, to improve the quality of secondary education across the nation. Under PRIME, BEP organised workshops for school leadership and school management committees (SMC), and provided training to subject-based teachers for non-governmental secondary high schools.[1] Later in the same year, the government allowed BRAC to set up pre-primary school centres within government primary school catchments areas to discuss with the community and the SMC the introduction of pre-primary classes in government primary schools (GPS) as well as in registered non-government primary schools (RNGPS) (Ryan, Jennings and White, 2007). Following the successful implementation of PRIME, in 2005 BEP renamed the PRIME program to 'Partnership with Primary Schools' (PPS) in order to expand its training programs across the GPS and RNGPS (Sabur and Ahmed, 2010). In response to this new BEP initiative and in acknowledgement of its continued success, the government authorised BEP to implement its proposed complementary training program in 608 GPS and RNGPS in one district in Bangladesh (Ryan, Jennings and White, 2007).

By 2008 BEP initiated a 'joint pilot project' with the government of Bangladesh to extend its training programs to 20 *upzillas* (sub-districts) in three districts involving 2,600 GPS and RNGPS. However, when news about this BEP pilot project became public, a number of organisations, including various associations of primary teachers, civil society bodies and academics, voiced their concern about the involvement of BRAC – an NGO – in the primary education system of Bangladesh. Many of them argued that BRAC's involvement in the primary education system was the first step towards privatising the primary education system of the country (Sabur and Ahmed, 2010). However, the government responded to criticisms over the BEP pilot project by arguing that its involvement would greatly help the government to implement the second phase of its Primary Education Development Program (PEDP-II), originally funded by eight donor agencies (*The Daily Star*, 2008).

Although the government eventually withdrew the BRAC project in 2008 in the face of continued resistance from various primary schoolteachers' associations, this scenario offers a useful visualisation of how the ruling political elite, NGOs and donor agencies have been working over the years in utilising what Ball and Junemann (2012) call 'network-governance' in shaping the education system of Bangladesh. Ball and Junemann (2012) argue that the way in which various new kinds of policy communities become involved in policy networks, validate their discourses and can influence policy can be identified as a new form of 'network governance'.

Similarly, Steiner-Khamsi (2008) had explained that 'donor logic' promotes policy diffusion from the developed world into the developing world. Donor logic, they argued, helps explain why and how international financial institutions (IFIs) and bilateral aid agencies influence and promote selective policies from their own systems as 'best practices' in the developing world. For her, every international organisation has its own policy strategy and its funds reflect its own policy strategy and vested interests rather than a sensitive, humanitarian or purely philanthropic response to local needs. She points out that 'the donor-logic of the Asian Development Bank and the World Bank is finance-driven, the logic of bilateral aid agencies is self-serving in a different way' (p. 11).

Against this backdrop, this chapter critically explores the competing yet often complementary roles the ruling political elite, NGOs and donor agencies have played in shaping the education system of Bangladesh over the past 30 years. This chapter argues that the network governance comprising the trio of ruling political elite, NGOs and donor agencies has shaped the education system within its colonial legacy in the post-1980s period in a manner which has resulted in education being used to serve their own political and economic interests and agendas.

This chapter also looks at how the notion of 'decolonisation' – an oft-quoted agenda in national-level decision making – has played out in policies of this period. Rather than simply marking a discontinuity with colonial-era education, in this chapter we consider decolonisation as a discursive response to counterbalance the colonial effect – in this case the divisive politics of British colonial rule, which had repercussions in the post-independence subcontinent, and can be achieved through what Mignolo (2011) calls 'delinking'. Delinking, he explains, is 'contained in the sphere of authority' and 'occurs at the level of economic control' (Mignolo, 2012) through external bodies of power and influence. More significantly perhaps in the context of the current study, delinking cannot occur from an economy of growth, or from just 'a type of economy' (such as capitalism), but from an antithetical response to the 'instructions' of external agents and donors such as the World Bank, the IMF and 'related institutions'. Decolonisation thus is 'the political delinking from economic decisions' (Mignolo, 2012) and a reaction to Mignolo's concern about what he calls the 'politization of civil society' and is achieved through religious-political and epistemic delinking.

This chapter begins with a brief discussion of the methodological approach we adopted in this analysis. It then critically considers scholarly literature that conceptualises the decolonisation of the education system and its rationale in the context of Bangladesh. Next it discusses various global initiatives and the nature of how donor logic has continued to shape the education system of the country. The analysis of global policy documents, for example, Education for All (EFA) and sector-review reports of various donor agencies explore the influences and changes they have facilitated in Bangladesh's education. This analysis is followed by a critical consideration of NGOs' involvement in orienting education towards vocationalisation. Finally, this chapter draws out the political and economic implications of such local and international agencies for the country's education system.

'Donor logic' and the reproduction of the neoliberal agenda in education

With the spread of neoliberal ideologies since the 1980s, international donor agencies have sought in various ways to establish relations between education and economic development. In the early 1990s, for example, the World Bank adopted the idea of influencing national policy 'through the power of its ideas' (Jones, 2004, p. 190). This influenced other donor agencies to shift their financing policies towards developing countries from lending of *credit* to lending of *ideas* (Steiner-Khamsi, 2006). In order to develop a global education policy, key donor agencies including UNDP, UNESCO, UNICEF, and the World Bank established the Inter-Agency Commission, which organised the World Conference on Education for All (WCEFA) in 1990 at Jomtien, Thailand. The WCEFA, a significant milestone in educational development in the twentieth century, adopted the idea of generating human productivity as the aim of basic education. Crucially, this report emphasised addressing four key issues in any national education policy – relevance, quality, equity, and efficiency – (Inter-Agency Commission, 1990). International donor agencies have since circulated their ideas through policy initiatives and advice, analytical sector reviews, academic articles, impact evaluations, baseline surveys, benchmarks and conferences (Steiner-Khamsi, 2012; Verger, Edwards and Altinyelken, 2014; Molla, 2014). The following sections present a chronological outline of how this was enacted over the past four and a half decades.

Post-independence to the 1990s

In Bangladesh, international attention was paid to the national education system for the first time in the early 1980s when donor agencies became active in the nation's education sector through their involvement in the development of education programs and projects. The World Bank financed the government's first Primary Education Project (PEP) (1980–1985) and second PEP (1985–1990) (Magnen, 1994). These programs focused on expanding access to the existing primary school system and improving the quality of education by providing in-house training for teachers across Bangladesh (Magnen, 1994). Following the world conference on EFA, the Bangladesh government adopted the first National

Plan of Action (NPA) on EFA in 1992, which provided the basis for soliciting assistance from various development partners (ADB, 2008). In 1991, after a long negotiation with the World Bank and financial support from ADB, SIDA, UNDP, UNFPA and NORAD, the government developed the General Education Project (GEP), aimed at supporting a number of key government policy objectives in primary and secondary education as part of the Fourth Five-Year Plan (1990–1995) (Magnen, 1994; USAID, 2002).

The GEP aimed at attaining four specific objectives – increasing equitable access to primary and secondary schooling; improving the quality of general education at these two levels; strengthening schools' management capacity; and developing policies and programs for the future (Magnen, 1994). Among other reforms, the GEP introduced a new syllabus, curriculum and books and in 1992 established a separate primary education division – the Primary and Mass Education Division (PMED), under the prime minister's own portfolio – to oversee the overall implementation of the GEP. The key policy changes brought about by the GEP were an NGO approach to primary education through the establishment of satellite schools; involvement of the community in school operations; and support for the NGOs-run non-formal education system (Magnen, 1994). Later in 1997, the GEP was renamed the Primary Education Development Program (PEDP) to allow various donors to operate under one umbrella, although it continued to pursue the same goals as the GEP.

Post 2000 – greater international involvement

By 2000, this involvement changed character, with a growing interest in providing policy direction using education sector reviews. The process began when the prime minister of Bangladesh, Sheikh Hasina, met President Wolfensohn of the World Bank in October 1997 and they agreed to formulate a long-term reform plan for the Bangladesh education sector (World Bank, 2000). In its education review report of 2000, the World Bank 'set(s) out a possible vision for education and training in Bangladesh through the year 2020, analyz[ing] the main issues in the sector, and present[ing] some principles and options by which to bring the vision into reality' (World Bank, 2000, p. xvii). Following this, a number of donor agencies such as the Japan Development and Cooperation Agency (JICA) and USAID produced their own education sector review reports in 2002 to provide policy direction for education in Bangladesh (World Bank, 2000; JICA, 2002; USAID, 2002).

Clearly based on neoliberal doctrines, the World Bank's report identified a six-prong course of action that needed to be adopted in the education policy to realise the vision for 2020. This course of action included strengthening basic education; promoting the market relevancy of the curriculum of secondary education; ensuring private providers in transferring skills in vocational and technical education; reforming higher education; adopting cost-effective output measures in distributing public finance in education; and introducing new public management (NPM) in managing the education system (World Bank, 2000).

Subsequently, the World Bank's review seemed to be identified as a key strategic plan in the education sector by both transnational agencies and the post-2000s governments of Bangladesh. The donor consortium, which international donor agencies formed in 1973 to coordinate their activities in Bangladesh (Faaland, 1981), used the policy directions of the World Bank's education sector review as the 'basis for preparation of an overall education policy note in February 1999 for discussions' (World Bank, 2000, p. xvii). Furthermore, to ensure education loans from international donor agencies, and in line with the Dakar framework of EFA, the government adopted a 20-year Education for All National Plan of Action II (NAP II) using UNESCO guidelines (Ministry of Primary and Mass Education, 2003). The key objective of this policy was to generate a knowledge-based society by enhancing learning and teaching life skills through formal, non-formal and informal education (Ministry of Primary and Mass Education, 2003). Similar to what the World Bank had argued in its education sector review in 2000, in generating foundations for a knowledge-based society through education, this policy also emphasised the need to reorient education content and curriculum in relation to global market demands and a decentralisation of school management systems.

Strategically, adopting NAP II based on 'donor logic' provided justification for transnational donor agencies to continue allocating education loans to this sector in the post-2000 period. Since then, with financial support from international donor agencies, successive governments have implemented a series of separate and co-financed projects to shape the education system in response to the demands of an increasingly globalised market economy. Some of these education projects included the Female Secondary School Assistance Project (FSSAP) II, approved in 2001; the Secondary Education Sector Improvement Project (SESIP), approved in 1999; the Teaching Quality Improvement in Secondary Education Project (TQISEP), approved in 2004; the Secondary Education Sector Development Project and Program (SESDP), approved in 2006; the Secondary Education Quality and Access Improvement, approved in 2008; and the Higher Education Quality Enhancement Project (HEQEP), approved in 2009 (ADB, 2008; World Bank, 2009, 2013). The first two projects were completed, whereas the latter three projects are still ongoing at the time of writing.

In the 2000s and until 2016, various governments formulated three education policies – the Bari Commission Report of 2002, the Miah Commission Report of 2004 and the National Education Policy of 2010 – in which the government reproduced donors' ideas and priorities. These education policies all emphasised the importance of expanding technological and business education across the country, transforming the population into human resources (Chowdhury and Kabir, 2014). However, the current National Education Policy 2010 seems to have provided a comprehensive policy direction on how to establish links among different education streams at the primary education level based on a neoliberal policy agenda, one that has potentially shifted the entire education system towards vocationalisation (Figure 9.1).

Along with other reforms, the latest education policy restructured both primary and secondary education systems so that the duration of primary education

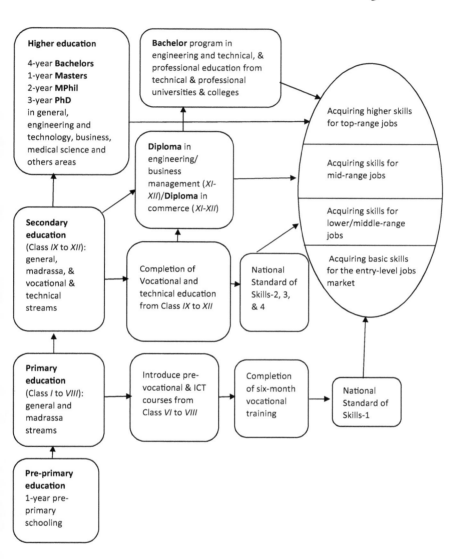

Figure 9.1 Education and employment pathways in Bangladesh

was extended from class V to class VIII to prevent early dropout and to create a pathway from the general education stream into the vocational education stream at the secondary level. In doing so, it introduced pre-vocational and ICT courses from class VI to class VIII in order to introduce technical and vocational education and training (TVET) values in job markets, and to help students understand why it was more productive to move into vocational education at the secondary level. The latest education policy argued that courses on pre-vocational and technical education at the primary education level would help students access better job opportunities 'if they discontinue their studies after the primary level' (Ministry of Education, 2010, p. 14). At the secondary level (class IX to class XII), along with other two streams – general and *madrassa* – it emphasised the need to shape vocational and technical education as a distinct stream just like the general stream.

To expand TVET across the country, the latest education policy also adopted a range of reform initiatives which included setting up at least one technical education institute in every sub-district; increasing the number of polytechnic, textile and leather institutes; encouraging public–private partnerships to set up new technical institutes; prioritising national budget allocation in vocational and technical sectors; ensuring continuous review and revision of TVET curricula in view of national and global job markets; and establishing a fully-fledged technical university offering bachelor degrees in the area of TVET (Ministry of Education, 2010). Although students with a diploma in TVET would be eligible to pursue a bachelor's degree in relevant courses, the latest education policy ensured that government would not to allow more students into the higher education system (ADB, 2015).

A year later, in 2011, to provide a policy framework outlining the mission and vision, objectives, priorities, strategies and governance of TVET operating in both formal and informal sectors, the government formulated the National Skills Development Policy 2011 (Ministry of Education, 2011) with financial support from the European Commission (EC) and the International Labour Organisation (ILO). The government planned to increase the number of TVET institutions and the number of students from 3 per cent to 20 per cent among all secondary students within the next 15 years, and introduced technical and vocational trade in the *madrassa* stream (Ministry of Planning, 2011). To accommodate such a large number of students in TVET, the government also introduced double shifts in existing technical schools, colleges and polytechnic institutes.

Donors' involvement in the education sector not only directs the policy trajectory of education in developing countries like Bangladesh, indeed, it also *justifies* the involvement of local NGOs and civil society bodies in the strategic direction of education through the adaptation of what is called the sector-wide approach (SWAp). In the second half of the 1990s, donor agencies all over the world used the idea of SWAp as 'one of several means for development agencies to achieve greater coherence in *their* approaches to providing development assistance' (UNESCO, 2007, p. 3). In Bangladesh, donor agencies adopted the idea of SWAp in PEDP II, where they emphasised the need for incorporating NGOs and civil society bodies in managing public sector development initiatives in primary education (ADB, 2008).

However, leading NGOs working in the education sector criticised the way in which the government realised the idea of SWAp. In a position paper prepared in 2008 by the Campaign for Popular Education (CAMPE) – an umbrella forum of NGOs focusing on advocacy and campaign network activities in education – it argued that 'the most critical feature of a sectoral approach is *sectoral thinking*, not a rigid administrative modality' (Ahmed, 2011, p. 17). The way in which the idea of SWAp was shaped by NGOs and civil society bodies in Bangladesh can be identified as what Ball terms 'network governance', to influence the overall direction of education in the country. In the following section we look closer into the roles of NGOs and ruling elites in the education system of Bangladesh and the political dimensions of such involvement.

NGOs, civil society and the politics of 'non-formal' education

In the early twentieth century, there were several initiatives to educate elderly people within the subcontinent's literacy movement in British India. In its first post-independence Education Commission Report in 1974, the government of Bangladesh emphasised the need for the eradication of illiteracy through informal education (Ministry of Education, 1974). This Report underscored the government's responsibility to set up education centres for elderly people in each sub-district and to ensure extensive involvement of the masses in a nationwide major intergenerational literacy movement. Although the idea of an 'informal' education envisioned the basic provision of agricultural and industrial skills to a large number of mostly elderly illiterate people, very importantly it also underlined the need of acquiring broad socio-political knowledge as a part of building a newly born state.

However, the growth of NGOs in post-independence Bangladesh soon enabled donors to promote their agenda and priorities in the nation's education policies. Although in their early inception in 1972, NGOs in Bangladesh were primarily engaged in providing relief through rehabilitation programs to assist war-affected destitute women (Karim, 2001), throughout the 1970s, international donor agencies focused on the idea of the non-formal education (NFE) approach to be introduced in developing countries to combat rural poverty (Rose, 2009). At that time, the World Bank commissioned a study titled 'Attacking Rural Poverty: How Non-formal Education Can Help' by Philips H. Coombs with Manzoor Ahmed, which emphasised the importance of reorganising and re-systematising non-formal education to increase rural employment, productivity and income in poor countries (Coombs and Ahmed, 1974). In that study, the World Bank identified non-formal education as an alternative *approach* rather than an alternative *provider* of education (Rose, 2009), and had a particular interest in identifying the possibility of future investment in the field of non-formal education (Coombs and Ahmed, 1974). The idea the World Bank had developed to eradicate poverty through a non-formal education system was eventually adopted by BRAC, the leading NGO in Bangladesh, in the mid-1980s, aiming to provide education to children who were excluded from the state-sponsored education system (Rose, 2009).

While through informal education the government focused on the mass education movement by involving all sections of society across the country, at its early stage in 1985, BRAC's non-formal education program concentrated on providing basic education opportunities through the pre-primary education system (Ahmed, Ahmed, Khan and Ahmed, 2007). Rose (2009) notes that over the years, this path of NGO-provided non-formal education became a solid, stable and sustainable parallel system to the formal education system in Bangladesh. Currently BRAC²'s NFPE is broadly known simply as the BRAC Education Program (BEP) involving pre-primary, primary, secondary and continuing education. In addition, along with BRAC, at least 1,315 other NGOs are now involved in offering non-formal education across the country (CAMPE, 2009). The share of non-formal primary education gradually increased over the decades, from 8.8 per cent in 1998 to 9.6 per cent in 2008 (CAMPE, 2015). In fact, Ahmed's (2011) study claims that on average more than a million children annually attend NGO-operated non-formal primary education programs each year, which are provided through more than 30,000 'one-room, one-teacher centres' across the country. In essence, the way in which NGOs adopted the non-formal education approach in its school systems secured the channelling of direct funds from donors.

However, it was not until 2000 that the government recognised non-formal education as a parallel system to the formal system, and several initiatives were taken by both transnational agencies and civil society bodies operating under NGOs to establish the idea of non-formal education as a legitimate and recognised alternative approach in Bangladesh. Following the declaration of Education for All (EFA) in 1990, and with the support of leading NGOs and international donor agencies, civil society bodies initiated a national NGO-EFA coalition – Campaign for Popular Education (CAMPE) – to ensure the continuation of NGOs' voice in the education policy formation process. According to its objective statement, CAMPE aimed to 'advocate and lobby to enhance NGO participation in educational policy making and other national and international educational activities/issues' (2016). CAMPE produces various education reports including the Education Watch Report each year as a part of campaign and advocacy in favour of EFA and the non-formal education system (2016). In a policy dialogue on the education sector in 2014, CAMPE invited top officials of the government and policy actors who were involved in the formation of the National Education Policy 2010, along with civil society members, in which it emphasised the need for decentralising the education sector (CAMPE, 2014). Paulson (2006) reports that in many cases, CAMPE reports were highly critical towards the formal education system and its quality. Significantly, NGOs and donor agencies were the key consumers of these reports.

In addition, donor agencies began to use the BRAC non-formal education program in their policy advocacy and to 'refer to it as a *counter* example to Government (in terms of cost per student, teaching quality, attendance etc. which made the relationship with government difficult)' (ITAD, 2012, p. 8). The World Bank also urged the government to build more partnerships with NGOs to bring success to EFA programs (Lewis, 1997) around the country. Indeed, the glorification of the BRAC non-formal education model and its success in removing illiteracy and ensuring quality of education, as well as the joint efforts of donors and NGOs, pushed the government to recognise the non-formal education system as an essential and complementary stream to formal education. Rather than seeing it as 'informal' education, the government now recognised the idea of 'non-formal' and 'continuing' education in its National Education Commission Report in 2003, as a way of generating human resources through educating outreach workers (Ministry of Education, 2003).

Over the years, the government also developed a number of policy documents with guidelines for shaping the idea of non-formal education and related activities within non-formal programs across the country. These non-formal education policy documents include the Non-formal Education Policy (NEFP) 2006, Mapping on Non-formal Education Activities in Bangladesh 2009 (with support from CAMPE and UNESCO) and the Non-formal Education Law 2014. In its National Education Policy of 2010, the government focused on 'some basic education or vocational training to use their skills in real life situations through the non-formal schooling' (Ministry of Education, 2010, p. 20). In 2013, with technical support from the Bangladesh Technical Board and financial support from the Bangladesh National Commission for UNESCO, the government finally developed a curriculum for non-formal vocational education (pre-vocational *I* and pre-vocational *II*) to provide policy direction on how students of the non-formal education system could transition into vocational and technical education (Bureau of Non-formal Education, 2013).

Despite several attempts by the government in shaping non-formal education, most non-formal NGO schools were not operated under government rules and regulations and had not adopted the national curriculum into their systems (Hossain, 2004). BRAC itself claims its non-formal education approach as unique; it does not seek to be involved in policy dialogue and negotiations on its version of the non-formal education system (ITAD, 2012). By the early 1990s, BRAC education 'was comparable to the state education system in terms of coverage and presence in rural Bangladesh' (Hossain, Subrahmanian and Kabeer, 2002, p. 11), and BRAC had developed its own curriculum from class I to class V, focusing on the acquisition of 50 government-mandated competencies and life skills. To achieve these competencies and life skills, BRAC used BRAC books for class I to class III, and NCTB books and BRAC supplementary materials for class IV to class V (Ahmed, Ahmed, Khan, and Ahmed 2007). However, in the case of secondary-level education, BRAC seemed to be more active in working with the government (ITAD, 2012). Paulson (2006) argues that the move to work with the Ministry of Education was part of shifting BRAC's role as a provider to become involved in the formal education system.

The ruling elite and the politics of education

The previous two sections analysed the ways in which the colonial education system persisted and indeed was in some ways even reproduced in the post-independence education system in Bangladesh. In this section, we focus on the role of the ruling elite in terms of how their interests manifested in the development of the nation's education system over a period of nearly four decades.

Before looking into this matter, we attempt to briefly understand the historical and political processes of adopting the (neo)colonial Pakistani education system in Bangladesh (from 1947–1971). Lingard (2009) argues that an understanding of historical processes can be useful in understanding current policy processes. When the British left the Indian subcontinent in 1947, they split it into two countries and Bangladesh became part of Pakistan, based on a predominantly religious two-nation theory (Chowdhury and Kabir, 2014). However, the continued persistence of the economic, linguistic, cultural and political hegemony of West Pakistan (now the state of Pakistan) cumulated in the War of Independence in 1971 in which East Pakistan split and emerged as the independent nation of Bangladesh on the basis of secular-socialistic principles.

Before independence, the state under Pakistani rulers formulated several policy documents, for example, the 1957 Educational Reforms Commission for East Pakistan, the Commission on National Education in 1958 (Government of Pakistan, 1958) and the New Education Policy in 1970 (University Grants Commission, 2009). In the first National Educational Conference held in Karachi in 1947 after the British exit, the Pakistani rulers reassessed the British education system and set up Islamic religious ideology as a vision for the entire education system. The Commission on National Education in 1959 asserted that the fundamental value of education was 'to preserve the Islamic way of life [. . .] The moral and spiritual values of Islam combined with the freedom, integrity, and strength of Pakistan should be the ideology which inspires our educational system' (Government of Pakistan, 1958, p. 11). In other words, the leadership of the day positioned religion and tradition, as well as a number of divisive past British traditions in the education system, to construct a particular version of Pakistani nationalism, ignoring the diverse socio-political and economic factors existing across different regions in Pakistan. As a new state, Pakistan designed its education system from its colonial past to construct 'citizens' 'in the same image – obedient, loyal, hardworking and able to subordinate themselves to authority' (Saigol, 2003, p. 12).

As discussed earlier, although the donor-NGO nexus – in the name of creating the foundations for a knowledge economy – had helped reproduce the colonial agenda through vocationalisation of education, the ruling elite in post-independence Bangladesh aimed at shaping education based on their *own* brand of ideological perspectives. Hossain, Subrahmanian and Kabeer (2002) argued that the political elite in Bangladesh had long been in conflict over 'the definition of national identity', and 'the process of national identity creation [. . .] played out in education policy through the compulsion of successive governments to imprint their own brands of nationalism on the population' (2009, p. 1). The formation of the first Education Commission, led by eminent professor Qudrat-I-Khuda, just after independence, was strategically important to transition the education system to one espousing socialist political views and ideas 'in order to establish a non-discriminatory, egalitarian and just society' (Chowdhury and Kabir, 2014, p. 7). It viewed education as a way of building Bengali nationalism and facilitating the reformation of society (Ministry of Education, 1974). The prescribed school textbooks – particularly the history books – were written in a way that could help students inculcate the Bengali national identity (Riaz, 2011). Although the Khuda Commission report advocated for a uniform education system in line with the constitution, it did not, however, provide a clear policy direction on how religious education institutions, namely *madrassas*, were to be blended into mainstream general education (Riaz, 2011).

With building up one's own form of nationalism becoming political capital (Hossain, Subrahmanian and Kabeer, 2002), successive authoritarian military regimes (from 1975 to 1990) now adopted the idea of the 'Bangladeshi' (rather than 'Bengali') nationalism, and the idea of 'secularism', which was one of the four pillars in the constitution, was substituted with 'absolute trust and faith in the Almighty Allah' (Riaz, 2005, p. 174). Similar to what Pakistani rulers did to its education system throughout the Pakistani regime, Bangladesh's post-independence military regimes adopted the idea of imbibing Islamic sentiment into the education system. Effectively dissolving the Khuda Commission, General Ziaur Rahman (1975–1981) formulated his own committee on curriculum and syllabi in 1978, which declared, 'Islam is a code of life, not just the sum of rituals. [. . .] So the acquiring of knowledge of Islam is compulsory for all Muslims – men and women' (Ministry of Education, 1978, cited in Riaz, 2011, p. 121). The state under General Zia *re*introduced religious studies at various levels of primary and secondary education. In this continuation, the government under General Ershad (1981–1990) formed the Bangladesh National Education Commission (BNEC), headed by Professor Mofizuddin Ahmed in 1987, in which 'religious education for the first time was made compulsory in order to create "religious sentiment" and human and moral values for the young generation' (Chowdhury and Kabir, 2014, p. 7).

In the interest of retaining the momentum of the populist political mandate to rule the country, post-1990 democratically elected governments nourished the sentiment with which the two authoritarian military rulers had injected Islamic sentiment as a political agenda into the education system. Since the 1990s, partisan practice became a determinant factor in developing education policy and practice, and the parties in power promoted the proliferation of Islamic education institutions into the mainstream education system. Although in her first tenure, Prime Minister Begum Khaleda Zia (the widow of General Zia, 1991–1996) did not form any education commission or policy, similar to her predecessor (and husband) General Zia, she instilled the idea of *Bangladeshi* (rather than Bengali) nationalism and 'deliberately obliterated discussion of various aspects of the Bengali nationalist struggle and its leaders and textbook descriptions of the identity of the opponents of the war of independence became vague' (Riaz, 2011, p. 123). In her second regime (2002–2006), Begum Zia formed two education commissions led by Professor M. A. Bari and Professor Moniruzzaman Mia in 2002 and 2003, respectively, in which religious education was extended to class II. In 2000, the BNP government adopted a policy for primary education in which the first objective out of 22 was the 'indoctrination of students in the loyalty to and belief in the Almighty Allah, so that the belief inspires the students in their thought and work, and helps shape their spiritual, moral, social and human values' (Kabir, 2004, cited in Riaz, 2011, p. 122).

In her first (1996–2001) and second tenures (2009–2014), Prime Minister Sheikh Hasina (daughter of Sheikh Mujibur Rahman) formulated two national education policies in 2000 and 2010 respectively on the basis of the Khuda Commission report (Ministry of Education, 2000, 2010). As discussed previously, the Khuda Commission report had attempted to 'decolonise' the education system by adopting a unified and secular education system in 1974. These state-formulated education policies made concessions with non-secular/religious bodies of interest (Riaz, 2011) in two specific ways. First, in her first regime, Sheikh Hasina's government did not bring any changes into the previous government's extension of religious education to grades one and two (Riaz, 2011). Second, it emphasised moral and religious education as part of building the moral character of the learners (Ministry of Education, 2010). Although four main streams of religions education – Islam, Hinduism, Buddhism and Christianity – were recommended at both the primary and secondary education levels (Ministry of Education, 2010), this in practice meant Islam was to become the dominant religious subject for all students because lack of resources such as textbooks and teachers meant that students from religious minorities often had to opt to learn Islam (Riaz, 2011) – a process that in practice exemplifies the use and displacement of secular categories through the conflation of religion with Islam.

Along with injecting religious sentiment into the mainstream education system, the governments under both authoritarian military dictators and democratic regimes facilitated the flourishing of the *madrassa* education system across the country, which was originally adopted in post-independence Bangladesh as part of 'the legacy of the spectacular resurgence of Islamic religious education in India during the late nineteenth century' (Ahmad, 2004, p. 102). Although through the first Education Commission the government had emphasised the need for reformation of the *madrassa* education system to merge with mainstream education (Ministry of Education, 1974), over the next three decades, the *madrassa* education system became the fastest growing sector in Bangladesh in terms of total numbers and students (Asadullah and Chaudhury, 2009). In fact, between 1972 and 2004, the number of government-supported (Aliya) *madrassas* increased by 732 per cent (from 1,412 to 11,746), whereas the number of privately managed *madrassas* (Qwami) increased to 50,000 (Riaz, 2008). Around 3,900,000 students are currently enrolled in different education levels – Dakhil, Alim, Fazil and Kalim – in the *madrassa* education institutions (BANBEIS, 2015) across the country – further evidence of the anti-secular movement that informed successive governments in expanding the education system.

Although this chapter has argued that the Bangladeshi education system is still quintessentially steeped in colonial aspirations, there are significant key differences in terms of the critical preoccupations of education. While British rulers introduced the English education system as a means to furthering political and economic interests, the Indian leaders along with the English-educated class saw in the English language the 'key to the West' (Basu, 1974, p. 73). English as the new language arrived with the promise to Indians of a new worldview, and the Indian English-educated class quickly became the driving force in Indian politics and shaped English education to generate new political life and ideas. It recognised English as the medium of expression that would ultimately forge the unity of *all* Indians (Basu, 1974).

Indeed, the establishment of the University of Dhaka by British rulers in East Bengal in 1921 helped an East Bengal–based intelligentsia to emerge, which produced a politically unintended consequence at the end of the British regime and during the first years of the Pakistani regime (1947–1971). Once the British departed, East Bengal became part of Pakistan; however, the political leaders and educated class felt no basic difference between the British and the Pakistani rulers. The political leaders and educated class of then East Pakistan saw higher education as a catalyst to achieve their political goals during the Pakistani regime (Kabir, 2010). Consequently, the role of education in society changed, turning against the Pakistani rulers. Similar to what education did for India, the development of the East Bengal–based intelligentsia created the climate and the actors for a social movement to push forward the establishment of a new country – Bangladesh – in 1971 (Basu, 1974).

Discussion and conclusion

> *It is necessary to build convincing arguments for people to realize that 'development' is an option, justified by actors, categories of thought, institutions, the media, etc. It is one option and not the only option, which carries with it its own splendors, together with certain miseries (e.g., the rhetoric of modernity and the logic of coloniality). This is the struggle for the control of knowledge.*
>
> (Mignolo, 2012)

This chapter has critically explored the complex relationship of the fine threads connecting historical antecedents and determinants, and the government's preoccupation vis-à-vis the current personality of the education market, as reflected in policies and priorities of successive governments in post-independence Bangladesh. We have seen how donors have sought legitimation through espousing ideas, priorities and agendas propagated through international projects and policies such as EFA, and how this has resulted in an increase in privatisation, investment and decentralisation. Symptoms have started to appear that increasingly indicate an ideological friction between the spirit of desecularisation and indoctrination on one hand, and the spirit of liberation and national identity on the other. The push for an apolitical and desecularised education has resulted in a loss of critical thinking and an education no longer based on the spirit of intellectual curiosity. Through what Mignolo (2012) has termed the 'politicization of civil society', it has been suppressed and subdued by the more pragmatic, neoliberal, politically motivated, instrumentalist, market-driven, quick-fix agendas.

This discussion demonstrates how the Bangladesh education system has been shaped by the persisting binary of mutually opposing forces – the global market and its own form of political ideology – over the past four decades. In the 1980s, a nexus between donor agencies and NGOs emerged which would influence the government into reforming the education system based on neoliberal doctrines. The manner in which these donor agencies dictated to the government to reform the education system in turn helped transfer the education system into a mode of vocationalisation. Similar to the economic role of the colonial education system in British India, the current role of education became primarily to increase the productivity of human resources to serve the global market (Table 9.1).

It can be seen that the current push towards religionisation is a direct response to the education system's move towards vocationalisation – an effort to reclaim and protect an identity in the face of global pressures. The momentum of market-driven vocationalisation and politically imposed, ideology-based religionisation has resulted in a critical-intellectual vacuum. True, an ideology-based education was antecedent in the colonial era, however, what seems to have been lost in the space of a few decades is the critical reflexivity which ultimately supported the movement towards freedom and independence.

This chapter has argued that, similar to the colonial political agenda, the education system post-independence was significantly forged and fashioned by the

Table 9.1 From colonial to post-colonial: the shifting of the education system of Bangladesh

		Education system in British India (1835–1947)	Education system in Pakistan regime (1947–1971)	Post-independence education system in Bangladesh (1971–)
Key actors		– Catholic missionaries – British rulers	– Pakistan rulers	– Donor agencies – Government/ ruling elite – NGOs – Civil society bodies
Purposes	**Political tool**	– To serve British colonial rulers to continue British rule in the Indian subcontinent	– To serve Pakistani rulers to continue Pakistani rule	– To generate a generation to serve the party in power – To create an apolitical attitude/ acritical market ideology
	Economic tool	– To supply skilled manpower for the British economy	– To supply skilled labour for the Pakistani economy	– To supply semi-skilled and skilled labour force for market – Vocationalised
Target groups		– Elite	– Elite	– Mass

vested interests of the ruling elite. Based on the four constitutional pillars of nationalism, socialism, secularism and democracy, the first Education Commission report had aimed to decolonise the education system where education was to be used as an instrument in nation-building. However, the political turmoil in 1975 facilitated the ruling elite to merely espouse and *re*produce the colonial political agenda in education, which became the subject to be produced in its own form of nationalism and through which religious sentiment was re-instilled as a political agenda. The political interests of post-1975 governments, by design and deliberation, virtually eliminated the accumulated spirit of the historical process of the emergence of Bangladesh as an independent country, demonstrated through the massive sacrifice of lives in the War of Independence against Pakistan.

The colonial antecedents and determinants, the current personality of the education market and the ruling elite's priorities as reflected in educational policies have shaped education to construct an acritical generation to serve the market and to allow the ruling elite to continue their domination in the society. The generation produced through such education has become largely cynical towards the spirit of independence, is often motivated by partisan politics and has adopted a market-driven attitude and quick-fix solutions as its mantra. The terrorist attack on 2 July 2016 at a café in Dhaka, which left 20 people dead including 18 foreigners (*The Daily Star*, 2016), suggests that the nation's education system has failed to enlighten this generation in the *zeitgeist* and true spirit of a democratic, secular and modern education. It is undeniable that the emergence of radicalism could be a result of global power politics (Riaz, 2016), and the lack of criticality in the local education system has created opportunities for local radical groups to fill the vacuum with religious fanaticism for the young generation.

This chapter in no way argues against educating the masses in the spirit of local sensitivities. However, it questions to what extent the Bangladeshi education system has been decolonised on the basis of the rhetorically ubiquitous 'spirit of liberation' as many claim. It argues that the original source of the *re*colonisation of the Bangladeshi education system that has occurred through tri-(ideological) power – colonial aspiration, market hegemony and an own-form of political supremacy – has been connected through the idea of network governance emerging between donor agencies, NGOs and the ruling political elite. It also suggests that it is important to develop a 'secular' education system in order to truly enlighten the generation with the most enduring needs of this day and age.

Notes

1 Although registered non-government secondary schools are managed by the SMC, they are still funded by the government. The government provides 100% of the salaries of teachers and other facilities and expenses of the schools. This secondary school system follows the national curricula, textbooks and examination system.
2 We refer to the BRAC Education Program (BEP) as an NGO education approach since donor agencies and other NGOs in Bangladesh have since modelled on the BEP across the country and beyond.

References

ADB, 2008, *Education sector in Bangladesh: what worked well and why under the sector-wide approach*. Available at www.oecd.org/countries/bangladesh/42228468.pdf. Accessed 15 July 2016.

ADB, 2015, Innovative strategies in technical and vocational education and training for accelerated human resource development in South Asia Bangladesh. Available at https://www.adb.org/sites/default/files/publication/167320/tvet-hrd-south-asia-bangladesh.pdf. Accessed 15 July 2016.

Ahmad, M. 2004, 'Madrassa education in Pakistan and Bangladesh'. In S. Limaye, R. Wirsing and M. M. Honolulu (eds.), *Religious radicalism and security in South Asia* (pp. 101–115). Honolulu, HI: Asia–Pacific Center for Security Studies.

Ahmed. M., 2011, *The sector-wide approach in Bangladesh primary education: a critical view*. Dhaka: Institute of Education and Development, BRAC University. Available at https://assets.publishing.service.gov.uk/media/57a08ae340f0b652dd000974/PTA57.pdf. Accessed 25 April 2016.

Ahmed, M., Ahmed, K. S., Khan, N. I., and Ahmed, R., 2007, *Access to education in Bangladesh: country analytical review of primary and secondary education*. Dhaka: Institute of Education and Development, BRAC University. Available at www.create-rpc.org/pdf_documents/Bangladesh_CAR.pdf. Accessed 25 April 2016.

Asadullah, M. N. and Chaudhury, N., 2009, 'Holy alliances: public subsidies, Islamic high schools, and female schooling in Bangladesh'. *Education Economics*, *17*(3), 377–394. doi:10.1080/09645290903142593.

Ball, S. J. and Junemann, C., 2012, *Networks, new governance and education*. Bristol: Policy Press.

BANBEIS, 2015, *Madrassa education*. Available at http://banbeis.gov.bd/data/images/chap06.pdf. Accessed 15 July 2016.

Basu, A., 1974, *The growth of education and political development in India, 1898–1920*. New Delhi: Oxford University Press.

Bureau of Non-formal Education, 2013, *Curriculum for Pre-Voc level- 1 (for non-formal vocational education*. Dhaka: Ministry of Primary and Mass Education. Available at www.bnfe.gov.bd/site/page/d92efefd-b946-4c1a-bec9-755a045000fa/. Accessed 25 April 2016.

CAMPE, 2009, *Directory of NGOs with education programme in Bangladesh* (vol. II). Dhaka: CAMPE. Available at www.campebd.org/Files/25022014040047pm Directory_of_NGOs_with_Education_Programme___Volume_II.pdf. Accessed 30 October 2016.

CAMPE, 2014, *Annual report 2014*. Dhaka: CAMPE.

CAMPE, 2015, *Moving from MDG to SDG: accelerate progress for quality primary education*. Bangladesh: CAMPE.

CAMPE, 2016, *Objectives of CAMPE*. Available at www.campebd.org/page/Generic/0/3/4. Accessed 12 July 2016.

Chowdhury, R. and Kabir, A. H., 2014, 'Language wars: English education policy and practice in Bangladesh'. *Multilingual Education*, *4*(1), 1–16. doi:10.1186/s13616-014-0021-2.

Coombs, P. H. and Ahmed, M., 1974, *Attacking rural poverty: how nonformal education can help*. Baltimore, MD and London: Johns Hopkins University Press.

The Daily Star, 2008, 'BRAC not "NGO-nising" any primary school'. Available at http://archive.thedailystar.net/newDesign/story.php?nid=40818. Accessed 25 January 2016.

Faaland, J., 1981, *Aid and influence: the case of Bangladesh*. London and Basingstoke: The Macmillan Press Ltd.

Government of Pakistan, 1958, *Report of the commission on national education*. Karachi: Ministry of Education.

Hossain, N., 2004, 'Access to education for the poor and girls: educational achievements in Bangladesh'. Paper presented at the Estudio de caso preparado para la Conferencia Mundial sobre la Reducción de la Pobreza en Gran Escala: A Global Learning Process y conferencia sobre el tema), Shanghai.

Hossain, N., Subrahmanian, R. and Kabeer, N., 2002, 'The politics of educational expansion in Bangladesh'. IDS Working Paper no. 167. Available at https://open docs.ids.ac.uk/opendocs/bitstream/handle/123456789/3929/Wp167.pdf. Accessed 15 July 2016.

Inter-Agency Commission, 1990, *Meeting basic learning needs: a vision for the 1990s. Background document for the World Conference on Education for All*. Jomtein: Inter-Agency Commission.

ITAD, 2012, *Support to civil society engagement in policy dialogue Bangladesh country report, additional annex I: Case study reports*. Available at www.entwicklung.at/fileadmin/user_upload/Dokumente/Evaluierung/Evaluierungsberichte/2013/2012004CSO_Bangl_AnnexI.pdf. Accessed 15 July 2016.

JICA, 2002, *Bangladesh education sector overview*. Available at www.jica.go.jp/activities/schemes/finance_co/approach/pdf/eban.pdf. Accessed 15 July 2016.

Jones, P. W., 2004, 'Taking the credit: financing and policy linkages in the education portfolio of the World Bank'. In G. Steiner-Khamsi (Ed.), *The global politics of educational borrowing and lending* (pp. 188–200). New York: Teachers College Press.

Lewis, D. J., 1997, 'NGOs, donors, and the state in Bangladesh'. *The Annals of the American Academy of Political and Social Science*, 554, 33–45.

Lingard, B., 2009, 'Researching education policy in a globalized world: theoretical and methodological considerations'. *Yearbook of the National Society for the Study of Education*, 108(2), 226–246.

Kabir, A. H., 2010, Neoliberal policy in the higher education sector in Bangladesh: autonomy of public universities and the role of the state. *Policy Futures in Education*, 8(6), 619–631. doi:dx.doi.org/10.2304/pfie.2010.8.6.619.

Karim, L., 2001, 'Politics of the poor? NGOs and grass-roots political mobilization in Bangladesh'. *Political and Legal Anthropology Review*, 24(1), 92–107.

Magnen, A., 1994, *Donor co-ordination in education: a case study on Bangladesh*. Paris: UNESCO.

Mignolo, W., 2011, *The darker side of Western modernity: global futures, decolonial options*. Durham, NC: Duke University Press.

Mignolo, W., 2012. Delinking, decoloniality and dewesternization: interview with Walter Mignolo (Part II). In *Critical Legal Thinking*. Available at http://critical legalthinking.com/2012/05/02/delinking-decoloniality-dewesternization-inter view-with-walter-mignolo-part-ii/. Accessed 20 October 2016.

Ministry of Education, 1974, *Bangladesh Shikkha commission report* [Bangladesh Education Commission report]. Dhaka: Ministry of Education.

Ministry of Education, 2000, *Jatiyo shikkha nity* [National education policy]. Dhaka: Ministry of Education.

Ministry of Education, 2010, *National education policy 2010*. Dhaka: Ministry of Education.

Ministry of Planning, 2011, *Sixth five year plan FY2011–FY2015: accelerating growth and reducing poverty (part 1)*. Dhaka: Ministry of Planning.

Ministry of Primary and Mass Education, 2003, *Education for all: national plan of action 2003–2015*. Dhaka: Ministry of Primary and Mass Education.

Molla, T., 2014, 'Knowledge aid as instrument of regulation: World Bank's non-lending higher education support for Ethiopia'. *Comparative Education*, 50(2), 229–248. doi:10.1080/03050068.2013.807645.

Paulson, N., 2006, *Bangladesh: civil society participation and the governance of educational systems in the context of sector-wide approaches to basic education*. Toronto: University of Toronto.

Riaz, A., 2005, Traditional institutions as tools of political Islam in Bangladesh. *Journal of Asia and African Studies*, 40(3), 171-196. doi: 10.1177/0021909605055072.

Riaz, A., 2008, *Faithful education: madrassahs in South Asia*. New Brunswick, NJ and London: Rutgers University Press.

Riaz, A., 2011, 'Islamist politics and education'. In R. Ali and F. C. Christine (Eds.), *Political Islam and governance in Bangladesh* (pp. 115–135). London and New York: Routledge.

Riaz, A., 2016, 'Who are the Bangladeshi "Islamic militants"?' *Perspectives on Terrorism*, 10(1): 1–17.

Rose, P., 2009, 'NGO provision of basic education: alternative or complementary service delivery to support access to the excluded?' *Compare*, 39(2), 219–233. doi: 10.1080/03057920902750475.

Ryan, A., Jennings, J. and White, J., 2007, *BRAC education programme. BEP 2004–2009. Mid term review NORAD*, Oslo, Norway.

Sabur, Z. U. and Ahmed, M., 2010, *Debating diversity in provision of universal primary education in Bangladesh*. Dhaka: Institute of Education and Development, BRAC University.

Saigol, R., 2003, *Becoming a modern nation: educational discourse in the early years of Ayub Khan*. Islamabad: Council of Social Sciences.

Steiner-Khamsi, G., 2006, 'The economics of policy borrowing and lending: a study of late adopters'. *Oxford Review of Education*, 32(5), 665–678.

Steiner-Khamsi, G., 2008, 'Donor logic in the era of Gates, Buffett, and Soros'. *Current Issues in Comparative Education*, 10, 10–15.

Steiner-Khamsi, G., 2012, 'For all by all? The World Bank's global framework for education'. In S. J. Klees, J. Samoff and N. P. Stromquist (Eds.), *The World Bank and education: critiques and alternatives* (pp. 3–20). Rotterdam: Sense Publishers.

UNESCO, 2007, *Education sector-wide approaches (SWAPs): Background, guide and lessons*. Paris: UNESCO. Available at http://unesdoc.unesco.org/images/0015/001509/150965e.pdf. Accessed 11 April 2016.

USAID, 2002, 'Bangladesh education sector review report no. 1'. Available at www.beps.net/publications/BANGLADESH%201%20Overview%20of%20Basic%20Education%20Sector.pdf. Accessed 15 July 2016.

Verger, A., Edwards Jr, D. B. and Altinyelken, H. K., 2014, 'Learning from all? The World Bank, aid agencies and the construction of hegemony in education for development'. *Comparative Education*, 50(4), 381–399. doi:10.1080/03050068.2014.918713.

University Grants Commission, 2009, *Handbook: universities of Bangladesh*. Dhaka: University of Grants Commission.

World Bank, 2000, *Bangladesh education sector review* (Vol. I). Dhaka: University Press Limited.

World Bank, 2009, *Higher education quality enhancement project.* Available at http://web.worldbank.org/external/projects/main?pagePK=64312881&piPK=643028 48&theSitePK=40941&Projectid=P106216. Accessed 24 September 2010.

World Bank, 2013, *Higher education quality enhancement project (Credit No.4544-BD) Amendment to the financing agreement.* Available at www-wds.worldbank.org/external/default/WDSContentServer/WDSP/SAR/2013/03/19/090224b08 19f7acd/1_0/Rendered/PDF/Official0Docum0ment00Credit045440BD.pdf. Accessed 10 September 2014.

10 Democratic transition in a post-colonial state

Dialogue and discord in Tunisia's post-revolutionary transition, 2011–2014

Jonathan Murphy and Virpi Malin

Introduction

This chapter explores the challenges faced in the development of a new democratic constitution subsequent to Tunisia's Arab Spring revolution of 2011. As a case study, it examines how and why dialogue took place in the constitutional process. The case is contextualised within a broader reading of the geopolitical dynamics within which the political transition occurred. It is argued that the neoliberal transformation of the state attempted by the Ben Ali regime engendered and exacerbated social tensions and led to the revolution, and that the successful post-revolutionary governance transformation rested on the suturing of social conflicts through an open-ended dialogic process. The Tunisian case both illustrates the destabilising trajectory of neoliberalism and models a pathway to peaceful construction of a democratic settlement.

This chapter proposes not only that 'Western models' of the state are unsuitable for transfer to post-colonial states, but that, in the actual context of the international crisis of neoliberalism and the rise of atavistic populism, the 'learning' should travel in the opposite direction. Through their constitutional process, Tunisians were able to surmount deep identitarian differences and construct an institutional order in which all could recognise a reflection of themselves. It is precisely this type of process that is required for Europe and North America to break free of its current cycle of mutual alienation and anger.

While there is a growing literature on the Tunisian revolution – and, in regard to the eventual constitutional settlement, on the role of the UGTT trade union (Yousfi, 2015) – there has been little if any consideration of the implications of the Tunisian transformation for broader thinking around democratic transformation. Further, there are few analyses of the relationship between neoliberalism and democracy, and specifically of the impact on democratic outcomes of social conflict and political instability generated by neoliberal policies.

This chapter focuses on both these questions. It argues that the open and inclusive dialogic model adopted after the revolution permitted a compromise to be found that enabled the transition's success. Further, it contends that neoliberalism not only played a significant role in destabilising Tunisia's development prior to the revolution, but also continues to undermine social relationships and the possibility for equitable development under the new democratic system. Tunisia's trajectory and challenges are relevant not only to the developing world, but also to the countries at the core of the global order, whose own institutions have gradually been hollowed out and undermined by neoliberalism. An open and comprehensive process for (re)building democratic institutions across the world can learn much from Tunisia's path.

This chapter is presented in three main sections, followed by a conclusion. In the first section, the argument is contextualised through situating Tunisia's development trajectory following independence within the broader geopolitical environment. The second section sets out the challenge facing Tunisia in building a democratic state after the revolution, and explores the key characteristics of the dialogic processes undertaken. The third section explores the significance of the Tunisian experience in the light of the existential challenges facing liberal democracy internationally, with growing discontent manifested at the same time by the rise of demagogic populism on one hand, and of nihilist movements committed to the destruction of Western civilisation on the other.

The conclusion asserts that the rehabilitation of democratic governance can take place only through authentic and inclusive dialogue on both national and international levels. This process will not be smooth as in a Habermasian vision of ideal speech state communication, but will rather depend on the successful navigation of a 'messy', agonistic process in which the subaltern asserts her right to speak, or in Freire's (1970, 2005) words, to 'name the world'. This is a key lesson brought by the Tunisian democratic transition.

The Tunisian context

Summary

In this first section, is argued that following independence from French colonialism in the late 1950s, and through the 1960s and 1970s, Tunisia was able to build the foundations of a modern state that allowed for considerable social and economic gains, including the establishment of a welfare state, economic infrastructure and inclusive citizenship. This achievement was facilitated by an international environment favourable to developmentalist policies. From the 1980s, the model came under increasing attack as neoliberal ideas became internationally hegemonic, and the country was pressured to adopt neoliberal policies of marketization, liberalisation, and insertion into an integrated global economic order. The neoliberal prescription unleashed unbalanced growth that undermined the social contract on which the independent developmentalist state had been founded. The accountability nexus between elites and population was broken, and the ruling clique took advantage of liberalisation and marketization to build a kleptocratic economy, while the welfarist and developmental roles of the state were undermined. The regime attempted to preserve its power through driving wedges between different segments of the population. The 2011 revolution culminated the destabilisation process and set off the Arab

Spring uprisings whose effects continue to impact both the Arab region and the global geopolitical order.

The conditions under which the post-colonial state emerged created a development dilemma that led to the sublimation of conflict under an authoritarian, state-building project whose stability was undermined by growing demands for citizen voice on one hand and increasing external pressure to harness state resources in the service of a globalised neoliberal project on the other. When this dynamic led to the unravelling of order and the overthrow of the Ben Ali regime in 2011, Tunisians were forced to find ways to rebuild the state through the suturing of divergent social imaginaries in the creation of a new constitution that could provide a foundation for the future.

From the beginning, and across the post-colonial world, the challenges of establishing both economically successful and accountable orders within the newly independent states could not be compared with the trajectories of countries at the core of the global economic order. Governance consent, including for the distribution of resources in a situation of overall penury, was secured generally, including in Tunisia, through the legitimacy of the independence movement that had inherited power, and through a social contract built on the relative asceticism of the post-colonial elite and the delivery of wider life opportunities to the former colonial subjects.

The possibility for the first generation of post-colonial leaders to deliver on this commitment was partly the result of a generally favourable geopolitical environment. Most countries in the developing world – including Tunisia – emerged from the collapse of the old imperialisms (of Britain, of France, of Portugal, and other lesser imperialisms) into a world dominated by the new superpowers of the United States and the USSR. The specificity of these new hegemons was that their claim to power was not built (at least explicitly) on an imagined racial superiority that fundamentally underpinned the old imperialisms, but rather on a belief in their governance models' inherent ideological superiority. Their competing metaphors for the public good were built around two types of equality, one of the autonomous individual, the other equality within the collective. Neither claim was ever fully realised, but they provided new master scripts that in practice, in the decades following World War II, led to a geopolitical balance that despite the uncomfortable shadow of the Cold War, provided stability and a certain margin for manoeuvre for the emergent elites of former colonies. Because there was competition between the superpowers for the loyalty of the newly independent states, post-colonial states could bargain with their mentor hegemons, and as in the case of Tunisia, chart a relatively independent national development strategy.

It is in this context that independent Tunisia charted its post-independence path under the astute President Habib Bourguiba, who managed to maintain positive relationships with the West, and particularly the former French colonial power, while pursuing a developmentalist economic strategy. The Bourguibist strategy entailed state-led economic and social development based on universal education, the abolition of 'feudal' social relationships and particularly the emancipation of women, state-led industrialization and the foundations of a welfare state. While these policies were implemented through an authoritarian, top-down approach, by the 1980s, Tunisia was widely viewed as an example of successful post-colonial development. What in retrospect might appear to be a surprising combination of socialistic (or perhaps more accurately, welfarist) policies and a largely pro-Western foreign policy was neither particularly unusual among post-colonial states, nor inconsistent with the then Keynesian-influenced developmentalist orthodoxy reigning at the World Bank and other international development and financial institutions.

The advent of neoliberal economic policies at the international level brought an end to the relative development freedom post-colonial states enjoyed, at the same time as oil price shocks compromised the viability of national industrial development strategies. Further, it could also be argued that by this time, the initial ascetic inclinations of post-colonial leaders had been blunted by the temptation of using their positions for personal benefit rather than for the selfless edification of the modern state. In the case of Tunisia, an increasingly authoritarian, erratic and aging Bourguiba was deposed in 1987 by a former intelligence officer converted to politician, Zinedine Ben Ali. While Ben Ali initially promised expanded freedoms, including for repressed political opponents ranging from leftists to Islamists, this brief thawing of political repression was quickly replaced by a systematic and cynical manipulation and suppression of opponents, including a particularly effective strategy of enlisting leftist support against Islamists who were presented as a threat to the secularist project. That cleavage remains a major defining feature of Tunisian politics.

The Ben Ali regime gradually revised its development approach to align with the new development thinking that swept through the international development institutions in the wake of neoliberalism's conquest of economic orthodoxy. This new mantra replaced state-led development with the edict that markets could solve all development problems. Instead of the state itself spearheading development, its role would be to create the conditions for the flourishing of markets, through eliminating controls on foreign capital, imports and exports, privatising state-owned industries and substantially reducing the state's proportion of GDP.

Opposition to the Ben Ali dictatorship was composed of two main strains of thinking; a secularist and largely left-wing opposition with perspectives ranging from social democratic to Marxist, and an Islamist opposition. While in the first years after independence, the left was perceived as the major threat by Bourguiba, and subject to substantial repression, by the end of the Bourguiba period and the assumption of power by Ben Ali, the Islamic movement was identified as the main threat to the autocratic power. Ennahdha and its predecessor, the Movement of the Islamic Tendency (MTI), were subjected to severe repression and most of its leadership was imprisoned, forced underground or exiled. Some elements of the leftist opposition were tolerated, although no serious opposition was permitted and the state exercised a stranglehold over public communications which was used to overwhelm opposition voices.

With the rise of jihadist movements from the 1990s (the first major bombing of Western interests was an attack against American troops in Yemen in 1992), the Ben Ali regime conducted an incessant and virulent communication campaign associating Islamism with terrorism, a perspective underlined by the bloody civil war between Islamists and the government that stretched through the 1990s in neighbouring Algeria. Thus, the association between Islamism and terrorism was inculcated in every Tunisian citizen during this period. However, this came at a price for the regime; for those not inclined to accept the government script, Islamism became seen as the main alternative to the corrupt authoritarian rule. The double-edged sword of the repression of the Islamists was that all those resisting dictatorship were classified as Islamists; for example, the secularist journalist and Ben Ali opponent Tawfik Ben Brik reports being arrested and interrogated in 1999 by the police who told him that while he was 'the most important intellectual in Tunisia', he had 'the same structure of thinking as the Islamists'.[1]

Given the limitation of naked repression, Ben Ali chose the tried and proven strategy of divide and rule. Faced with a leftist opposition on one hand that was weakening with the collapse of the Soviet Bloc and the increasing in-roads of neoliberal thinking into the European social democratic left, and the rising potency of Islamist ideas on the other hand that could capitalise on resentment towards the imperious impositions of the post-imperial order (crystallised most nakedly in Western policy towards Palestine), Ben Ali chose to pit the two against each other. Characterising Islamism as an existential threat, the regime produced a deluge of propaganda highlighting the perfidy of Islamist ideas, and embarked on waves of arrest, torture and exile, while simultaneously reaching out to a 'loyal' leftist opposition that was allowed to function within strict parameters (with even a few parliamentary seats reserved for them) as long as they explicitly preferred the Ben Ali regime to the Islamist enemy.

While this calculation paid off for a number of years, eventually the more insightful of the secularist opposition realised that their only hope to escape marginalisation and subjection to an increasingly catastrophic regime mismanagement and theft was to find some kind of working compromise with the Islamists. The roots of a possible democratic transition came about with the 18 October 2005 movement, which began as a hunger strike of leaders of key opposition forces, highlighting abuse of human rights and freedom of speech in Tunisia, timed to coincide with the World Summit on the Information Society organized in Tunis in November 2005. The hunger strike regrouped Islamist and secular political opponents of the government, as well as leading civil society activists. While not all opposition parties agreed to participate (for example, the Communist Party declined), the movement included representation from Ennahdha through to the far left and also involved most politically moderate opposition parties.[2] The organisations supporting the hunger strike founded a movement with a broad agenda for democratic transition in Tunisia. The agenda was built on an agreement on eight common democratic principles.[3] The disparate and often mutually suspicious opposition was beginning to coalesce around nodal points of commonality (Laclau and Mouffe, 1985: 112).

The political reconciliation articulated with growing grassroots citizen discontent, expressed in a number of uprisings in the regime's last years, particularly in the mining regions of the impoverished interior, which had been neglected by the governing coastal elites. Eventually, as is now well known, the uprising that began in the interior town of Sidi Bouzid after the self-immolation of a young vegetable seller in protest against police mistreatment and lack of opportunity led to waves of protests that an already isolated and discredited regime was unable to control. On 14 January 2011, Ben Ali fled to exile in Saudi Arabia, while many of his kleptocratic entourage were caught trying to follow him out of Tunisia.

Building a democratic state

Summary

This second section examines the situation inherited by Tunisia's successful revolutionary movement after the fall of Ben Ali. The unexpectedly rapid collapse of the regime spared the country generalised violence or civil war, as occurred later in several other Arab Spring countries, but left a society marked by deep cleavages. These cleavages, fostered by the neoliberal development model adopted by Ben Ali at the behest of the international financial institutions, included gross regional disparities, mutual distrust between the elites and the bulk of the population and profound conflict around the teleology of the state. These latter differences pitted modernist perspectives favouring construction of a secular state in the image of the Napoleonic state, against a cultural-spiritual imaginary that posited the state as a reflection of Tunisia's Muslim, Arabic identity. Overcoming these cleavages, or rather, establishing legitimate democratic institutions despite the differences, was the major task of the transition, and its success was the result of a lengthy, complex and often fraught dialogic process.

Tunisians had overthrown a corrupt and dictatorial regime, and embarked on a path towards a new democratic political system. Unlike in many previous cases, the destination of this path was not predetermined, whether through the teleology of the radical ideologies of the first half of the twentieth century and their Arab nationalist manifestations, or through the imperatives of regional transformations, such as occurred through the incorporation of former Communist countries of Central and Eastern Europe into the European Union after the collapse of the Soviet Bloc between 1989 and 1991. Tunisia was a small enough country and far enough away from any geopolitical hotspots that it was largely left to its own devices in navigating a democratic transformation, though of course external advice on the best road to democracy was freely and assuredly given by the same international institutions that had only months before lauded the 'economic miracle' of the previous regime.

The process that took place in the three years after the revolution can be divided into three discrete stages. In the first (the 'Habermasian') phase, after democratic elections to a constituent assembly in October 2011, political actors organised a structured and iterative dialogic process in which citizens and organisations across the country were invited to provide input into the constitutional process, on the basis of progressively more refined constitutional drafts. In the second phase, the process was halted after two leftist politicians were assassinated, presumably by Islamist terrorists. Opposition politicians walked out of the constituent assembly, and large street demonstrations were organised by the opposition with competing shows of popular force by Islamists in the governing coalition. In the third phase, which has drawn the closest international attention, a 'quartet' of key civil society organisations led by the UGTT trade union acted as intermediaries in facilitating a 'national dialogue' which eventually led to a political accord that was then returned to the constituent assembly for refinement, and adoption of a new constitution in January 2014. This in turn led to the holding of democratic elections for the presidency and the new parliament in late 2014, and the peaceful transfer of power to the elected president and governing coalition in parliament.

The entire constitutional process is interesting for many reasons, including notably the successful navigation of a peaceful transition within the Arab world, despite Tunisia having no democratic history, and its contradiction of an often-repeated trope regarding the 'unsuitability' of the Muslim and/or Arab world for democratic governance. However, in this section, attention is paid rather to the characteristics of the dialogic processes and implications for thinking about democratic transition.

After the January 2011 revolution, Tunisians were faced with building a new order in a context in which their society had been marked not only by the lingering effects of colonialism (Mamdani, 1996), but also by the corrosive impact of neoliberalism, in which state-building had been denigrated in favour of 'market fundamentalism', where corruption had become endemic and closely integrated with the marketization process, and in which the previous regime had explicitly exacerbated the 'secularist–Islamist' rift as a divide-and-rule strategy.

Unlike in many countries faced with sudden regime collapse, Tunisia did not descend into uncontrollable disorder. There are a variety of reasons for this, including notably the state structure that the first generation of independence leaders had constructed and that remained relatively functional despite the depredations of the later Ben Ali years, and in particular, the very rapid mobilisation of opposition forces, built on the mutual confidence forged through the 18 October 2005 accord, around a transition plan involving free elections to a constituent parliamentary assembly that would then draft a new constitution for the country.

Actors enter into dialogic processes bearing the marks of their previous experiences. In the case of countries emerging from dictatorship such as Tunisia, the imprint of authoritarian constraints on free speech and interaction is embedded within society and in social interactions (Moghaddam, 2013). Surprisingly, while there have been many celebrated studies of the interaction of authoritarianism and personality (Adorno et al., 1950), there has been very little scholarly discussion of the impact and constraints placed on dialogue when engaged actors have been marked by their passage through dictatorship with its repression of diverse ideas, prohibition of free discussion and normalisation of interpersonal brutality. Overcoming the dictatorial legacy includes not least the challenge of including victim and perpetrator in a democratic dialogue.

In the period 2011 to 2014, Tunisians learned for the first time to talk with each other in a climate unmediated by the constant threat of police reprisal, and unaided by the simple framing of the world into simple primary shades that had been the hallmark of the Ben Ali regime – and particularly his favourite, mauve shade in which regime propaganda was generally delivered. The process of designing a new political order which was reflected in the drafting of a new constitution was marked with numerous hair-raising moments; indeed, an analogy with an apparently out-of-control roller-coaster ride would not be an exaggeration. However, in the course of this process, Tunisians learned to talk with each other across boundaries that had intentionally been deeply carved across the national psyche – in an authoritarian regime, differences are never just a matter of opinion, but are potentially a matter of treachery deserving of punishment. Inevitably, opposition is itself constructed in the messianic terms that are necessary in order to resist overwhelming state pressure, as was the case with the emergent Islamic movements that sprang up across the Arab region, including in Tunisia, as an alternative to the brutality and declining material rewards that the first generation of mainly Arab nationalist regimes had brought: initial optimism for liberation from depredations of colonialism replaced by a dialectic of degeneration driven by economic liberalisation, the usurpation of power and resources by emergent post-colonial elites and the impossibility of satisfying public expectations for a reasonable standard of living.

Tunisia has no democratic tradition which could be called upon to provide an iterative anchor for the establishment of a democratic institutional structure; the country was starting from scratch. Furthermore, the country explicitly chose perhaps the most difficult road to establish a new democracy: the creation of a democratic framework anchored in a new constitution that would be written from a blank page, by a popularly elected constituent assembly. The new constitution adopted in January 2014 was not based on a single template, whether a past constitution or (as is the case in many former colonies) the constitution of an influential external power (in Tunisia's case, this would have been that of France). There was no preliminary 'official understanding' of what the new democracy should be like. So creating the constitution – 'naming' the democracy – meant that the different actors, including representatives of different parties across the ideological spectrum, had the possibility to name the world from their perspective. There was no 'truth' which actors needed to accept in order to engage in the dialogue around a new constitution, unlike many participatory processes in which participation effectively entails acceptance of the world as seen by those designing the dialogue (Cooke and Kothari, 2001). This absence of a pre-existing framework at the same time made progression through the constitutional process fraught with crises and uncertainty, but also invested the eventual constitutional agreement with an unusually deep authenticity and legitimacy.

In the immediate aftermath of the 2011 revolution, an interim government of former senior Ben Ali regime officials held power for a few weeks, but was faced by increasing popular contestation. The original idea of simply organising new elections was not acceptable, and there was a strong popular demand to build a new democratic order from scratch through the election of a National Constituent Assembly (NCA) whose role would be to draft a new constitution that would reflect the will of the people and assure democratic rights and freedoms.[4] This temporary parliament was elected on 23 October 2011 using a proportional representation system, in elections judged free and fair by national and international observers. The 'Islamist' Ennahdha Party won 89 of the 217 seats with about 37 per cent of the popular vote. The rest of the seats were divided between 19 other parties and eight independents. A government was formed between Ennahdha and two smaller, centre-left parties with a moderate secularist orientation.

The decision to elect a constituent assembly was somewhat controversial particularly among the legal elite. Tunisia, home to the Arab world's first constitution in 1861, has a well-developed constitutional justice expertise and even hosts the International Academy of Constitutional Law. These concerns were exacerbated when the NCA elections gave Ennahdha a plurality and the ability to drive, if not to control, the process. Fears grew among secularists that the constitution-drafting process would result in an Islamisation of the state, especially as the provisional government under Ennahdha leadership failed to effectively deal with (or in some minds, was complicit in) a number of Islamist extremist actions, including an attack on an art exhibition and on the American school, as well as permitting the visit to Tunisia of some extremist clerics who promoted regressive social practices, including female genital mutilation, child marriage and polygamy.[5]

The constitution-drafting process was initially intended to take one year. Six constitutional committees were established, one for each core chapter of the new constitution. Popular consultations were included in the process, and parliamentarians formed committees that visited all 24 governorates of the country and gathered input from citizens. A series of drafts was produced during 2012 and 2013 and released for public input. There was a passionate ferment of public debate, with the newly free and ideologically diverse media reporting any and all perspectives, disagreement and rumours.

From the beginning, the process was characterised by polarisation, and power asymmetries, with different actors each tending to feel that they were the one without power. The Islamists, who had been subjected to 30 years of repression under the old regime, felt that they were threatened by representatives of the former regime and its police state. Conversely, there was considerable distrust regarding the motives of Ennahdha among secularist opposition members and organised civil society, including the powerful UGTT trade union movement. The secularists felt that they were faced with an 'alien' force, an opponent convinced that it was speaking with the force of God on its side, one that wore a 'uniform' (Islamic dress such as the hijab) and for whom loyalty to its political party far exceeded the relatively loose and transitory political alliances typical of the secularists and the political left. Frequently, there was a rejection of the human equivalency of the other; conversations between secularists about Islamists culminated in denigration of their appearance, 'they are all ugly,' 'they pretend to be virginal but they have the worst morals of all under that veil.' On the other side, outspoken secularists were threatened by accusations of *takhfir*, apostasy, a particularly menacing and dangerous accusation because it can be interpreted as an invitation to murder the accused.[6]

The debate focused particularly on the identity of the state. During the election campaign, Ennahdha had committed not to propose sharia law as the basis for the new constitution, however Ennahdha leader Rachid Ghannouchi equivocated on this in early 2012 under pressure from hardliners within his party, causing uproar among secularists. Eventually, Ennahdha decided not to pursue sharia, and agreed to maintain the first clause of the old constitution, which states that the country's religion is Islam, but that the state is republican.[7] Another identity issue on which there was a very high level of contestation and mobilisation was the question of gender equality. While the broad idea of equality was accepted by mainstream parties, including the Islamists, conservatives within the NCA, including some members of Ennahdha, attempted to include a clause in the constitution that stated:

> The State assures the protection of the rights of women, her social gains, on the basis of complementarity with the man within the family and as associate of the man in the development of the homeland.[8]

While, again, Ennahdha eventually dropped the idea of complementarity (which had provoked division within the party) in favour of an unequivocal constitutional entrenchment of gender equality,[9] the sense that there was a consistent and repeated effort to Islamise the state and to roll back the modernist gains of the post-independence period continued to enrage secularists and deepened mistrust. The assassination of a leading leftist politician in February 2013 worsened tensions and led to massive street protests by secularist forces, who accused the Ennahdha-led government of at least laxity towards Islamist extremists, or even of complicity of some of its leaders in the assassination. Nevertheless, by June 2013 a fourth constitutional draft was published on which there was broad consensus apart from about 10 points of disagreement, and the Assembly plenary began debate on the constitution, leading towards a vote of the Assembly, with a two-thirds majority required for adoption.

However, the assassination of a second leftist leader on 25 July 2013 led to an explosion of citizen anger, daily mass demonstrations in front of parliament and an opposition boycott of the NCA, leading to the suspension of the Assembly's work for the last half of 2013 and effectively the first, Habermasian dialogic phase of the transition. The opposition did not restrict itself to protesting the assassinations, but in addition demanded the resignation of the Ennahdha-led government and agreement both on changes to the constitution to protect secularism, and on the process for organisation of elections immediately after constitutional adoption.

While there were widespread fears that the showdown would degrade into generalised violence or even a coup d'état, the crisis actually led to a broadening of the debate beyond the NCA and onto the streets. Initially two forms of legitimacy opposed each other; the legitimacy of the elected parliament (which was called into question by protestors because the parliament had exceeded its originally planned year to draft a constitution), and the popular legitimacy of the street, which claimed to reflect the original spirit of the 2011 revolution. After several months of blockage, a third actor inserted itself into the debate: four major Tunisian organisations, including the leading trade union central and the main employers' association, which came to be known as the Quartet.[10] The Quartet, which could be described as reflecting a corporatist legitimacy of organised Tunisian society, launched a process known as the National Dialogue. The Dialogue initially entailed separate consultations with all the political parties represented in the Assembly, as well as other major social actors. The process of agreeing on what the Dialogue would be about and establishing preconditions for the Dialogue to begin (particularly the principle that once the Dialogue had concluded, the government would resign and be replaced with a 'technocratic' government charged with organising elections) took several months of tense shuttle diplomacy, accompanied by varying levels of street mobilisation on both sides, before the different actors were able to even sit down together in the same room and discuss the content of the Dialogue. It was notable that the great bulk of energy was devoted to the establishment of mutual confidence based on respect for the legitimacy of the other rather than on the specific policy content. The points of policy disagreement on the content of the constitution, while significant in relation to a small number of its articles, assumed a secondary role. All the actors, even those vehemently committed to one camp or another, concurred that 'once we can agree on the terms for a dialogue, the actual constitutional debate can be concluded very quickly'. The core question that had to be addressed was how the different sides could trust each other. For the secularist opposition, its fear needed to be assuaged that an Ennahdha-led government would make use of its control of the state apparatus to assure victory in elections and its permanent continuation in power. For Ennahdha, it wanted confidence that if it let go of power, its leaders and supporters would not find themselves back in prison as in the Ben Ali era, or as was then occurring in Egypt, where the Muslim Brotherhood government had been overthrown by the army and its leaders were being arrested and activists slaughtered. At the same time, the actual process of dialogue proved both inclusive and ultimately extremely effective.

By the time agreement had been reached on restarting debate on the constitution at the NCA, on the resignation of the government and its replacement by a technocratic government and an election process and timetable, it was the beginning of January 2014. From this point, the process moved extremely quickly and in general very smoothly. The National Constituent Assembly established a 'compromise' committee that addressed articles in the proposed constitution that did not have consensus. The committee, which represented all the parties of the Assembly, hammered out agreements, while the Quartet continued to hold National Dialogue meetings that permitted a broader input into points of disagreement both in the constitutional process and on broader policy and governance matters. The Assembly made significant changes to the last constitutional draft, which mainly had the effect of strengthening human rights protections.

The gender equality provisions in particular were significantly strengthened, setting a progressive example in the region and beyond, and this time the great majority of Ennahdha women deputies and Ennahdha deputies as a whole voted for the strengthened clauses, a dramatic shift from the terms of the debate in 2012. After clause-by-clause voting, the final constitutional draft was voted on 26 January 2014, only three weeks after debate had begun in the plenary. The new constitution was adopted by 200 votes out of 216, with support from across the political spectrum.

The eventual success of the Tunisian constitutional process is well known and earned the Nobel Peace Prize for the architects of the National Dialogue, which channelled the latter stages of the constitutional process towards a positive outcome and enabled free and peaceful elections to be held for the new parliament and presidency created by the new constitution. These elections in turn led to a smooth and democratic transfer of power, the first in Tunisia's history. Tunisia's democratic transformation continues six years after the revolution, providing an important example of the possibilities for successful and nationally directed transition.

The Tunisian transition and the contemporary democratic context

Summary

This third section places the Tunisian democratic transition within a broader discussion about democracy and democratisation. The section begins by discussing what the Tunisian transition has revealed about what makes for authentic dialogue in a democratic transition. In contrast to a managed dialogue in which power always rests with those having the authority to speak, the 'messy', agonistic process in Tunisia stretched wide enough to accommodate perspectives that had been conditioned to exclude the other's legitimacy. The section goes on to explore how what actually happened in Tunisia contrasted with the hubristic certainty of Western-driven transition tropes. The section ends by arguing that in the current situation of crisis of Western democracy, it is Tunisia that can provide a conflict-resolution and democracy-promotion example for Western Europe and North America; this chapter is part of a rethinking of democratic development that attempts to de-Orientalise the democratic project.

There is considerable debate within political philosophy regarding how democracies should operate, and indeed what constitutes democratic dialogue. It has been long understood that for collaborative decision making to take place, the engaged actors need to interact according to some type of mutuality; in other words, where each feels free to contribute to the dialogue and that their contribution inheres in the final decision. The most commonly presented explanation of the desired condition for democratic dialogue within contemporary political philosophy derives from Habermas's (1975) proposition of an ideal speech state. However, Habermas has been sharply criticised by critical post-structuralists who argue that the ideal communicative state is a fantasy; interpersonal interactions always entail power and indeed according to Foucault, power is the capillary lifeblood of society. Building from this perspective, Laclau and Mouffe (1985) developed a less expansive but more dynamic understanding of democratic politics in which the fluidity and dynamism of power relationships underpin an always imperfect and conditional nature of democratic debate. In this approach, developed through a fusion of Foucauldian, Althusserian and Gramscian insights, the victorious (the 'hegemonic') perspective is constructed on the basis of conditional and temporary commonalities of interest established not through the victory of an impersonal and commonly acknowledged Reason, but rather through a messy and multi-layered process of debate, alliance-building, conflict, brinkmanship and compromise.

Unlike in the ideal of a more linear, deliberative approach, the agreement, the hegemonic order, is always qualified and temporary, not least because any process no matter how inclusive is marked by power relationships, will leave some feeling partly or completely excluded, and will be subject to continuing renegotiation including moments of qualitative break. However, this model of 'agonistic democracy' is differentiated from authoritarian rule and violent transformation through the acceptance by all actors of the Other's right to exist and to speak (Mouffe, 2013). The character of democratic as opposed to authoritarian systems could be represented on a continuum in which the most democratic systems are those permitting the greatest variety of different opportunities for construction of hegemony (meaning a wide range of democratic processes within a polity), as well as relative ease of reconstructing hegemonic alliances. In contrast, in an authoritarian system such as that of Tunisia under Ben Ali, a monolithic elite hierarchically organised under Ben Ali exercised overwhelming hegemony over decision-making and repressed, physically if necessary, alternative perspectives.

The challenge of the democratic transition in Tunisia, therefore, was to move from untrammelled hierarchic hegemony to the dynamic and interactive process of decision-making. This endeavour, particularly without external factors rewarding a democratic outcome, required the development through democratic dialogue of a system for democratic decision-making. Thus, it was a process that more or less had to be invented as it went along.

The international discourse of democratic development is almost entirely driven from Western sources, whether government-sponsored think tanks and NGOs, or academic 'transitologists'. In this idealised transition imaginary, the reason for authoritarianism is presented as resulting from a combination of two main factors; inadequate and underdeveloped democratic institutions, and a 'lack of capacity'. These circumstances are mutually reinforcing; weak institutions are weak because the actors in those institutions lack capacity, and the actors lack capacity because they function in institutions that do not support their development. As is typically the case in development theory generally, the solution is to 'teach' a better way; discourse is based on an adult–child metaphor. The 'adult', the Western expert, possesses knowledge that needs to be transferred to the developing country recipient, both in terms of comportment (working diligently, acting in the interests of constituents rather than self, etc.) and knowledge (learning how to read a budget, understanding which policies are good and which are bad according to the current development prescriptions, etc.).

The transparent clumsiness with which 'the right thing' is transferred by Western-dominated development agencies to governance practices in developing countries might seem shockingly self-interested to an external observer uninvested in the transaction; for example, the transnational financial institutions provide courses on various flavours of structural adjustment (essentially, opening markets and selling off state assets to transnational corporations, while reducing the policy powers of the developing country state) at well-equipped centres in attractive Western locales like Vienna and Paris. Such centres do not offer courses, for example, in 'inappropriate' options, such as the potential for states repudiating debts incurred by corrupt leaders who had profited from their status as preferred clients of the major Western powers.

When, in 2014, we started exploring how the constitution-building process had succeeded in an environment that was increasingly hostile to democratic development, it was still possible to characterise the Tunisian example within a framework that validated this Orientalist view of democratic development as a process that involves the civilising of those who 'through no fault of their own' lacked access to the received wisdom and confirmed experience of Western democracies. The 'problem' of radical populism that was manifested in various Western countries was worrying, of course, and the antics of Marine Le Pen or the US Tea Party could send shivers down the spine of civilised society, but Western elites were confident that ultimately these could be managed without too much difficulty. If the British advocates of a reimagined glorious Britannia free from the shackles of Brussels bureaucrats had started to disrupt right-wing politics in the UK, elites were still confident that citizens could be sold a stitched-up compromise that would keep them quiet for now. If Marine Le Pen's National Front was starting to win mayoralties in post-industrial France, a left–right alliance of decency would exclude it from national power. In the United States, the Tea Party was mainly a problem because it made the Republicans unelectable, so it was a cloud with a silver lining.

The Brexit vote of June 2016 certainly roiled Europe. Still, though, it could be put down to the insular peculiarity of the British and their failure to get over the loss of empire. But Donald Trump's victory in November's American election stopped liberals in their tracks. If the citadel of neoliberalism had fallen to an demagogue with a campaign built around scapegoating, something possibly serious might be up. The ease with which core Western institutions such as the European Union could be brought down, the readiness of large swathes of Western populations to support political ideas that directly contradict liberal 'fundamental values' on which the post–World War II order was constructed – accords like 1948's Universal Declaration of Human Rights – opens a gaping hole in the smooth certainty with which the democratic development discourse has been peddled in developing countries. And not before time.

The crisis of Western democracy revolves around the dilemma that is at the heart of any system of inclusive governance: how can different interests and perspectives be included in a situation that is inherently overdetermined, as Althusser (1967) put it? In other words, the variety of different social imaginaries in any society is so great and so diverse that they cannot all be entirely satisfied, while at the same time, resources are inherently finite. Democratic systems in a number of Western countries were able to manage these divergences and frictions through complex trade-offs reflected in temporary compromises made more durable through democratic institutional frameworks that provided voice to all (although never as equitably as pluralist models pretend). However, democracy practitioners rarely consider the advantages that Western countries have had: control of most global resources first through imperial domination and then through use of imperialism's accrued economic (and social and human) capital as well, often, of overwhelming military advantage. The wealth of the American system was built, first, on the subjugation of original peoples and the exploitation of the lands from where they had been cleared, and then in a next stage through the projection of the American economic model in the tank tracks of American military superiority.

The Tunisian transition is, by contrast, an example of a democratic transition that did not occur under the umbrella of some dominant power, was not driven by the conditionalities attached to participation in a supranational alliance such as the European Union and that successfully confronted deep cleavages within the population.

The Tunisian transition occurred through a dialogic process, but one that does not fit the presumptions of the classic Western model of dialogue as articulated particularly by Habermas. Neither, however, was the Tunisian process without structure; its success and even uniqueness derived from its ability to relentlessly challenge the limits of legitimate order, without crossing over into mutual destruction.

Conclusion

Despite the manifold roots of conflict and the underlying battle for hegemony between different groups and interests that underpins all state-building processes, throughout the Tunisian constitutional process, the more profane divergences were sublimated into a master narrative of secular versus religious social imaginaries, in which supporters of either narrative were characterised by the other as wicked, and thus ineligible to participate in democratic discourse.

At first glance, this existential battle around Islam and the state might appear far removed from the problems roiling Western societies; it is commonplace in Western accounts to perceive conflicts in Muslim societies as being special to those societies. But if we step back from a culturalist approach that essentialises religion as 'reason in and of itself' (an approach which presumably secularist thinkers should *a priori* reject), we can read the conflicts in Tunisia and in the core capitalist countries as deriving from the same problematic: the loss of social cohesion in societies that have been torn apart by a generation of market fetishism in which mutuality has been derided and individual enrichment lauded at the expense of the collective good. This ideology, neoliberalism in its essence, leads inherently to conflict and the breakdown of the welfare state that had under-pinned growth and stability in the West, as it also had in Tunisia.

Beyond providing an opportunity to highlight the considerable achievement of the Tunisian people in establishing a democratic order in less than favourable circumstances, this chapter also presents what could be called a subversion of Ori-entalism. Whereas the Orientalist developmentalist narrative presents the Other as fundamentally flawed and in need of correction, the Tunisian example emerges as one that symbolises not simply the triumph of democracy against adversity, but a path, a lesson, a model for Western nations, for so long the self-assured purvey-ors of development lessons. For, as discussed in the third section of this chapter, they are suddenly confronted with the collapse of the certainties of the post-war liberal order, the rise of populist authoritarianisms, the fracturing of state and transnational institutions and the promise of a new global arms race by the new demagogic president of the United States.

It has been argued in this chapter that the cleavages now being so sharply felt in the West are already well known in the developing world. Far from being the out-come of the defectiveness of the post-colonial (in need of fatherly correction by development institutions), the conflict and regime collapse that led to the 2011 Tunisian revolution derives from the same cause as the explosions of discontent that have been witnessed over the past few years in the developed societies, from Occupy Wall Street, Syriza and Podemos, through to Marine Le Pen, Brexit and Donald Trump. The cause, in short, is neoliberalism, a totalitarian ideology that spread like wildfire from the small Bolshevik-like cells of the Mont-Pelerin Soci-ety, Ayn Rand's Objectivism, and the Chicago School, until within a few years it had captured the interests and imaginations of elites internationally. Like every good idea, however, the West feels constrained to impose it insistently and puni-tively upon the Oriental Other, a pattern that extends back to forcible conver-sions to Christianity through to catastrophic colonial agricultural projects like the African groundnut scheme. Whereas the neoliberal medicine was introduced rela-tively cautiously in the West, with judicious backtracking when resistance became too strong such as was the case with Margaret Thatcher's 'poll tax' in Britain, the perceived untrustworthiness and incompetence of post-colonial governance required that the medicine be applied forcibly, a tactic that became possible as the Cold War ended and poor countries became dependent on Western sources for access to development capital.

With the possibility for looking back in international retrospective, the neolib-eral fantasy tends to follow a certain critical path. The dismantling of economic controls in statist development approaches often leads to a short-term economic boom, as profit-making opportunities attract foreign capital, and public wealth is transferred to the market typically at vastly discounted prices. In the short term, money washes into economies providing investment opportunities (and also effectively corrupting developing country elites by tempting them to convert their social capital into personal economic capital at the expense of their leader-ship legitimacy).

This is what happened in Tunisia. Under neoliberalism, overall economic growth indicators remained relatively strong through to the last few years of the Ben Ali regime, as was also the case in Egypt, the next Arab Spring country to explode. But behind the façade, resources were being funnelled into the pockets of the Ben Ali clan and entourage, while social and economic development projects were increasingly converted into patronage schemes and the opportunity in the case of infrastructure projects to squeeze further state funds through contracts tendered to cronies in return for kickbacks and the cover-up of shoddy cost-cutting delivery; roads that fall apart within a few years of the ribbon-cutting fanfare.

Post-colonial regimes like that of Tunisia hit the wall of the neoliberal contradiction sooner than Western regimes. There are simply fewer resources to nourish a supportive middle class, and the technologies of manufacturing consent are less developed and institutionalised. But the rapid rise of populist contestations, nationalist demagoguery and xenophobia in numerous Western countries suggests that the crisis of neoliberalism is generalised, and that we are entering the period of what Techau (2016) calls 'sophisticated state failure'. While the resources and technology available to wealthy states remain enormous, the network of governance institutions is broad and sophisticated, and the processes of formal democracy continue to function, the scope of alternatives provided within mainstream politics has narrowed to the extent that all mainstream politics is discredited, and an increasing proportion of citizens, if they do engage with the electoral system at all, select candidates they feel will blow up the system. The only way that this existential crisis can be overcome is for Western states to follow Tunisia's example, through embarking on a journey of inclusive social dialogue; not one mediated by elite-driven 'deliberative processes' that will always generate 'acceptable' conclusions, but one in which all may speak, and in which the only constraints are the common desire not to fall into the abyss.

Notes

1 Tawfik Ben Brik, 'La convocation', *Nouvel Observateur*, 15 May 2014, accessed at http://tempsreel.nouvelobs.com/monde/20140515.OBS7277/tunisie-la-convocation.html.

2 Reporters sans frontières, 'A quelques heures de la clôture du SMSI, le "Mouvement du 18 octobre" met un terme à sa grève de la faim', 18 November 2005, accessed at http://fr.rsf.org/tunisie-a-quelques-heures-de-la-cloture-du-18-11-2005, 15536.html.

3 Collectif 18 octobre à Paris Pour les Droits and les Libertés en Tunisie, 'Plate-forme politique pour une action commune', 2006, accessed at http://nachaz. org/index.php/fr/textes-a-l-appui/politique/102-2012-09-11-12-11-20.html.

4 Isabelle Mandraud, 'La Tunisie va connaître de vraies élections libres', *Le Monde*, 20 April 2011, accessed at www.lemonde.fr/tunisie/article/2011/04/20/la-tunisie-va-connaitre-de-vraies-elections-libres_1510254_1466522.html.

5 Hedia Barakhet, 'Tournée du "Cheikh" Nabil El Aouadhi – Ces prédicateurs qui nous divisent. . .', *La Presse*, 30 January 2013, accessed at http://fr.allafrica.com/ stories/201301300902.html.

6 After one notorious incident, secularist MPs insisted on the inclusion of a clause in the new constitution that makes it illegal to accuse someone of apostasy: 'Constitution tunisienne: l'opposition obtient l'interdiction de l'accusation d'apostasie', *Jeune Afrique*, 6 January 2014, accessed at www.jeuneafrique.com/Article/ ARTJAWEB20140106081515/.

7 'Tunisia's Ennahdha to oppose sharia in constitution', *Reuters*, 26 March 2012, accessed at www.reuters.com/assets/print?aid=USBRE82P0E820120326.

8 Sarah Diffalah, 'Les femmes seulement 'complémentaires' de l'homme ?', *Nouvel Observateur*, 9 August 2012, accessed at http://tempsreel.nouvelobs.com/ monde/20120809.OBS9325/tunisie-les-femmes-seulement-complementaires-de-l-homme.html.

9 Dominique Lagarde, 'Nous avons fait preuve d'un certain laxisme face aux salafistes', *L'Express*, 21 September 2012, accessed at www.lexpress.fr/actualite/ monde/afrique/tunisie-nous-avons-fait-preuve-d-un-certain-laxisme-face-aux-salafistes_1162293.html.

10 The UGTT trade union central, the UTICA employers' association, the Tunisian Human Rights League and the Tunisian Bar Association.

References

Adorno, T. W., Frenkel-Brunswik, E., Levinson, D. J. and Sanford, R. N. 1950. *The authoritarian personality*. New York: Harper and Row.

Althusser, L. 1967. Contradiction and over-determination. *New Left Review*, 41, 15–35.

Cooke, B. and Kothari, U. eds., 2001. *Participation: the new tyranny?* London: Zed Books.

Freire, P. 1970. *Pedagogy of the oppressed*. New York: Seabury.

Freire, P. 2005. *Pedagogy of the oppressed*. 30th anniversary edition. New York: The Continuum International Publishing Group Inc.

Habermas, J. 1975. *Legitimation crisis*. Boston, MA: Beacon Press.

Habermas, J. 1984. *The theory of communicative action. Volume I: Reason and the rationalization of society*. Boston, MA: Beacon Press.

Habermas, J. 1990. *Moral consciousness and communicative action*. Cambridge, MA: MIT Press.

Habermas, J. 1996. *Between facts and norms: contributions to a discourse theory of law and democracy*. Cambridge, MA: MIT Press.

Laclau, E. and Mouffe, C. 1985. *Hegemony and socialist strategy*. London: Verso.

Mamdani, M. 1996. *Citizen and subject: contemporary Africa and the legacy of late colonialism*. Princeton, NJ: Princeton University Press.

Moghaddam, F. M. 2013. *The psychology of dictatorship*. Washington, DC: American Psychological Association (APA).

Mouffe, C. 2013. *Agonistics: thinking the world politically*. London: Verso.

Techau, J. 2016. Sophisticated states are failing – politicians need to take risks. *Financial Times*, 16 April, accessed at www.ft.com/content/f519492e-022b-11e6-99cb-83242733f755.

Yousfi, H. 2015. *L'UGTT, une passion tunisienne. Enquête sur les syndicalistes en révolution (2011–2014)*. Paris: Karthala.

11 Theorising the state (or its absence?) in anti-corporate protest
Insights from post-colonial India

Nimruji Jammulamadaka and Biswatosh Saha

The door could soon be shut on Vedanta's mining plan in Niyamgiri. The Environment Ministry has decided that the claim of even one village council for cultural or religious rights over the hills provides the legal mandate to the Central government to reject the proposal under the Supreme Court orders.

(20 August 2013, *The Hindu*)

The National Green Tribunal (NGT) on Thursday cleared the way for OPG Power Ltd's 300 megawatt (MW) thermal power plant in [the] Kutch region of Gujarat. [. . .] The bench dismissed the appeal against the SEIAA decision, and slapped a fine of Rs 10,000 on the appellant for 'exhibiting continuous litigative mind' and doing so with 'impunity'. The bench said had the appellant not been a villager, they 'would have put a burden of heavy costs' on him.

(19 July 2013, *Down to Earth*)

These news reports capture the range of variation in responses to anti-corporate protest in India. The first pertains to the protest of an indigenous community against the Vedanta mining company on the east coast of India. This protest has also gone transnational and has seen recent success, as is evident from the Supreme Court judgement referred to earlier. The second report, as the administrative tribunal's ruling reveals, has had limited success. It pertains to a protest by a rural community against industrial activity on the Bhadreshwar coast of western India.

How does one make sense of these two diametrically opposite outcomes of anti-corporate protests? Sight of these conflicts played out every day in courts, corridors of government and the community (and brought into our homes through the television and newspapers) triggered a deep concern and pushed us towards making sense of these conflicting developments- success in one case and failure in another. This concern has occupied us for the past few years and as management and organisation studies (MOS) scholars teaching in a management school, we turned to the tools of our trade to make sense of this world around us. This chapter is an explication of our quest and the sense we have made so far in explaining these developments. Along the way we have discovered that anti-corporate protests in post-colonial states are not just protests against corporations in the light of the neoliberal turn of the state, but are also enactments seeking to decolonise the state that carries the legacy of the colonial moment. We share these reflections too with you.

We are deliberately writing this chapter as a narrative account, because it is not only difficult, but also morally impossible for us to isolate ourselves from these developments in the spirit of objective research. Not only do we live in the society that we are writing about, our life histories enabling us to relate to the worldviews of these communities who are being displaced, but we also belong to the tribe that actually teaches corporations how to manage themselves more profitably. Our narrative is organised as follows. We begin by briefly sketching the theoretical departure points and method of our exploration, followed by a brief description of the two anti-corporate protests that form the substance of this exploration. We then engage with the findings, at which point our reflexivity and post-colonial sensibility come forth. From here on, we shift gears and, following a critical hermeneutic approach, venture into a deeper engagement with context and history in locating these two protests. Our journey finally brings us to a realisation of the role of anti-corporate protest in the foment of post-colonial state-building. We conclude by highlighting the peculiar condition of the post-colonial state and its political opportunity structure.

Theoretical departure points

Studies of social movements (SM) (understood as those directed against the state) coming from the discipline of sociology had initially focused on explaining the conditions under which movements and mobilisation occur, especially the nature of the state that impacts mobilisation (Eisinger, 1973; Tilly, 1978; Kitschelt, 1986; Kriesi et al., 1995). The state has been characterised as either open or closed under the rubric 'political opportunity structure' (POS). This rubric has expanded to include social, political, legal and economic aspects of society (Costain, 1992; Marks and McAdam, 1996; Wilson and Cordero (2006). *'Political opportunity theory is explicitly concerned with predicting variance in the periodicity, content and outcomes of activist efforts over time across different institutional contexts'* (Meyer, 2004). Further, factors which influence mobilisation can also influence movement outcomes (Amenta et al., 2010). Arguing that states and SM affect each other recursively, Amenta and colleagues' (2010) review of research highlights resource mobilisation and mobilising structures, framing strategies and political opportunities as the key determinants that impact SM outcomes. Research finds a curvilinear relationship between openness of the state and the ability to mobilise, the argument being that open structures provide enough channels to voice discontent and thereby preclude effective mobilisation (Meyer, 2004).

MOS has engaged closely with SM studies (Davis et al., 2005); beginning with resource mobilisation theory (Zald and McCarthy, 1987; Edwards and McCarthy, 2004), more contemporary efforts have focused on explaining questions within MOS using SM concepts. Such research appears to have taken two directions. The first direction has focused on explaining the emergence of new industries and the adoption of management practices through an SM lens (Rao et al., 2000; Schneiberg and Soule, 2005; Walker and Rea, 2014). The second direction has sought to understand the shift of target of SM from the state to the corporation (Van Dyke et al., 2004; King and Pearce, 2010; Soule, 2012; de Bakker et al., 2013). This work has argued that the global spread of neoliberalism (Centeno and Cohen, 2012) has weakened states (Smith and Fetner, 2010) and made corporations powerful, thus directing SM against corporations and corporate irresponsibility (King and Pearce, 2010). Studies of anti-corporate protests have shown how protests impact corporations' internal policies and behaviour (Den Hond and Bakker, 2007; King, 2007; King and Soule, 2007; Weber et al., 2009; Quellier, 2013). Studies have looked at resources and mobilisation by anti-corporate protests (Keck and Sikkink, 1998; Haug, 2013; Yaziji and Doh, 2013;Della Porta and Tarrow (2004)). Environmental protests have been identified as an important sub-set of such anti-corporate protests (Banerjee, 2008, 2011; Özen and Özen, 2009; Hieneman-Piper, 2011; O'Brien, 2012; Kraemer et al., 2013; Bertels et al., 2014). This sub-set of studies has pointed to state repression as a key issue impacting POS of anti-corporate protest. Literature on such protests in the developing world has suggested that they seek to influence action through national and international solidarity and alliance building. The ideas of 'translocal resistance' (Banerjee, 2011) and the 'boomerang model' (Keck and Sikkink, 1998; Kraemer et al., 2013) are developments in this line. The boomerang model has become particularly important given that societies in nation-states of the periphery within the core–periphery divide are seen as weak or ineffective at mobilizing SM (due to state repression); peripheral states are also conceived as increasingly ineffective in the face of globalisation (Smith and Fetner, 2010). Versions of the boomerang model point out that in addition to solidarity, international activist partners provide material resources and 'much needed' exposure for local protests globally thereby influencing power-holders located in the global North and through them indirectly those in the South (Smith and Fetner, 2010). These international pressures interact with and complement national factors and influence movement success (Kraemer et al., 2013).

These studies on anti-corporate protest, especially on the environment, offer us a useful departure point. With these background understandings of the weakened state, the role of transnational and national advocacy networks in shaping movement outcomes and, taking a cue from the SM literature which has identified mobilisation, framing and POS as the key elements impacting movement outcomes (McAdam et al., 2003; Amenta et al., 2010), we venture into an exploration of protests by the Dongria-Kondh community of Niyamgiri against Vedanta and the fishing and farming community of Bhadreshwar-Mundhra against Adani.

A brief note on the method

The two anti-corporate protests that we have examined are the one against Vedanta in Niyamgiri and the one against Adani in Bhadreshwar-Mundhra. It intuitively appeared to be a good idea to look at them comparatively, when we began studying them in 2009. We discovered both of them around the same time (end of 2008), one as a member of a mailing list of concerned citizens, and the other as a member of the alumni of a school. In both these mails, the people at the forefront of the protests had written about their struggles to mobilise support. In both cases, company operations and public protest began around the same time. Both had enormous ecological and human consequences. These two sites are on either side (east and west) of the country. Both sites offered several locational advantages to the firms in question. The Niyamgiri hill has high-quality bauxite deposits and Vedanta expected the cost of mining and processing bauxite in India to be much lower compared to other parts of the world. Similarly, the Mundhra coast is well suited for a port (Adani's plan) and has in fact been one for centuries. Thus the two protests seemed highly comparable.

In 2009, when we first began observing them, the outcomes of these protests were unclear. As we write, outcomes in the case of Niyamgiri are in favour of protestors, and in the case of Mundhra, the outcomes appear to be going against the protestors or seem far away in the future and unclear. Our data comprise nine different sources: press reports, reports of activist groups, emails from advocacy groups, websites, annual reports and other company publications, websites of activist groups and challenger groups, government ministry documents related to these projects, the government pollution control board's documents on these projects, reports of court decisions, legal documents from the beginning of these protests until 2013. In all more than 250 different types of documents were examined, some of the documents ran into several hundred pages. For the anti-Adani protest, data were initially quite sketchy, so key protest leaders were contacted to confirm our assessments derived from published reports. We have also actively observed the struggle unfolding in the media over the past five years. Our data collection, analysis and literature review was an ongoing reflexive process over a period of three to four years. In analysing the data, we first prepared detailed descriptions of the two protests and established basic facts about the two. We adopted the structured focused comparison approach to comparing cases[1] described by George and Bennett (1979)George and Bennett (2005). According to this approach, '*questions asked of each case must be of a general nature; they should not be couched in overly specific terms that are relevant to only one case but should be applicable to all [. . .] subclass of events with which the study is concerned*' (p. 86). This method also requires adequate theoretical preparation to generate and evaluate various alternate hypotheses satisfactorily (George and Bennett, 2005; Bennett, 2010; Collier, 2011). As suggested, the process-tracing technique has been used in evaluating the data collected. Process tracing '*is defined as the systematic examination of diagnostic evidence selected and analysed in light of research questions and hypotheses posed by the investigator*' (Collier, 2011: 823). Unlike grounded theory approaches, where there is an emphasis on coding and theme generation, process tracing involves investigating data for clues to establish causal inferences and to discard alternate explanations (Bennett, 2010; Collier, 2011). We therefore developed various alternate explanations from existing literature on anti-corporate SM and teased them within the data to examine the effectiveness of these explanations. In developing these explanations, we asked general questions about alliances, framing, protest tactics, strategies and mobilisation for each protest and carefully evaluated explanations and accumulating support for arriving at our inference.

Background to the two protests

Against Vedanta at Niyamgiri

Niyamgiri is a hill on the east coast of India in the state of Odisha. It is home to around 7,000 people of the endangered indigenous community known as Dongria-Kondhs. The hill is a site of religious significance for them. Vedanta Alumina Limited (VAL), headquartered in London, embarked on a massive $2 billion plan to establish the world's largest integrated alumina mining and refining complex with mining at Niyamgiri. In June 2002, the district administration began the process for land acquisition, wherein during public hearings, the villagers explicitly asked for the project's cancellation. Thus began the struggle against VAL by the people of Niyamgiri (see Table 11.1 for basic details of the protest). Their struggle coincided with the presence of various national and international NGOs

Table 11.1 Basic details of the anti-Vedanta and anti-Adani protests

	Anti-Adani	Anti-Vedanta
Location	The coast of the Mundhra region in the Kutch district on the western coast of India	Niyamgiri Hill in the Eastern Ghats mountain range on the east coast of India
Nature of the project	India's largest private port and Special Economic Zone (SEZ) for industries, special focus on thermal power generation plants	World's largest Integrated Alumina mining and refining project
Name of the key firm	Adani Port and SEZ Limited (APSEZL)	Vedanta Alumina Limited (VAL)
Other firms involved	Yes, several other companies which are located inside the SEZ	No, only VAL
Location of key firm's headquarters	India	London, UK
Value of the project	$ 1.6 billion US	$ 2 billion US
Total area	approximately 6,500 hectares currently	approximately 1,500 hectares
First licence issuance	in early 1990s to Adani for salt making	in 1997 to Sterlite for mining

	Anti-Adani	Anti-Vedanta
Official assessment of displacement	land acquired from 14 villages, several hectares of coastal area	12 villages affected, 60 villages to be relocated
Ecological features to be impacted	Marine National Park, Mangrove forests	Protected Wildlife Sanctuary and Elephant Corridor
Environmental impact	Sea pollution, destruction of fishing habitat, mangrove coastline, farmlands, salination of farmlands, deposition of fly ash, threat of extinction of endangered species of corals and other marine life listed in IUCN red data book	River pollution, leaching of minerals into the soil, threat of extinction to endangered species listed in IUCN red data book
Size of community affected	8,000–10,000 fisherfolk, about 15,000 salt making workers in addition to peasants	7,000 approximately
Nature of community getting affected	Farmers, herdsmen, fisherfolk, salt pan workers	An indigenous group called Dongria-Kondh Dongria-Kondhs (hill dwellers)
Does policy prohibit such industrial and economic activity in these locations?	Yes (Coastal Regulation Zone)	Yes (Forest Act)
Is environmental clearance required?	Yes	Yes
Protests began from	2005	2002
Protest organisation of the affected	Machimar Adhikar Sangharsh Sangathan (MASS)	Niyamgiri Suraksha Samiti (NSS)

in the nearby areas working on different projects. Informed and assisted by these NGOs, the indigenous community formed an organisation called the Niyamgiri Suraksha Samiti (NSS) to focus its protest.

Against Adani at Mundhra

The Bhadreshwar–Mundhra coast, with its extensive mangrove forests, rich corals and fisheries on the western coast of India in the state of Gujarat, has been home to a thriving community of fisherfolk, farmers and salt workers. In 1995, the Adani conglomerate secured a licence from the Ministry of Environment and Forest (MOEF) to set up a port for handling general cargo and petroleum products and began commercial operations. APSEZL (Adani) announced plans for a $1.6 billion[2] investment to develop the Mundhra area into the largest private port in India as a Special Economic Zone (SEZ). In addition to Adani's power plant, 10 other companies were setting up power plants in this SEZ. The multi-product SEZ project was planned over 13,500 hectares, with 6,473 hectares under current operations. While there was general discontent with Adani's activities amongst the community, it was after the SEZ came into effect in 2005 and the government of Gujarat transferred several thousands of hectares of common land to Adani for the development of the project that serious protests emerged (see Table 11.1). The local fishing communities were adversely impacted by these developments because their access to the sea was cut off and the quality of their catch suffered. They were also displaced. They formed the Macchimar Adhikar Sangharsh Sangathan (MASS) in 2007 to fight against Adani. Grazing lands from 14 villages were acquired for the SEZ and the villagers were protesting against the acquisition.

Comparing the two cases: initial explanations

We began our examination of the two cases using the framework of POS (Kriesi, 2004; Meyer, 2004) and the adjusted and elaborated boomerang model proposed in the context of the anti-Vedanta movement by Kraemer and colleagues (2013). Meyer explains POS as '*exogenous factors [that] enhance or inhibit a social movement's prospects for (a) mobilizing, (b) advancing particular claims rather than others, (c) cultivating some alliances rather than others, and (d) employing particular political strategies and tactics rather than others, and (e) affecting mainstream institutional politics and policy*' (2004: 126). An examination of the data for the first parameter of mobilising reveals that in both cases, mobilisation ran into thousands of protestors showing that there was legitimacy accorded to both movements in the respective communities.

In both cases (see Table 11.2), there was opportunity for public protest, but there was also the absence of protection for the life of protestors. Since both protests were located within one country, we felt that the political culture of state repression or its absence would be common to both. Demographically, whereas anti-Vedanta protestors belonged to a single ethnically homogenous indigenous community (since only this group was affected), anti-Adani protestors belonged to diverse rural communities of fisherfolk, salt pan workers, cattle herders and farmers. Indigenous protests, including armed insurgency against industrial activity, have been on for more than 150 years in the eastern parts of India (Guha, 1989; Damodaran, 2006); if this demographic characteristic was the cause, several tribal protests should also have met with success. However, most such protests have not achieved their goals, including other protests in Odisha itself. Therefore, we felt that demographic difference was an insufficient explanation for outcome differences. Further, the two cases of mobilisation appear to have drawn

Table 11.2 Comparison of the anti-Vedanta and anti-Adani protests

	Adani	*Vedanta*
Legal means of protest		
Cases in High Court and SC	Village *panchayats*, MASS 2010 onwards	Wildlife Society of Orissa, Lokshakti Abhiyan, Academy of Mountain Environics in late 2004 in the Supreme Court
Representations to district collectors*	Yes	Yes
Representations to State Pollution Control Board, state authorities*	Yes	Yes
Representations to MOEF*	Yes	Yes
Protest Tactics		
Local protest tactics*	local demonstrations with thousands participating, sit-ins, one lasted 32 days to gain access road to sea for fishing	local demonstrations with thousands participating, sit-ins, blockades
Disruption of annual meetings	No	Yes, in London
Divestment by international investors	No	Yes, Joseph Rowntree Charitable Trust in 2010, Church of England in 2010, Norwegian Pension Funds in 2007 among others
Networking		
Key organisation	MASS trade union of fisherfolk	NSS organisation of the indigenous people
National alliances	Local: KNNA, Others: Fishing groups in India like Fishmarc, NAPM, Groups Against SEZs	Local: LSA, Academy of Mountain Environics, Orissa Wild Life Society, Others: NAPM, MMP, Indigenous Rights groups,
International alliances	No, one-page rap sheet on Adani by Greenpeace	Yes, Greenpeace, Amnesty International, Oxfam, Human Rights Watch, ActionAid, Survival International. Several international campaigns, documentaries, reporting and funding

(*Continued*)

Table 11.2 (Continued)

	Adani	*Vedanta*
Nature of claims made: framing		
Frame A	Adverse lifestyle impact: Centuries-old, traditional, foot-based fishing practices being destroyed	Adverse lifestyle impact: Centuries-old indigenous culture being destroyed
Frame B	Adverse impact on livelihoods, displacement: fisherfolk, salt workers, cattle herders, farmers' livelihoods are suffering. Direct cause – land acquisition; Indirect case-ecological destruction	Adverse impact on livelihoods and displacement: Centuries-old forest dwelling livelihoods suffering due to ecological damage
Frame C	Adverse impact on environment. Destruction of mangroves, coral reefs, intertidal zone, salination of land and air pollution	Adverse impact on environment. Destruction of watersheds, soil, water and air pollution
Frame D	These communities are not recognised as indigenous. As rural communities did not have an analogous claim to that found in the anti-Vedanta case	As violation of indigenous community rights: Dongria-Kondhs recognised as an indigenous community in India
Frame E:	Violation of traditional rights of fisherfolk and salt pan workers	Violation of traditional rights of communities living in the forest
Wider awareness (no. of articles, coverage examined from 1 March 2004 to 1 March 2014)	key words used: Adani, Mundhra, protest	key words used: Vedanta, Niyamgiri, protest
Sympathetic news media *Down to Earth* magazine	50, 2007 onwards	150, 2005 onwards
General news media *The Hindu*: progressive national daily	1, 3 articles, keywords: Adani, Sunita Narain committee	2006 onwards. 60
The Economic Times: a national business daily	0	32

	Adani	*Vedanta*
The Times of India: a national daily	0	21
India Today: a national news magazine	0	2010 onwards, 15
Political openness in the federal structure		
Centre–state relations	Centre–state coordination for pollution control. Land acquisition a state issue.	Centre–state coordination for pollution control. Land acquisition a state issue.
Party at centre	Congress	Congress
Party in the state	BJP (a national-level party opposed to Congress)	BJD (a state-level party opposed to Congress)
Nature of centre–state political party relations	Gujarat: BJP in power, Congress in opposition for past several years. State government sponsored project actively	Odisha: BJD in power, Congress in opposition for last several years. State government sponsored project actively
State Repression		
Fear of life, lack of protection from state for perceived threats to life of protestors	Yes. Some activists killed under suspicious circumstances	Yes. Some activists killed under suspicious circumstances.
Freedom to assemble and blockade	Yes. On occasion police restricted assemblies.	Yes. On occasion police restricted assemblies.
Backdrop of armed conflict	No	Yes. Rampant Maoist insurgency
Affecting mainstream institutional politics	No electoral impact. One ruling party elected representative (MLA) expressed public support.	Became an electoral issue with Congress rallies in the area. Rahul Gandhi, a key Congress leader led rallies

* We have tried to compute the number of representations and local protests. Due to incomplete coverage of such events by news media, our computations would have been inaccurate. Hence we only examined for presence or absence of the mechanism and not intensity of use.

from the same popular ethic and collective memory of protesting for justice existing in India. India has had several hundred years of history of mobilising against authority both by peasants and indigenous groups (Shah, 1990, 2002; Oommen, 2010a, 2010b).

Our data examination for the second parameter of POS 'advancing of particular claims' revealed that both protests were making substantially similar claims as similar framing strategies were being used (see Table 11.2, section on frames). The anti-Vedanta protest differed on one count, Frame D (see Table 11.2). It framed their struggle as one for the protection of indigenous rights. This was an observation we could not dismiss easily, so holding on to it as part of a 'preliminary explanation',[3] we explored the third parameter, 'nature of alliances'. Our analysis (see Table 11.2) suggested significant differences in the alliances and networks in use in the two protests. Whereas the anti-Adani protest was characterised by national networks and alliances, the anti-Vedanta movement had, in addition to the national networks and alliances, a very strong presence of international human rights and environmental advocacy groups. Extensive lobbying and demonstrations by these transnational advocacy groups (TAGs) outside India even led to divestments from Vedanta citing 'abuse of human rights of indigenous people'. Even signature campaigns directed at the president and prime minister of India were organised by these TAGs. Support of TAGs and the framing of the issue as 'human rights of indigenous groups' appeared to be the second element working in favour of the anti-Vedanta protest. This strengthened our 'preliminary explanation'. Moving to the next parameter of POS, i.e., 'particular political strategies and tactics employed', we could see from the data that both protests were using protest marches, demonstrations, sit-ins, blockades, research reports, filing court cases, submitting memoranda and representations to the government. In addition, anti-Vedanta protests were using two other protest tactics – disruption of annual board meetings in London and pressuring ethical investors to divest from Vedanta. These two tactics again used the 'indigenous rights' frame. Given the federal structure and multi-party politics of India, we also examined the role of the government in power at the federal centre and in the states of Odisha and Gujarat. As explained in Table 11.2, in both cases, land acquisition was a subnational (provincial) matter and thus if electoral inter-party rivalry had to be influencing protest outcomes, then the outcome should have been more favourable to the anti-Adani struggle since the BJP (Bharatiya Janata Party), the ruling party in Gujarat, was a national-level party as compared to the BJD (Biju Janata Dal) in Odisha, which was only a regional party. BJP was a bigger electoral threat to Congress which was in power at the centre in Delhi. Since the anti-Adani protest did not have any such favourable outcome, this explanation was discarded and thus at this juncture, it appeared that our data was pointing towards a confirmation of the 'elaborated boomerang model' discussed in the literature. With this accumulating confirmatory evidence, we moved to examine the last parameter for assessing POS i.e., 'affecting mainstream institutional politics'. Prima facie, our data showed that the anti-Vedanta protest had become an electoral issue and the ruling Congress party was organizing rallies in the area (Table 11.2). No such actions were seen in the anti-Adani protest. We also assessed popular interest in the protests through newspaper reports in key national dailies in India (Table 11.2). The data showed an absolute lack of coverage in popular press for anti-Adani protests, whereas the anti-Vedanta struggle had received substantial coverage. Coverage of anti-Adani protests was limited to some sympathetic outlets like the magazine *Down to Earth* published by the environmental organisation Centre for Science and Environment. This stark difference provided further support to our 'preliminary explanation', and we reasoned that the TAGs' framing of the anti-Vedanta protest as 'indigenous rights' had brought it high visibility, more resources, electoral interest and, finally, better outcomes at Niyamgiri.

It appeared that the absence of TAG support in the anti-Adani protest was the key factor that could be contributing to poor outcomes. But we still needed to explain the reasons for the absence of TAG support in the anti-Adani protest from within the boomerang framework to accept this 'preliminary explanation'.

Literature on the TAG's corporate targets suggests that MNCs with strong images, reputations to protect and leadership positions make for productive targets of anti-corporate campaigns because they bring focus to the whole sector (Lund-Thomsen and Nadvi, 2010; King and Pearce, 2010). Adani was a company headquartered in India as against Vedanta, which was headquartered in London.[4] Thus, it appeared logical that Vedanta provided a target with high visibility as against Adani for TAGs. For an anti-mining protest like anti-Vedanta, one could have allied with all the anti-mining protests globally, whereas Adani was a regular case of land acquisition and thus presented limited opportunities for transnationalisation of the protest or its 'externalisation' (Dellaporta and Tarrow, 2004). The rural fishing and farming communities of Mundhra, unlike the Dongria-Kondhs, did not present an opportunity to use the 'indigenous rights' frame due to their peasant status. The people of Mundhra would not have made good demonstration specimens (representatives of Dongria-Kondhs dressed in all their tribal regalia were paraded in front of corporate and government offices) at annual general meetings, a tactic the TAGs were using actively in the Niyamgiri case to buttress their 'indigenous rights' frame. They had also orchestrated 'tribal festivities' for this purpose.[5]

Our preliminary explanation of the boomerang impact of TAGs now received greater support because we were not only able to observe how it benefitted the anti-Vedanta protest, but also to establish why the anti-Adani protest could not have had TAG support. The analysis until now confirmed TAG support as the crucial factor whose presence appeared to lead to beneficial outcomes in the anti-Vedanta protest and whose absence seemed to suggest poor outcomes for the anti-Adani protest. This factor offered a comfortable fit with existing literature and therefore we decided to accept this as the explanation for our quest.

Despondency of the once-colonised: the effect of location

While we felt compelled to accept this explanation, we could not get over a deep sense of anguish and despondency. We remained disturbed because if we as free citizens could not influence our own democratically elected government and needed outside support which was unpredictable and likely unavailable in most cases,[6] what kind of democracy were we in? What did our independence mean, was this really *swaraj*? Our discontentment found resonance in the work of decolonial theorist Walter Mignolo. Writing about 'post-occidental reason' Mignolo says *'the possibilities of theorizing colonial legacies could be carried out in different directions: from a strictly disciplinary location [. . .] finally, from the site of someone for whom colonial legacies are entrenched in his or her own history and sensibility'* (2000: 111). He suggests *'de-linking'* as the strategy through which the epistemic and spatial breaks necessary in process of *'theorizing from the colonial sensibility'* are effected. 'De-linking' stems from a recognition of geopolitical and historical conditions of coloniality and the experience of the colonised as not only fundamentally different from but also constituted by Eurocentric modernity (Mignolo, 2000, 2005, 2006). This recognition involves not positing a linearity of progress that denies coevalness using *colonial difference*, but accepting the '*other*' as different from a '*paradigm of coexistence*' (Mignolo, 2005, 2006). Conceptually, 'de-linking' firstly involves '*detaching from the rules of Eurocentric knowledge*' and secondly, '*bringing into existence new and distinct politics of knowledge/understanding*' from the experience of coloniality (2006: 18). 'De-linking', however, does not mean discarding Eurocentric knowledge; instead, it is about simultaneously maintaining respect for and effectuating departures from such knowledge (2006: 6–7). Thus, inspired by the possibilities of actively engaging with our discontentment, we felt obligated to revisit our data, not limiting ourselves to the '*disciplinary perspective*' (following Mignolo, 2000: 111), but from the perspective of our collective lived experience of the post-colonial[8] condition.

Empirical pointers to location's relevance

Our first observation was of the deep divergence in the framing of the anti-Vedanta protest as 'indigenous rights' by the TAGs and 'as a case of environmental violations and abuse' within India. All the interventions which stopped Vedanta's operations on one hand and supported the local community on the other were coming from MOEF, not the ministry of tribal affairs (except after the final judgement). Secondly, our analysis of the course of events on the ground at Niyamgiri following the TAG campaign against Vedanta leading up to divestments showed that it had limited ground-level impact. The divestments did not halt Vedanta's construction plans. While divestments were happening, Vedanta had completed construction and started operations. Even the share prices of Vedanta had not suffered severely during that period.[9] At Mundhra, there was hardly any attempt to engage with shareholders even by the domestic activist community. It probably might not have seemed like a meaningful tactic given our discovery of its uncertain contribution to movement outcomes at the ground level. A third divergence was in the locus of the decision; while the TAGs directed signed petitions to elected representatives (legislature), hoisting them as the locus of decision-making, the actual decisions on the ground were being made by the courts (judiciary) and government departments (executive).

These divergences told us that something more was happening and that the differential protest outcomes in the two cases were not exclusively due to TAG support. The TAGs' involvement might have helped the Dongria-Kondhs in some way, but it definitely could not be the sole reason. Setting aside the role of TAGs as the differentiator, we decided to further explore the role of courts and government administrative departments where the actual decisions were being made, i.e., the state. To inform ourselves conceptually, we went back to the literature on SM, but this time instead of focusing on anti-corporate protests, we broadened our horizon to include aspects of state and law. Amenta and colleagues (2002), suggest conceptualising the state as constituted by various arms like bureaucracy, policy, legislation and elected representation instead of as a monolith, to develop nuanced explanations of opportunity structures for SM. Other studies have highlighted the growing importance of courts in securing SM outcomes through the legal opportunity structure in a wide range of SM ranging from anti-nuclear protests to movements around employment and disability rights (Epp, 1998; Hilson, 2002; Pedriana, 2006; Wilson and Cordero, 2006). After this review, we found ourselves in a paradoxical situation; on one hand viewing the state as neoliberal, weak and ineffective and on the other seeing it as a powerful site for sustained claim making. We crawled our way out of this paradox by deploying '*de-linking*' following Mignolo. A recent review in the *Annual Review of Sociology* finds that '*current discussions of postcolonial sociology question the applicability of Western social scientific concepts and theories to the global South*' (Steinmetz, 2014: 77).

Postcolonial state

We therefore decided to examine the 'postcolonial state' and not the state as such. Postcolonial political scientists examining South Asia have argued that the state in the post-colonial condition is not a direct outcome of an ascendant bourgeoisie, but an imperial implant (Alavi, 1973) and therefore the state (which has a highly developed bureaucratic machinery that predates colonial transfer of power at independence) is autonomous from class capture and becomes the site of intense negotiations of different class interests through passive revolution (Alavi, 1973; Kumar, 2005; Kaviraj, 2010; Chatterjee, 2011). '*The characteristic feature [. . .] in India [was] the relative autonomy of the state as [a] whole from the bourgeoisie and the landed elites; the supervision of the state by an elected political leadership, permanent bureaucracy, and an independent judiciary*' (Chatterjee, 2011: 217). Partha Chatterjee (2011) suggests that in the Indian post-colony, the state is far from neoliberal. He says the Indian state has sought to attenuate the ill effects of state-supported primitive accumulation and therefore donned a developmental and welfare role. A regime of governmentality is in vogue where the state manages populations through disbursing welfare; '*[C]ontrary to those who argue that the state, in its recent neoliberal heartlessness, has withdrawn from the welfare role [. . .] its arms, bearing the instruments of coercion as well as of looking after populations, are now able to reach more corners of the territory and more sections of the people than any formal governmental structure has ever done in Indian history*' (Chatterjee, 2011: 92–93).

Revisiting our method

With the comfort that this conceptualisation of the post-colonial state provided for us, we realised that our method too would have to be revised to incorporate these contexts in detail. We therefore adopted from this stage on in our quest the critical hermeneutics approach, which provides an '*interpretive approach for understanding texts*' (Prasad, 2002: 12, 2005; Prasad and Mir, 2002; Gopinath and Prasad, 2013). Contemporary hermeneutic analysis regards not just written documents, but *'social and economic practices, culture and cultural artifacts, institutional activities and structures and so on'* as texts (Ricouer, 1971, cited in Prasad, 2002). Thus, we regarded the two anti-corporate protests as the *'text'* we were seeking to understand. In the hermeneutic method, the *'text'* exists in a relationship with its *'context'* (Phillips and Brown, 1993), and an understanding of the *'text'* therefore moves along *'multiple levels of comprehensiveness and in so doing work[s] towards expanding and broadening our own hermeneutic horizons'* (Gopinath and Prasad, 2013: 12). The expanding levels of the *'context'* in which our *'protest text'* was located, were identified as the immediate legal and bureaucratic framework impinging on the two protests and the wider national struggles against land acquisition. Hermeneutical analysis also invokes an engagement with history as a part of the *'context'*. Therefore, we examined the historical backdrop of environmental conflict and judicial activism in India. Interpretation in the hermeneutic approach involves constantly moving between the whole and the part, the text and the context, through the researcher's own situatedness through a dialogue with the text. For providing a critical perspective to the interpretive act of *'moving between the context and the text'*, we relied on post-colonial theory as it is aligned with our historical situatedness and ethico-political sensibilities. In revising our method, we did not disregard the findings of structured focused comparison of the two cases done so far, but added on to this core by emphasising two more aspects: a) the legal and government angle and b) the geopolitical and colonial history.

Discovering the data again: location leads us to law

Upon realising that the MOEF was making the decisions, we explored this in greater detail. Environment clearances were required by both companies. Legally mandated environment impact assessments (EIA) submitted by the firms in both cases were problematic. Yet, MOEF was far clearer in denying clearance to Vedanta citing violations, whereas it permitted Adani with some riders on conservation and protection of livelihoods. What could explain this divergence on seemingly similar issues? Quickly we noticed that the MOEF's correspondence with state governments, firms and other interested parties – whether autonomous scientific agencies or even activists – was not on its own accord, but pursuant to the implementation of various court pronouncements. So, we explored the legal dimension further. At both Niyamgiri and Mundhra, filing public interest litigations (PILs) and writs in the court on behalf of the community was one of the first things done. Multiple suits had been filed and counter filed by the protestors and the companies.[10] Court decisions impacted the ebbs and flows of protest strategies. While the Vedanta project was permitted initially even after environmental violations with directives to spend on CSR in the verdict on the first PIL filed in late 2004, the subsequent appeals (made in 2008) under the Forest Rights Act (FRA) went in favour of the Kondhs (see opening quote). The first set of PILs in the Mundhra case challenged the acquisition of 1,000 acres of common grazing land from the Zarpara village (*Alabhai vs. State*). The villagers argued that their *gramsabha* (village council) had unanimously rejected such acquisition, and that the *sarpanch* (elected village head) had surreptitiously signed over the land. The High Court (HC) ruled against the village community and held that '*the Collector resumed the land in the Government which was hitherto allotted to Panchayat for its Gauchar purposes* [. . .] *Sarpanch got the resolution passed without following proper procedure. We cannot accept this objection for a variety of reasons.*' HC held that the proper procedure provided in the 1894 Land Acquisition Act[11] and the 2004 SEZ Act for government resuming possession of lands vested in the village had been followed as there was nothing on record to the contrary. The Supreme Court (SC) upheld this verdict. Examination of both the protest judgements revealed that different Acts were being applied to the two cases, and their outcomes emerged as different.

What were these different laws? Well, the Niyamgiri hills and the Dongria-Kondhs were covered under Schedule V of the Constitution of India, the *Samata* judgement and also the Forest Rights Act of 2006. The basic provision of special status, i.e., Schedule V, was a creation of the colonial British administration. It was created to quell tribal rebellion against the British for felling trees and dispossessing tribals of their forests. According to this provision, indigenous land cannot be sold to a non-indigenous person. Subsequently, the Forest Rights Act enacted in 2006 broadened the scope to include those depending on forests and also incorporated *gramsabha* as the body that decided on the collective rights of the community. The state's eminent domain had a limited sway here. In Mundhra, however, the Land Acquisition Act of 1894 and the SEZ Act of 2005 among others were being used. The 1894 Act, a British creation based on the principle of the state's eminent domain for acquiring land for 'public purpose', laid out an administrative procedure for completing the acquisition. Basically, the 1894 Act did not recognise any 'rights' of local village communities to their lands. A contest by landowners (*gramsabha* and village community had no *locus standi*) was possible only with regards to procedure. Amendments to the Act after independence brought in compensation and expanded the scope of 'public purpose' to include land acquired for private industry. The SEZ Act built on this and, in line with the global turn to neoliberalism, explicitly stated the state's right to acquire lands for private industrial and economic development and listed a slew of fiscal and other benefits to be passed on to the large corporate sector.

With the *gramsabha*'s 'rights-based claim' not finding acceptance in courts due to the absence of a constitutional basis, the anti-Adani protest entered into a strategy of legal entanglement. Several writs, PILs and complaints were filed with courts, quasi-juridical authorities and bureaucratic departments (see Table 11.3 for details) on matters of procedure, violation of rules and directives. The creation of the National Green Tribunal provided a new and timely forum to make more nuanced appeals. Each of these led to commissioning delays in the project. This strategy produced modest gains in the form of government mandating a fresh EIA for project expansion; one of the power plants, OPG, changed its technology to a less polluting one. This legal entanglement also triggered a process

Table 11.3 Indicative list of appeals made in the anti-Adani protests

Type of Appeal	Body to which Appeal Was Made	Appeal Against	Appeal Made by	Nature of Appeal	When
PIL	High Court	Adani SEZ, state and central govt.	Shiracha villagers	violation of procedure	1st June 2013
PIL objection at environmental hearing	High Court pollution board	SEZ, Centre SEZ	Navinal villagers Tunda villagers	violating procedure impact on people, env.	1st June 2013 1st July 2013
PIL	High Court	SEZ, port	Navinal villagers	adverse impact environment	1st May 2013
PIL	High Court	SEZ, state,	Zarpara villagers	violation of procedure, violation of rights/ justice	22nd Jun 2011
Writ Written appeal	High Court District collector	12 companies OPG, Adani, Tata, SEZ	Navinal villagers fisherfolk, salt pan workers, farmers	violation of procedure adverse impact on livelihoods, environment	early 2012
PIL	High Court	Gujarat govt.	Navinal villagers	adverse impact, violation of rights/justice	1st February 2011
Complaint Memorandum	SEIAA District Collector	Pollution Board SEZ	Husain villager villagers and fisherfolk	violation of procedure against land acquisition	1st May 2012 2004

Source: compiled by authors from newspaper reports and other protest documents of dialogue and negotiation outside the courts between the communities and the companies. OPG's technology change could be attributed to some of these negotiations.

The context

Broader struggles against land acquisition

Indeed, the protesters against Adani were aware of the legal difference and built solidarity with other anti-land acquisition struggles, especially those against SEZs happening all over the country. Wide protest and legal entanglements had severely constrained SEZ functioning in India. Government data show that of the 436 SEZs which had received formal approval until March 2015, only 199 are operational and a total of only 3,937 firms are working there. While more than 2 *lakh* hectares were to be acquired for all SEZs (Singla et al., 2011), as per government's SEZ website about 53,000 hectares of land has been acquired by 2015.[12] The constitutional validity of the SEZ Act itself has been challenged in the courts. Government took cognizance of the simmering discontent towards these policies. '*Land acquisition for Special Economic Zones (SEZ) has given rise to widespread protest in various parts of the country. Large tracts of land are being acquired across the country for this purpose. Already, questions have been raised on two counts. One is the loss of revenue in the form of taxes and the other is the effect on agricultural production*' (Expert Group Report, Planning Commission, p. 13, cited in Singla et al., 2011). These nationwide protests called for a complete overhaul of the land acquisition policy in India, criticising not only the SEZ Act, but the 1894 colonial act too. Even courts started remarking on the limitations of the colonial act. SC in a 2011 judgement quashed land acquisition under the 1894 act made by the Uttar Pradesh government in Noida by invoking the 'urgency clause'(and bypassing the due process of inviting objection from landowners) to benefit private industry. The SC bench noted: '*courts should view with "suspicion" the action of the government in acquiring land for private parties in the name of urgency.*'[13] All these popular protests, intermittent judicial directives and the stalled commercial projects led to a rethink within the government, and eventually the Scheduled Tribes and Other Traditional Forest Dwellers (Recognition of Forest Rights) Act (FRA) in 2006 and a massively revised Right to Fair Compensation and Transparency in Land Acquisition, Rehabilitation and Resettlement Act,(LARR) in 2013 were enacted in place of the old colonial laws. Both these laws recognise the rights of the local community and their *gramsabhas* or councils over their resources and necessitate their consent for divesting them of their lands (see Table 11.4).

Why now? historical background of these struggles and activism

While the expanded understanding of the context helped us situate the two protests within a colonial legal framework, what we were struck by was the timing.

Table 11.4 Restoration of rights usurped at the colonial moment

Clause	Recognitions
LARR, 2013	
Preamble: Purpose of the Act	'Voice' in the acquisition process to *panchayats* and *gramsabhas* (local governance institutions recognised through the seventy-third constitutional amendment)
Prior Consent Clause	Quasi-group voice to affected families
Definition of project-affected persons	Livelihood rights from land apart from property rights
Definition of project-affected persons	Group and individual rights to forest recognised, expanding the meaning and significance of forest rights
FRA, 2006	
Preamble: Purpose of Act	Traditional knowledge/skill of forest dwelling-tribal communities
	Historical errors and injustice during colonial, early post-colonial periods
Rights clause	Both collective (traditional) and individual rights
Duty of forest right holder or collective body in areas with forest right holders	Vests collective local body with the responsibility to preserve 'culture'

Source: compiled by authors from the respective Acts

Whereas the Act in question was enacted in 1894, why were the protests peaking now, almost a century later? On examining the history of ecological and land-related conflicts in India, we see that noted historians Gadgil and Guha (1994, 1995) say, *'in contemporary India, conflicts over nature* [. . .] *raise important questions around distributive justice* [. . .] *the fate of these conflicts is intimately connected to the development process as a whole'* (1994: 103). But this *'development process'* anchored and undertaken by the state was largely unchallenged in independent India (post 1947) until the 1970s and early 1980s. Nehruvian temples of modern India, i.e., big dams and industries, displaced several million, yet there was no pronounced protest, in fact, neither state nor civil society even kept track of the displaced then. These were probably seen as sacrifices to be made for building a nation out of a colony. In fact, Dr. B. R. Ambedkar (one of the constitution's drafters and a champion of caste liberation), was the chairman of the committee that decided to build independent India's first dam – Hirakud on Mahanadi – displacing thousands, including indigenous groups and the poor. Specific protests against projects were handled on a case-by-case basis, depending on the intensity of protest, some were shelved, others continued. It was only after the realisation that the fruits of 'development' were unevenly distributed and the conditions of ecological and development refugees were dismal that the '*development process*' was challenged in the early and mid-1980s and a national debate began about its relevance and desirability (Gadgil and Guha, 1994).

Judges become activists

An intriguing aspect of court entanglement in the protests was the promptness and faith with which protesters at Niyamgiri, Mundhra and other movements in the country readily approached courts for remediation on grounds of environmental fallouts or lack of due process. We were curious to know whether this recourse to legal intervention was a naïve response and a failure to recognise that courts operate within the bounds of law and that the law itself was not supportive of the protestors. Further examination of the use of courts suggested that this might not be the case. Court rulings revealed that the legal recourse was being used extensively and courts were sympathetic to protestors (Dwivedi, 1997; Sahu, 2007). The recourse to courts appeared to be a behaviour emerging from a deeply held belief and tradition in India about the state as a responsive and a legitimate protector of rights. India has also had a very deep history of social boycott, protest and civil disobedience in pre-colonial times and earlier to ensure that the state (rulers) lived up to and delivered on its duties of welfare of the people (Majumdar, 1922; Dharampal, 1971). There have of course been situations and court rulings which went against the communities, and in those cases, the courts supported the larger national development interests, for instance the Sardar Sarovar dam project on the river Narmada. But these were decisions in favour of the state and not in favour of specific corporations. And these decisions tied into the larger development debate in the country.

In many cases, approaching a court was the first means of protest. The PIL provided a way for courts to engage in activism. The PIL route had opened after the firm establishment of powers of judicial review, after the 1975 Emergency, when a ruling majority enacted draconian laws [to amend the constitution without limitation] and SC struck down the twenty-fourth amendment (see Table 11.5). SC articulated in the process a 'basic structure doctrine' that limited the legislature's power to amend the constitution. Amendments were possible as long as they did not disrupt the 'basic structure' built around fundamental rights. It was with this counter majoritarian check on democracy, in the interest of democracy, that SC acquired wide legitimacy as an arm of the state, and the post-Emergency phase of judicial activism began through the uniquely Indian innovation in jurisprudence (Bhagwati and Dias, 2012) in the form of public interest litigation (PIL) (see Table 11.6 for the specifics of the doctrinal and processual innovations). The eminent legal scholar Sathe (2001) says, '[*P*]*ost-emergency judicial activism was probably inspired by the Court's realization that its elitist social image would not make it strong enough.* [. . .] *Therefore consciously or unconsciously, the Court began moving in the direction of the people* [. . .] *reconceptualizing the judicial process by making it more accessible and participatory.*'

Public recourse to courts was a behaviour emerging from a deeply held cultural belief in the state as responsive and a legitimate protector of rights. Mishra

Table 11.5 Evolution of judicial activism in India

Time	Mandate/Power to Act	Significance for the Court	
		Legal	*Political*
Founding of constitution – exception of the colony (British ACT)	Written 'bill of rights' (fundamental rights) adopted; SC and HC provided power of 'writ' (Article 32) to address constriction of fundamental rights	Powers of interpreting 'rights' granted to courts	insistence on bill of rights as exception of the colony.
	Grants SC powers for judicial review of colonial law (and new enactments) to test for inconsistency with fundamental rights (article 13)	Judicial review powers formalised	Limited entry into legislative domain
1950s	Follows British tradition – SC works as a *positivist* court	Establishes sanctity of constitution	Defers to legislative and administrative programs of the State
	Agrarian land reforms context, interprets 'right to property' to include compensation when the state acquires private property		Courts seen as siding with landed class.
	Constitutional amendments (with two-thirds majority in Parliament) dilutes the 'compensation clauses'		Judiciary power curtailed by legislature
Late 1960s	*Golaknath v. Punjab* case, constitutional amendment by Parliament cannot constrict fundamental rights	articulates 'basic structure doctrine' – Parliament cannot amend the 'basic structure of the constitution'	Judiciary attempts check legislature power
	Twenty-fourth constitutional amendment removes limitations on Parliament to amend constitution		Judiciary power weakened
	Full SC bench strikes down twenty-fourth amendment		Judiciary checks legislature power; Gains institutional mass legitimacy

Late 1970s	*Indira Gandhi v. Raj Narain* strikes down a constitutional amendment validating prime minister's election	'Basic structure doctrine' reaffirmed	SC gains new legitimacy
1980s onwards	Liberal interpretation of 'personal liberty' and 'procedure established by law' in Article 21	Doctrinal and processual innovation through PIL (expanded fundamental rights through doctrine of interrelationship of rights)	Judiciary politicized significantly: Executive and Legislative action affecting 'personal rights' opened up for judicial review through writ; increased access to Courts for 'masses'

Source: reconstructed from, Sathe (2001, 2002); Balakrishnan (2008, 2010); Bhagwati and Dias (2012)

Table 11.6 Innovation in jurisprudence by the Supreme Court of India

Doctrine	Conventional	Modification and Innovation
'Standing' – who can move the court?	Petitioner whose legal rights are threatened	NGOs, activists and individuals on behalf of others if rights violated
Procedure of filing petition	Formal petition and court fee	letter written to Supreme Court
Evidence	Judges play no role in generating evidence	proactive ascertainment of facts by Court through Court appointed commissions of enquiry to aid groups without this ability
Writ of Mandamus	issued to compel public authority to fulfil legally duty	issued to mandate acts within the discretionary power of the government through directives to administration
Monitoring compliance	No active role usually	Court appointed monitoring agencies, matter kept sub-judice
Judicial proceedings	Court plays a neutral role	Collective problem solving approach to bring social issues to the focus of the executive and legislative branch of the government

Source: reconstructed from Sathe (2001)

(2004) has suggested how '*polity in Ancient India was the main instrument for social reform, economic progress, and welfare of the people, national integration and nation building*' (p. 9). Historian Ramchandra Guha (1989) illustrates this belief through accounts of community protest against corrupt state functionaries in Tehri in colonial India, while leaving the political role of the ruler/state intact. This cultural belief seems to have compelled judicial activism (evident from references to ethos in judgements) to secure institutional legitimacy for judiciary as a constituent of the state. Even the villagers of Zarpara contesting Adani pitched their arguments on such a protection of rights first, only to lose, and then shifted tactics to legal entanglement. Similarly, even when police were used to favour Vedanta at Niyamgiri, the protests did not challenge the state's legitimacy. While the community identified police and government collusion with the company, its faith in the state's process remained intact and it continued to seek justice from state authorities.

Critical interpretation of our findings

What began as an exploration of POS of two protests brought us to judicial activism and the state. The significance of 'judicial review' to legal theory and thus the state became obvious to us when juxtaposed against the principle of 'separation of powers' between judiciary, legislature and executive arms of the state. Whereas in English common law, this means that judges will not 'make law' but defer to the Austinian sovereign power of Parliament to legislate, Indian judicial review (explained in Table 11.5) in contrast recognises prerogatives of the judiciary (subject to conditions) to play a quasi-executive or quasi-legislative role by subjecting acts of executive or legislative branch of the state to judicial oversight. Even in the colonial period, Indian courts had the power of review (though rarely used), since the 'colonial difference' in a subordinate dominion could not allow the Indian government to enjoy sovereign powers.

The explicit power of 'judicial review' sneaked into the constitution of independent India also due to exigencies of the post-colonial condition at the founding moment of the post-colonial state – requiring a continuing negotiation between the continuity of colonial laws and the gradual elaboration of constitutional principles. A 'written bill of rights', as well, was a negotiated concession going against the English tradition for the colony which had to learn constitutional ways. Over time, judiciary expanded its jurisdiction over executive and legislative action through power of writ (applicable on violation of fundamental rights) and PIL through expansive interpretation of rights and their interrelationship – as several rights were gradually interpreted as extensions of fundamental rights. The power of judicial review made the Indian SC the most powerful apex court in the world. It also made it a political institution akin to the legislature, rupturing the principle of separation of power of the arms of the state, because the ultimate determination of a 'basic structure' is a political judgement (Sathe, 2001).

What we gather, therefore, from our quest to understand the outcomes of the two anti-corporate protests is that these are not simply protests directed at companies, but struggles situated in the specific history of the post-colonial condition. These protests are stages that not only instantiate the coloniality of the state, but also provide the necessary social legitimacy and political will to secure a decolonial transformation of the state. Acts of the state via the invocation of the 'eminent domain of the state' annexing community resources following the global neoliberal turn open up the colonial legacy for scrutiny. There is some historical evidence to believe that pre-colonial legal systems were fairer, though we do not go into those details here. Thus, a review of the history and contexts of these two protests actually reveals that the state, far from being either an elitist ally or even a disengaged regulator, has actually been consistently responding to the claims being made on it by its citizens. It inherited a legal system, planning system and a development philosophy from its colonial rulers, and the state and the public went with it for some time in larger public interest in the early decades after independence (in 1947) in the 1950s and 1960s, until its ill effects were obvious.

The laws being redrafted at this moment in history attest to both the continuation of the colonial encounter and ongoing decolonisation, i.e., the restoration of the rights usurped at the colonial moment. The post-colonial state is not frozen in time, nor is it a unitary, monolithic entity. It is also categorically different from the Western nation-state in the delineation of the nature of powers between legislature-judiciary-executive, but it is a contest over the nature of state itself. The post-colonial state in this sense is 'being made' in an ongoing manner through ongoing negotiations of public claim making and still-continuing processes of decolonisation. At the moment of independence, while the colonisers left, the post-colonial state inherited a colonial system from its colonial rulers. The state and the public have been working with it and slowly transforming it even as they continue to integrate with contemporary globalisation. The strangeness of the post-colonial condition is heightened by the fact that even decolonial gains are actually materialised only by leveraging the colonial difference instilled in the 'bill of rights' and 'judicial review' at the moment of the transfer of power. This strangeness of the coexistence of coloniality/decoloniality is aptly captured in philosopher Neurath's expression: 'rebuilding a ship while sailing in it'.

Notwithstanding the practical benefits in establishing solidarity amongst all anti-corporate struggles transnationally and translocally, and the temptation to merge all these struggles into the grand flow of the global anti-globalisation/anti-corporate protest in the pursuit of solidarity, it is necessary to recognise these struggles as situated in the specific histories of these nations and their states as being enacted and built through ongoing negotiations of public claim making and still continuing processes of decolonisation. The colonisers may have left, but they left behind their legacies of legal, political, social and economic systems which often have and continue to conflict with pre-existing and indigenous notions of all these and other categories. In fact, some of these conflicts are at the levels of these categories itself. Ways of life which do not recognise fragmentation of the person into a public and a private being, or into a political, economic, legal and social being, have been and continue to be in conflict with this economic, political and legal systems anchored in such fragmentation. The land acquisition law was enacted by the British in 1894; the opposition then was towards the coloniser. That the public recognition of the full extent of its oppressiveness happened much later, almost 75–100 years later when 'eminent domain' was being invoked to acquire land for SEZs, long after the British left, is evidence of this. In a country where the king did not own the land summarily, but royal lands were specifically designated and earmarked (Mukherjee, 1919; Ghoshal, 1930), eminent domain has become a difficult notion to digest. The notion of eminent domain conflicts with traditional notions. That this law is being redrafted now attests to both the continuation of the colonial encounter and the ongoing decolonisation – as is also the case of the Forest Rights Act, which, while respecting the native tradition of local ownership rights, simultaneously reinforces the coloniser's category of the tribal as a static category that needs to be preserved and curated as a solution to its endangerment.

Conclusion

We never anticipated this direction for our quest, when we began searching for explanations of the outcomes of these two anti-corporate protests. We were able to overcome the limitations of our disciplinary focus in MOS only after we took into account our post-colonial sensibility and geopolitical location in explaining the interaction of anti-corporate protests with state. SM literature has broadly held that 'open structures', by providing adequate opportunities for citizens to voice discontent, pre-empt large-scale mobilization and therefore movement success. This openness in structures comes from spatial and functional decentralisation and separation of powers between the three arms of the government – legislature, executive and judiciary (Eisinger, 1973; Kitschelt, 1986; Kriesi, 2004). It is because of differences in categories that we could not capture the nuances of these two anti-corporate protests within the conventional categories like POS of MOS and SM literature. For in the post-colonial condition, the openness of POS is a precondition for a mobilisation redefining the nature of the state and making decolonising claims on the nature of the state. Our findings from India suggest that in a post-colonial context, it is the opposite. The openness, ease of access and fuzziness in the separation of powers between the three arms of the state arising from continuing contests for legitimacy enables popular mobilisation and creates necessary political conditions for the state 'grappling with the global neoliberal turn' to engage in decolonising actions and restoration of rights of local communities usurped in colonisation. We hope that our inquiry contributes to an understanding of the dynamic at the meso level of SM mobilisation, i.e., at the national level between the local and global levels- that anti-corporate protests in post-coloniality are attempts not just to secure interests against corporations, but directed at building the state. It might therefore be prudent for SM and MOS scholars to recognise this foment of state-building under globalisation in the post-colonies in gauging the relationship of SM with the state and corporations. It is also important to be open to the strategy of delinking if necessary in order to overcome the constraints imposed by disciplinary categories of social sciences in order to develop more nuanced and empowering explanations of phenomena. Other scholars examining state-building in the colonies have similar findings. Bebbington and his colleagues, commenting on rural development in Latin America in the context of anti-mining movements, find '*that the institutions, structures and discourses that govern asset distribution, security, and productivity are not pre-given. They are struggled over, re-worked, and co-produced through the actions and interactions of a range of market, state, and civil society actors* [. . .] *our cases make clear that social movements also co-determine the forms taken by institutions, structures and discourses*' (Bebbington et al., 2008: p. 2902, emphasis added). Similarly, Ivor Chipkin's recent work (2013) on corruption in state institutions in South Africa also argues that it is most appropriate to see it as a contest over 'state-building' rather than as a corruption of the state or the absence of the state. Our findings on enactment of the state resonate with theirs within the specificities of the post-colonial Indian context.

Notes

1 That has been used in political science research.
2 1 dollar equals approximately 50 INR.

3 Following Collier (2011) and Bennet (2010), who suggest accumulating evidence as one of the strategies for testing explanations.
4 Though Adani is headquartered in India, it does have operations in other countries. Similarly, while Vedanta is headquartered in London, it is almost an Indian company, owned and managed by non-resident Indian Anil Agarwal.
5 These tactics met with severe criticism amongst domestic activist communities and others, as essentialising tribal culture and representing it as static (Kraemer et al., 2013).
6 Interest of international groups depended on several strategic considerations of Northern NGOs (Jammulamadaka and Varman, 2010; Banerjee, 2011).
7 A vernacular term meaning self-governance. This was the rallying call of the independence struggle.
8 We use post-colonial to indicate the historical fact of colonisation and independence and postcolonial to indicate the theoretical body of knowledge.
9 Such a lack of impact on share prices was seen even in the Nike case, where activist criticism did very little to the share prices, and the company acted seriously only after its revenues slumped from a consumer boycott (Zadek, 2004).
10 Even official reports acknowledged that the companies strategically used the rules and their loopholes to illegitimately pursue what was otherwise legal.
11 Land is a sub-national state subject and Gujarat and Odisha have separate procedures prescribed. These procedures, though, have to confirm to the 1894 Act.
12 www.sezindia.nic.in. Accessed 2 April 2015.
13 *Times of India*. 18 April 2011.

References

Alavi, H. (1973). Peasant classes and primordial loyalties. *The Journal of Peasant Studies*, 1(1), 23–62.
Amenta, E., Caren, N., Chiarello, E. and Su, Y. (2010).The political consequences of social movements. *Annual Review of Sociology*, 36, 287–307.
Amenta, E., Caren, N., Fetner, T. and Young, M. P. (2002). Challengers and states: toward a political sociology of social movements. *Research in Political Sociology*, 10, 47–83.
Bakker, F. de, Den Hond, F., King, B. and Weber, K. (2013). Social movements, civil society and corporations: taking stock and looking ahead. *Organization Studies*, 34(5–6), 573–593.
Balakrishnan, Justice, K. G. (2008). Growth of public interest litigation in India. Fifteenth Annual Lecture. Singapore Academy of Law. 8 October, available at http://supremecourtofindia.nic.in/speeches/speeches_2008/8%5B1%5D.10.08_singapore_-_growth_of_public_interest_litigation.pdf.
Balakrishnan, Justice, K. J. (2010). The role of the judiciary in environmental protection. D.P. Srivastava Memorial Lecture. High Court of Chattisgarh, Bilaspur. 20 March, available at http://supremecourtofindia.nic.in/speeches/speeches_2010/dp_shrivastava_memorial_lecture_20-3-10.pdf.
Banerjee, S. B. (2008). Necrocapitalism. *Organization Studies*, 29(12), 1541–1563.
Banerjee, S. B. (2011). Voices of the governed: towards a theory of the translocal. *Organization*, 18, 323–344.
Bebbington, A., Bebbington, D. H., Bury, J., Lingan, J., Muñoz, J. P. and Scurrah, M., (2008). Mining and social movements: struggles over livelihood and rural territorial development in the Andes. *World Development*, 36(12), 2888–2905.
Bennett, A. (2010). *Process tracing and causal inference*, available at http://philsci-archive.pitt.edu/8872/.

Bertels, S., Hoffman, A. J. and DeJordy, R. (2014). The varied work of challenger movements: identifying challenger roles in the US environmental movement. *Organization Studies, 35*(8), 1171–1210.

Bhagwati, P. N. and Dias, C. J. (2012). Judiciary in India: a hunger and thirst for justice. *NUJS Law Review, 5*(2), 171–188, April–June.

Centeno, M. A. and Cohen, J. N. (2012).The arc of neoliberalism. *Annual Review of Sociology, 38*, 317–340.

Chatterjee, P. (2011). *Lineages of political society: studies in postcolonial democracy.* Ranikhet: Permanent Black.

Chipkin, I. (2013). Whither the state? Corruption, institutions and state-building in South Africa. *Politikon: South African Journal of Political Studies, 40*(2), 211–231.

Collier, D. (2011). Understanding process tracing. *PS: Political Science & Politics, 44*(4), 823–830.

Costain, A. N. (1992). *Inviting women's rebellion: a political process interpretation of the women's movement.* Baltimore, MD: Johns Hopkins University Press.

Damodaran, V. (2006). Indigenous forests: rights, discourses, and resistance in Chotanagpur, 1860–2002. In G. Cederlof and K. Sivaramakrishnan (Eds.), *Ecological nationalisms: nature, livelihoods and identities in South Asia.* Ranikhet: Permanent Black.

Davis, G. F., McAdam, D., Scott, W. R. and Zald, M. N. (Eds.). (2005). *Social movements and organization theory.* Cambridge: Cambridge University Press.

dellaPorta, D. and Tarrow, S. (2004). Transnational processes and social activism: an introduction. In D. dellaPorta and S. Tarrow (Eds.), *Transnational protest & global activism* (pp. 1–17). Boulder, CO: Rowman & Littlefield.

Den Hond, F. and De Bakker, F. G. (2007). Ideologically motivated activism: how activist groups influence corporate social change activities. *Academy of Management Review, 32*(3), 901–924.

Dharampal (1971). *Civil disobedience and Indian tradition: with some early nineteenth century documents.* Varanasi: Sarva Seva Sangh Prakashan.

Doors may close on Vedanta. *The Hindu,* (2013) available at www.thehindu.com/news/national/12th-gram-sabha-too-votes-against-vedanta-mining/article 5039304.ece.

Dwivedi, O. P. (1997). *India's environmental policies, programs and stewardship.* Great Britain: Macmillan Press Ltd.

Edwards, B. and McCarthy, J. D. (2004). Resources and social movement mobilization. In D. Snow, Soule, S. A. and Kriesi, H. (Eds.), *The Blackwell companion to social movements* (pp. 116–152). Oxford: Blackwell.

Eisinger, P. K. (1973). The conditions of protest behavior in American cities. *American Political Science Review, 67*(1), 11–28.

Epp, C. R. (1998). *The rights revolution: lawyers, activists, and supreme courts in comparative perspective* (pp. 5–6). Chicago: University of Chicago Press.

Gadgil, M. and Guha R. (1994). Ecological conflicts and the environmental movement in India. *Development and Change, 25*, 101–136.

Gadgil, M. and Guha, R. (1995). *Ecology and equity: the use and abuse of nature in contemporary India.* London: Routledge.

George, A. L. and Bennett, A. (1979). *Case studies and theory development.* New York: Free Press.

George, A. L. and Bennett, A. (2005). *Case studies and theory development in the social sciences.* Cambridge, MA: MIT Press.

Ghoshal, U. N. (1930). *The agrarian system in ancient India*. India: University of Calcutta.

Gopinath, C. and Prasad, A. (2013). Toward a critical framework for understanding MNE operations: revisiting Coca-Cola's exit from India. *Organization, 20*(2), 212–232.

Green tribunal clears way for OPG power plant in Gujarat. (2013). *Down to Earth*, available at www.downtoearth.org.in/content/green-tribunal-clears-way-opg-power-plant-gujarat.

Guha, R. (1989). *The unquiet woods*. New Delhi: Oxford University Press.

Haug, C. (2013). Organizing spaces: meeting arenas as a social movement infrastructure between organization, network, and institution. *Organization Studies, 34*(5–6), 705–732.

Hieneman-Piper, J. (2011). The structural violence of globalization: an urgent call for action. Paper presented at the *Academy of Management Annual Conference*, San Antonio, August.

Hilson, C. (2002). New social movements: the role of legal opportunity. *Journal of European Public Policy, 9*(2), 238–255.

Jammulamadaka, N. and Varman, R. (2010). Is NGO development assistance mistargeted? An epistemological approach. *Critical Review, 22*(2–3), 117–128.

Kaviraj, S. (2010). *The imaginary institution of India: politics and ideas*. New York: Columbia University Press.

Keck, M. E. and Sikkink, K. (1998). Transnational advocacy networks in international politics: introduction. In M. E. Keck and K. Sikkink (Eds.), *Activists beyond borders: advocacy networks in international politics* (pp. 1–36). Ithaca, NY: Cornell University Press.

King, A. (2007). Cooperation between corporations and environmental groups: a transaction cost perspective. *Academy of Management Review, 32*(3), 889–900.

King, B. G. and Pearce, N. A. (2010). The contentiousness of markets: politics, social movements, and institutional change in markets. *Annual Review of Sociology, 36*, 249–267.

King, B. G. and Soule, S. (2007). Social movements as extra-institutional entrepreneurs: the effect of protest on stock price returns. *Administrative Science Quarterly, 52*, 413–442.

Kitschelt, H. P. (1986). Political opportunity structures and political protest: anti-nuclear movements in four democracies. *British Journal of Political Science, 16*(1), 57–85.

Kraemer, R., Whiteman, G. and Banerjee, B. (2013). Conflict and astroturfing in Niyamgiri: the importance of national advocacy networks in anti-corporate social movements. *Organization, 34*(5–6), 823–852.

Kriesi, H. (2004). Political context and opportunity. In D. Snow, Soule, S. A. and Kriesi, H. (Eds.), *The Blackwell companion to social movements* (pp. 65–90). Oxford: Blackwell.

Kriesi, H., Koopmans, R., Duyvendak, J. W. and Giugni, M. G. (1995). *The politics of new social movements in Western Europe: a comparative analysis*. Minneapolis and London: University of Minneapolis Press/University College of London Press.

Kumar, V. B. (2005). Postcolonial state: an overview. *The Indian Journal of Political Science, 66*(4), 935–954.

Lund-Thomsen, P. and Nadvi, K. (2010). Global value chains, local collective action and corporate social responsibility: a review of empirical evidence. *Business Strategy and Environment, 19*, 1–13.

McAdam, D. (2003). Beyond structural analysis: toward a more dynamic understanding of social movements. In M. Diani and D. McAdam (Eds.), *Social movements and networks: relational approaches to collective action* (pp. 281–298). Oxford: Oxford University Press.

McAdam, D., Tarrow, S. and Tilly, C. (2003). Dynamics of contention. *Social Movement Studies*, 2(1), 99–102.

Majumdar, R. C. (1922). *Corporate life in ancient India*. Poona: Oriental Book Agency.

Marks, G. and McAdam, D. (1996). Social movements and the changing structure of political opportunity in the European Union 1. *West European Politics*, 19(2), 249–278.

Meyer, D. S. (2004). Protest and political opportunities. *Annual Review of Sociology*, 30, 125–145.

Mignolo, W. D. (2000). *Local histories/global designs: coloniality, subaltern knowledges, and border thinking*. Princeton, NJ: Princeton University Press.

Mignolo, W. D. (2005). *The idea of Latin America*. Cambridge, MA: Blackwell Publishing.

Mignolo, W. D. (2006). De-linking: Don Quixote, globalization and the colonies. *Macalester International*, 17(1), 8, available at http://digitalcommons.macalester.edu/cgi/viewcontent.cgi?article=1321&context=macint.

Mir, R., Marens, R. and Mir, A. (2008). The corporation and its fragments: corporate citizenship and the legacies of imperialism. In A. G. Scherer and G. Palazzo (Eds.), *Handbook of research on global corporate citizenship* (pp. 527–551). Cheltenham: Edward Elgar.

Mishra, K. K. (2004). The study of ancient political traditions. *The Indian Journal of Political Science*, 65(1), 9–20.

Mukherji, R. K. (1919). *Local government in ancient India*. India: University of Calcutta.

O'Brien, T. (2012). Environmental protest in New Zealand (1997–2010). *The British Journal of Sociology*, 63(4), 641–661.

Oommen, T. K. (Ed.). (2010a). *Social movements I: Issues of identity*. New Delhi: Oxford University Press.

Oommen, T. K. (Ed.). (2010b). *Social movements. 2. Concerns of equity and security*. New Delhi: Oxford University Press.

Özen, Ş., and Özen, H. (2009). Peasants against MNCs and the state: the role of the Bergama struggle in the institutional construction of the gold-mining field in Turkey. *Organization*, 16(4), 547–573.

Pedriana, N. 2006. From protective to equal treatment: legal framing processes and transformation of the women's movement in the 1960s. *American Journal of Sociology*, 111(6), 1718–1761.

Phillips, N. and Brown, J. L. (1993). Analyzing communication in and around organizations: a critical hermeneutic approach. *Academy of Management Journal*, 36(6), 1547–1576.

Prasad, A. (2002). The contest over meaning: hermeneutics as an interpretive methodology for understanding texts. *Organizational Research Methods*, 5(1), 12–33.

Prasad, A. and Mir, R. (2002). Digging deep for meaning: a critical hermeneutic analysis of CEO letters to shareholders in the oil industry. *Journal of Business Communication*, 39(1), 92–116.

Prasad, P. (2005). *Crafting qualitative research: working in the postpositivist traditions*. New York: ME Sharpe.

Quellier, S. (2013). A market mediation strategy: how social movements seek to change firms' practices by promoting new principles of product valuation. *Organization Studies, 34*(5–6), 683–703.

Rao, H., Morrill, C. and Zald, M. N. (2000). Power plays: how social movements and collective action create new organizational forms. *Research in Organizational Behavior, 22*, 237–281.

Sahu, G. (2007). Environmental governance and role of judiciary in India. Unpublished PhD thesis, Institute for Social and Economic Change, Bangalore.

Sathe, S. P. (2001). Judicial activism: the Indian experience. *Washington University Journal of Law and Policy, 6*, available at http://openscholarship.wustl.edu/law_journal_law_policy/vol6/iss1/3.

Sathe, S. P. (2002). *Judicial activism in India: transcending borders and enforcing limits.* New Delhi: Oxford University Press.

Schneiberg, M. and Soule, S. A. (2005). Institutionalization as a contested, multilevel process. In Davis G. F., McAdam D., Scott W. R., Zald M. N. (Eds.) *Social movements and organization theory* (pp. 122–160). Cambridge: Cambridge University Press.

Shah, G. (1990). Dalit movements and the search for identity. *Social Action (New Delhi), 40*(4), 317–335.

Shah, G. (Ed.). (2002). *Social movements and the state.* New Delhi: Sage.

Singla, S., Atmavilas, Y. and Singh, E. (2011). Special economic zones in India: policies, performance and problems. *ASCI Journal of Management, 40*(2), 21–59.

Smith, J. and Fetner, T. (2010). Structural approaches in the sociology of social movements. In B. Klandermans and C. Roggeband (Eds.), *Handbook of social movements across disciplines.* New York: Springer.

Soule, S. A. (2012). Social movements and markets, industries, and firms. *Organization Studies, 33*(12), 1715–1733.

Steinmetz, G. (2014). The sociology of empires, colonies, and postcolonialism. *Annual Review of Sociology, 40*, 77–103.

Tilly, C. (1978). *From mobilization to revolution.* New York: McGraw-Hill.

Van Dyke, N., Soule, S. A. and Taylor, V. A. (2004). The targets of social movements: beyond a focus on the state. *Research in Social Movements, Conflicts and Change, 25*, 27–51.

Walker, E. T. and Rea, C. M. (2014). The political mobilization of firms and industries. *Annual Review of Sociology, 40*, 281–304.

Weber, K., Rao, H. and Thomas, L. G. (2009). From streets to suites: how the antibiotech movement affected German pharmaceutical firms. *American Sociological Review, 74*(1), 106–127.

Wilson, B. M. and Cordero, J. C. R. (2006). Legal opportunity structures and social movements: the effects of institutional change on Costa Rican politics. *Comparative Political Studies, 39*(3), 325–351.

Yaziji, M. and Doh, J. P. (2013). The role of ideological radicalism and resource homogeneity in social movement organization campaigns against corporations. *Organization Studies, 34*(5–6), 755–780.

Zadek, S. (2004). The path to corporate responsibility. *Harvard Business Review, 82*, 12.

Zald, M. N. and McCarthy, J. D. (Eds.). (1987). *Social movements in an organizational society: collected essays.* New Brunswick, NJ: Transaction Publishers.

Index

For Product Safety Concerns and Information please contact our EU
representative GPSR@taylorandfrancis.com
Taylor & Francis Verlag GmbH, Kaufingerstraße 24, 80331 München, Germany